BUTE
A GUIDE

David McDowall

THE LAIRD PRESS

First published by The Laird Press
31 Cambrian Road, Richmond, Surrey TW10 6JQ
www.thelairdpress.com

British Library Cataloguing in Publication Data
A catalogue record for this book is available from the British Library

ISBN 978-095278477-7

Designed and typeset in Monotype Plantin & Formata
by Peter Moore

Printed in China
The Hanway Press Ltd, London & Lion Production Ltd

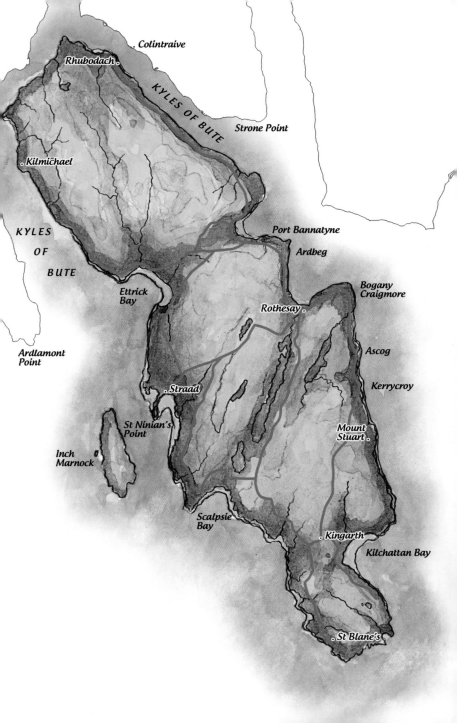

Colintraive

Rhubodach .

KYLES OF BUTE

Strone Point

. Kilmichael

KYLES

OF

BUTE

Port Bannatyne

Ardbeg

Bogany
Craigmore

Ettrick
Bay

Rothesay .

Ardlamont
Point

Ascog

. Straad

Kerrycroy

St Ninian's
Point

Mount
Stuart .

Inch
Marnock

Scalpsie
Bay

. Kingarth

Kilchattan Bay

. St Blane's

ARGYLL AND BUTE

4 SOUTH END

The Isle of Bute

❛ is ane elegant and trimme Ile, x miles lang, eivin and plane, induet with gret fertilie, decored with ane ancient and magnifik castel, quhairfra first sprang, as we have of ane alde traditione, the claim od the Kingis hous, to wit, the Stuardes, and familie. ❜

Bishop John Leslie
History of Scotland (1566)

❛ A true conservationist is a man who knows that the world is not given by his fathers, but borrowed from his children. ❜

John James Audubon (1785-1851)

Contents

(the best walk in each section is starred)

Acknowledgements

THE ILLUSTRATIONS AND MAPS

The illustrations have been reproduced by kind permission of the Ballast Trust (Dan McDonald Collection), p.121; Bute Museum, Rothesay, pp.21, 22, 23, 25, 27, 28, 43, 49, 51, 53, 57, 58, 62, 64, 68, 80, 93, 98, 99, 108, 113, 119, 122, 123, 124, 125, 155, 175, 182, 193, 201, 202, 203, 205, 207, 211, 249, 267, 272, 273, 274, 285, 287, 301, 307, 338; Sheila Cowan, p.218; Michael Curtis-Green, p.110; Dan Edgar, p.168; Dumfries and Galloway Libraries, Information and Archives, p.271; Ronald Fisher, p.127; Alec Galloway, p.184; Beryl and Tony Harrison, p.87; John Hogarth, p.76; Angela Kidner, pp.130, 326; Nigel Laird, p.265; John McCallum, pp.27, 281; McGrory Collection, Argyll and Bute Library Service, pp.24, 48, 290; McLean Museum and Art Gallery, Inverclyde Council, p.303; North Ayrshire Council Museums Service, p.296; from a private collection, p.243; Scottish National Portrait Gallery, p.165; Colin Zavaroni, pp.34, 35. The Bute overview map is the work of Jo Moore; the Ordnance Survey maps are reproduced by permission of Ordnance Survey on behalf of hmso, © Crown Copyright 2009. All rights reserved. Ordnance Survey Licence number 100049205. Permission was sought for images or text on pp.94, 181, 291, and remained untraced in the case of p.194.

THE WORDS

Bute was extensively written about in the nineteenth century, principally by (i) the retired town clerk of Rothesay, John Blain, in about 1816, yet his manuscript was only published in a version edited by William Ross, *Blain's History of Bute*, 1880; (ii) John Eaton Reid, *History of the County of Bute*, 1864, which also deals with Arran and the Cumbraes; (iii) the minister of Rothesay parish, J.K. Hewison, *Bute in the Olden Time*, 1893 (2 vols). In the twentieth century far less has been published in book form, but this is more than offset by the material published in *Transactions of the Buteshire Natural History Society* since 1908, and also *The Buteman* newspaper which is a rich seam of anecdotal material. In addition to all the foregoing, there has been a stream of useful small publications, many published by BNHS, not forgetting the interviews carried out by Brian Barr and published by Bute Sons and Daughters. I must register my substantial debt to all of these publications.

THE PEOPLE

Without the help of many individuals, my efforts would have amounted to little. In the first place, I must record my great debt to the helpfulness of librarians and archivists. Not only have they found what I wanted but they often knew what I needed long before I realised it myself. I am particularly indebted to Jean McMillan, Archivist of the Bute Museum, who endured more pestering from me than was remotely reasonable, looking out both papers and illustrations to meet my purpose, generous to a fault with her time and considerable knowledge. I was also a regular caller at the Rothesay Public Library where again I was met with great helpfulness, particularly from Patricia Pollock, Patricia McArthur and Janice McLaughlin. On the mainland I owe a debt of thanks to Eleanor Harris of the Argyll and Bute Library Service, Dunoon; Dr Margaret Mackay at the School of Scottish Studies, Edinburgh University; the staff of the National Library of Scotland on George IV Bridge and in the Map Library; the Scottish Record Office; the Royal Commission on the Ancient and Historic Monuments of Scotland; The British Library; the National Archives, Kew; and, finally, the London Library.

Others helped me with advice or in practical ways: Ronald and Ina Fisher; Alec Galloway; Susan Hothersall; Jamie Jauncey; David Kilpatrick at the Bike Shed who gave me all sorts of useful information and, of course, repaired my bike; Alistair McDonald; Robin McDowall; Alister McFarlane; Ross McLaughlin; Stuart Nisbet; Alison and Richard Ramsay; Emma Selkirk; Billy Shields (Bute's Countryside Ranger); Frances Wilkins; and Elspeth Wills.

I owe a different kind of debt to the people whom I interviewed for information about their own lifetime and knowledge. In truth, they have made this book and they can rightfully claim it as their own. Their personal reminiscences give this book the immediacy I could not possibly bring to it myself. They focus on the particular, a welcome rescue from the pretentiousness of generalisation. I have listed as many as I can remember interviewing and if I have forgotten anyone I hope they will forgive me. All of them, however modest they may think their contribution and even if they are not quoted, added to my insight and understanding: Ann and Tom Boag; Robert Currie; Sheila and Dugald Cowan; Annie Dougall; Dan Edgar; Ian Fisher; Mary Gellan; Bobby Gordon; Beryl and Tony Harrison; Brian and Janet Hill; John Hogarth; Tommy Hughes; Campbell Leitch; Duncan Lyon; Colin McArthur; James McMillan; John McMillan; Malcolm McMillan; Donald MacQueen; Tommy Rae; Bobby and Beck Reid; Ronald Robertson; Ian Sinclair; Bobby Speirs; John Thomson; Colin Zavaroni.

Cheryl and Darrell Wood first welcomed my wife and myself to Bute. It was with Darrell, Bute's Development Officer, that the idea for this book was slowly developed over a period of four years. Margaret and Iain Gimblett gave me initial encouragement. Before leaving Bute, they introduced me to Dan and Nicky Edgar who gave me great support throughout. Dan introduced me to several Brandanes (as the people of Bute are called) with a story to tell, gave sage advice, reminisced about his childhood and kindly read much of the text in draft. I owe him much.

Everywhere I have gone in Bute I have been met with kindness and consideration. It was a delight, therefore, to come across the words of James Robertson, a plant collector who made his name in the Far East, who having visited Bute in 1768 remarked, 'Whether from a virtuous inclination or from some other Circumstances, I cannot say, but…. they are Civil to strangers.' Kindness to strangers remains a Brandane characteristic.

Once again, I am hugely appreciative of the skill with which Peter Moore has designed and laid out this book, and very grateful to Jo Moore for providing the delightful overview map.

My sons, Angus and William, enthused about Bute and walked extensively across the landscape, providing useful advice and encouragement. Above all my dear wife, Elizabeth Laird, not only encouraged me with a faith in the outcome which I myself lacked but also read the text in draft, editing it, testing the walks and yet again critically reading the finalised version.

That there are still errors of both fact and judgement I cannot doubt, despite the best efforts of all the above. I am solely responsible for them.

David McDowall
October 2009

How to use this guidebook

Do not be put off by the length of this book. It is designed to make it easy to pick as little or as much as you want. 'Explorations' are for places to savour, not covered in the more prescriptive walks. For the walks, follow the instructions in bold type together with the marked routes on the OS map. The rest is commentary to be read before, during or after your walk, or not at all. I hope that the commentary will help evoke how the landscape once looked and how people lived on it.

Like Caesar's Gaul (but there all resemblance ends) I have divided Bute into three parts: (i) Rothesay and the central portion of the island; (ii) Kingarth and the south end; (iii) the north end. These divisions roughly accord with the old parish boundaries of Rothesay, Kingarth and North Bute. Each section contains an introductory portion, followed by three or four prescribed walks. In addition there are 'exploration' pieces on Scalpsie, Kilchattan and Ettrick bays and other locations which simply indicate what may be seen and where you may care to wander, rather than directed walks. If you are short of time, I have starred the most rewarding walk in each section (though I hope my choice will be hotly contested by those who use this book).

A fourth section of the book comprises background pieces. I hope they will be helpful for those who wish to know more. The Contents page will indicate how to cherry-pick this section. Alternatively, use the index.

WHY CHOOSE BUTE?

Almost any landscape carries its own rewards. Except where the landscape is wholly urbanised, geology, ecology and human intervention have worked together to create a landscape, a kind of notice board on which are pinned all sorts of reminders of what has gone before, in natural and in human history. Many of these reminders seem illegible or nearly so, and require considerable digging out (ask any archaeologist) but unless you are bereft of imagination, the rewards are beyond riches. For one discovers that 'There is a kind of natural magic in landscape…. the sense that there is always another story embedded – slightly askew – just beneath the surface of the story that is being told.'

Bute's landscape is a particular gem because it contains an astonishing multiplicity of layers indicating a rich and varied past, from the prehistoric traces – stone circles and tombs – through the age of the sea kings to the drovers, industrial barons, farmers and fishermen of the nineteenth and twentieth centuries, to today's dairy farmers maintaining herds of Canadian Holstein cattle. One reason for this enormous variety is that unlike any other island in Western Scotland, it has so much fertile terrain. Indeed, the distant name origin of Bute may indicate an 'island of corn'.

In researching this book I have been aware of the value of remembering the recent past, particularly what is carried in the memory of people who have lived on this landscape. Much of the commentary is not mine at all. Instead there are the voices of the islanders, the 'Brandanes', who have farmed the land, fished the seas or earned their livings by other means. I hope that as you read this book and walk Bute's landscape you will feel that you have had an encounter with the people, past and present, of this remarkable island.

WHY WALK?

The slowness of walking and the way it integrates us with the landscape make it a uniquely civilising activity, offering calm, a sense of reconciliation and connectedness, balm in a troubled age. This is what one compulsive walker, Rebecca Solnit, has to say:

> Even past and present are brought together when you walk as the ancients did…. each walk moves through space like a thread through fabric, sewing it together into a continuous experience – so unlike the way air travel chops up time and space as even cars and trains do. This continuity is one of the things I think we lost in the industrial age – but we can choose to reclaim it.
>
> *Wanderlust: A History of Walking* (2001)

One cannot say fairer than that.

PRACTICAL POINTS

When walking, always wear appropriate footwear and clothing. Do not take sunny weather for granted but make use of it and reserve indoor activities, notably the Museum, the Castle and the house at Mount Stuart for when the weather does not lure you outside.

GETTING AROUND

Having a car is helpful, but not necessary. Even during school holiday time one can get to many places by bus, or you can hire a bike from the Bike Shed, 23-25 East Princes Street (www.thebikeshed.org.uk). And there are taxis to retrieve you from distant places if necessary, current phone numbers for four firms, using the 01700 area code: 502275; 505050; 505044; 504224, but one may check at the taxi rank opposite the harbour.

USEFUL WEBSITES

The best website is www.bute-gateway.org, which should tell you all you wish to know with links to further points of enquiry. A visit to Mount Stuart merits a glance at www.mountstuart.com, the most essential information being that the house and gardens are open from 1 May - 30 September each year. The paddlesteamer *Waverley* calls at Rothesay each summer. If you are interested in a day trip, one can book on line at www.waverleyexcursions.co.uk.

CODE OF BEHAVIOUR FOR WALKERS

I could hardly do better than quote a Quaker exhortation:

> We do not own the world, and its riches are not ours to dispose of at will. Show a loving consideration for all creatures, and seek to maintain the beauty and variety of the world. Work to ensure that our increasing power over nature is used responsibly, with reverence for life.
>
> *Advices and Queries* No. 42, The Society of Friends.

Specifically:

(1) Never leave litter.
(2) If using a car, park it with consideration, especially for wide farm traffic.
(3) Always close gates properly behind you.
(4) Always use a stile when one is available.
(5) Try to keep to established footpaths where practicable.
(6) Try to avoid climbing over drystane dykes or wire fences, except where necessary.
(7) Always keep your dog leashed if there are any livestock around.
(8) Remember that dogs (like humans) upset most wildlife. Control them appropriately.
(9) In all things respect the people and landscape of this island.

Glossary

A few Scots or local words in the text may be unfamiliar, as listed below:

Brandane	a native of Bute
But-and-ben	a two-room cottage, the 'but' is the kitchen (in which one slept) the 'ben' is the better room or parlour
Butt	a small parcel of land, separated from its 'parent' farmland
Drystane dyke	a drystone or unmortared wall
Fank	sheep or livestock pen
Fermtoun	a hamlet usually of three or four families with its open field (in-field/out-field) system
Gaidhealtachd	the Gaelic-speaking lands
Harling	mortar and gravel finish to building exteriors, usually whitewashed
Howking	grubbing up or digging out (potatoes)
Kye	cattle
Policies	the pleasure grounds of a country mansion
Runrig	the ridge and furrow traces of open field ploughing
Smiddy	a smithy
Whin	gorse, or furze

PART I

Rothesay and central Bute

This section provides commentary for exploring Rothesay itself, and four walks, of which the pick, in my view, is the walk out to St Ninian's Point. The other three walks are relatively short and allow you to explore the rural hinterland to Rothesay, but on Walk No.1, also to explore the High Victorian villas of the seafront from Craigmore back into town. Skim the walks before setting out, so as to know which anecdotes are best kept till the end of the walk.

ST MARY'S CHAPEL • ROTHESAY

Sketch View from North East·

Rothesay town

INTRODUCTION

Rothesay's recent history gives understanding to what can now be seen. Short background pieces follow about the town's principal sites. A longer history of the royal burgh since its foundation may be found on p.247.

The town entered into years of great prosperity from the early 1800s as a result of the agricultural revolution (p.258), the rise of the herring fishery (p.283) and the manufacture of cotton goods (p.299). The end of the cotton industry in the 1860s and the decline of the herring industry at the end of that century were both more than offset by the rise of tourism. Tens of thousands of visitors poured off the Clyde steamers coming 'doon the watter' from Glasgow (p.304), between May and September each year. They brought great prosperity to the town.

With the Second World War the Royal Navy established a major submarine training base in Bute. The sailors' training was centred on Port Bannatyne while their disposable income was expended in Rothesay. The spending power of naval personnel became the mainstay of the Rothesay economy from each autumn until the summer holiday season. In September 1957, however, the Third Submarine Squadron left without warning and, save for a miniscule presence until 1970, the Navy never returned. Over the next three years the population of Rothesay fell by 20 per cent, from 10,000 to just under 8,000.

The second economic cataclysm began four years later with the collapse of Rothesay as a holiday destination. At the end of July 1948, *The Buteman* had still been able to report 'Tuesday's heat brought 10,000 day trippers to Rothesay.' By the early 1960s, however, going 'doon the watter' had become dowdy. With the post-war economic recovery at the end of the 1950s, many people in the Clyde catchment area bought cars and used them to explore Britain instead. By 1963 people were also beginning

STREET PLAN OF ROTHESAY

A Victorian Water closet
B Discovery Centre / Winter Garden
C Rothesay Castle
D Bute Museum
E The Old Sheriff Court
F The Mansion House
G Bute Fabrics

to seek cheap continental holidays and discover the delight of predictable sunshine and warmth. As a holiday destination Rothesay could not compete with the exotic. Instead, the population became infected by the 1960s *zeitgeist*, not merely by joining the 'car-owning democracy' but, among young adults at any rate, by taking a wholly new interest in personal appearance, heightened by the possibilities of shampoo. That same year *The Buteman* carried a revealing piece on a new crisis to hit Rothesay, dandruff: "'Those who are most concerned with dandruff," says Mr McCombe [fittingly, for he was a hairdresser], "are the 30-year olds."' It was as if dandruff had not previously existed.

By 1965 Rothesay's population had dipped below 7,000, since when it has only slightly increased, principally by drawing in people from the countryside, and by the advent of retirees from the mainland. In our

Rothesay Pier in the 1890s, three steamers anxious to offload their passengers.

lemming-like flight to sunny climes, we have collectively forgotten the treasures on our own doorstep.

THE PORT

> Before the town and castle is ane bay of sea, quhilk is a gude heavin for ships to lye upon ankers.
>
> Donald Monro, *Description of the*
> *Western Isles of Scotland,* 1549

It was the anchorage that made early human settlement inevitable but we do not know the arrangement of quays before the eighteenth century. In the 1750s, however, it was decided to provide improved facilities for the growing herring fishery. To imagine the scene, one must dismiss the whole of the seafront as it exists, and mentally bring the sea inshore till it more or less laps Montague Street. That is the extent of the land reclamation that has taken place over the past 250 years.

A single pier was constructed in the late eighteenth century but had to be replaced in the 1820s for three reasons: its progressive dilapidation under the rigours of stormy seas demanded extensive repair work; the herring busses had to queue for a berth to offload their catch; the quayside

Rothesay Harbour, looking towards Battery Place, before construction of the Esplanade in 1870. The large sailing vessel appears to be aground in McLea's boatyard (see p.26).

was very crowded because of the gutting, curing and packing herring barrels [see opposite]. Cooperage was the principal trade until this was displaced by the cotton industry in the 1820s. The *Rothesay Directory* of 1875 still listed numerous basket makers, cartwrights, coopers, cork cutters and coal merchants, now disappeared.

The first steamer, *The Comet*, arrived in 1812. Before then the journey to the mainland had been made in a half-decked sailing packet, an uncomfortable journey in adverse weather. It is said (but it is difficult not to be sceptical) that when the people of Rothesay saw *The Comet* approaching, a monster belching smoke, they fled inland. By 1830, however, not only were steamships a common sight but they were bringing custom in the form of visitors. Rothesay's life as a holiday resort had begun.

There were at this time about 600 dwellings in the burgh and visitors could find accommodation in perhaps half of these. The terrible pressure on accommodation was still almost a century away. During its heyday, however, Rothesay pulsated with life through the summer months, only to retreat into hibernation at the end of August.

Herring barrels festoon Rothesay Esplanade, a normal sight before 1939.

THE VICTORIAN WATER CLOSET

The Harbour Trust commissioned a public toilet for the massive number of passengers coming to the pier in 1899. More than a century later it still boasts the most elegant urinal in Britain. Imagine the delight of the first users, many of them probably unused to anything flushed, let alone with such a heavy dose of municipal pride. The urinals were supplied by Twyfords, a name that still greets us in our more intimate moments, at the princely sum of £530.

At Mount Stuart the Late Victorians knew how to celebrate the dignities of aristocratic existence. Here they demonstrated a similar sure-footedness in celebrating this the most humble physical necessity of the common man. 'Man', however, is the operative word, for in keeping with a general male belief in those days that ladies had no business to be out and about for long enough to need a public privy, no provision was made for women. In fact, all over Britain, women had to plan journeys with care, in order to avoid a crisis. This shaming deficiency has since been rectified. Restoration of the toilets in the early 1990s cost almost £300,000.

ESPLANADE

The Esplanade itself was constructed along the foreshore from 1870, the result of two individual donations of £500 (about £20,000 in today's money), and a third similar sum raised by 40 subscribers, in due course swallowing up the boatyard adjacent to the pier (see below). There was also a fish stall here on the shore, run by 'Old Granny' Deas. Her proper name was Elizabeth and she was the widow of Thomas Deas, a fisherman who had drowned at sea in the 1850s. They had both come over from Fifeshire. The Marquess of Bute used to look after widows he heard about, and ensured her livelihood by setting her up with a stall here. Her daughter, Catherine, married another fisherman, Robert McArthur of Daisy Cottage, St Ninian's Bay. Their great great grandson, Colin McArthur, lives in the same cottage and makes his living from the sea. He goes out from Rothesay Harbour almost every day to fish for prawns in his vessel, *Mo Mhairi* (p.78). At the west end the new Esplanade covered over a grimmer feature, the Gallowscraig, a rocky outcrop where criminals and witches had once been executed (on witches, see p.316). Even after the Esplanade had been built, the herring catch was cured and packed into barrels along the seafront (p.290).

The Discovery Centre (originally the Winter Garden), is a gem of late Art Nouveau style. It was made principally of steel and glass and completed in 1924. The steel was produced at the then world-famous Saracen Foundry in Glasgow. The Winter Garden was a concert and music hall

A Kintyre fish stall, similar to those in Rothesay, c.1890.

The Winter Garden, opened in 1924 and ready for its first event.

which offered holiday-makers a sense of fantasy – pagoda-roofed towers and a pleasure dome – where on rainy days they could seek entertainment from Glasgow's best comedians. Where a steep dome might have implied solemnity, pomposity even, the flattened one here cleverly suggests fun.

We are lucky to have it still. With the collapse of tourism in the 1960s, the Winter Garden went into steep decline. By 1982 it looked dilapidated and without a purpose. The Council decided to demolish it, a decision that today is difficult to believe. Voluntary action is the hallmark of a vibrant society. A group of local people came together, backed financially by the 6th Marquess, to present a powerful counter-argument on the basis of which central government allowed this group, now formed as a Trust, to redeem the Winter Garden to serve future generations of holiday-makers. We owe them our gratitude. Their lease runs out in 2084.

The Winter Garden was built on the site of a nineteenth century shipyard. In 1852, soon after the construction of Victoria Street, it had been

Sketch of Robert McLea's boatyard adjacent to the pier, before it was closed in 1872, published in The Buteman *in 1904.*

decided to lease the foreshore west of the port as a shipbuilding ground. It was here that Robert McLea, a master boatbuilder, produced fine smacks and schooners, for coastal trade and for fishing, and pleasure craft for the new industrial middle class. He reckoned to build at least five substantial wooden vessels each year. His yard was closed in 1872 for construction of the new Esplanade and the widening of Victoria Street. The new Esplanade had a lawn on which a bandstand was built, and a burgh in possession of a bandstand was naturally in want of a band. The band of the 1st Bute Artillery Volunteers, presumably in dark blue with scarlet Austrian knots on their sleeves, and stand-up collars to match, came to the rescue, playing light classical numbers and the popular tunes of the moment. In the words of *The Buteman*, 'the whole of the music was rendered in a most pleasing way.'

GUILDFORD SQUARE

The annual St Bruix Fair, held since 1585, or possibly earlier, was still being held in Guildford Square eighty years ago. It was named after St Brioc, born around 410 in Cardigan, Wales, and believed to have come to Rothesay, hence the association. The Gaelic and patronymic name for Rothesay was Cill a'Bhruic, the church of St Brioc. With the ascendancy of the Catholic Church in the Early Middle Ages, the parish was re-dedicated to St Mary and St Brioc was brushed aside. His name survived through the fair. Originally it was an annual event for buying and selling cattle and horses, yet in due course it aggregated other attractions.

St Bruix Fair, c.1900. By this time the fair has long ceased to fulfil its original purpose as a livestock market.

Guildford Square, the hub of Rothesay in about 1895. Note the horse-drawn tram, advertising Sunlight Soap. Duty-free chemically-made soap had only been available for a generation, the first generation in Britain to be clean.

In the early nineteenth century items for sale included tubs, pails, shoes and underwear. By the 1860s there were plenty of amusements too:

> As usual there was congregated in Guildford Square and neighbourhood a motley assemblage of dealers in lemonade, iced creams, sweeties &c, &c, and a very large number of shooting galleries, instruments for weighing, testing the strength, galvanic batteries, &c…. musicians, vocal and instrumental were as numerous as ever, and of

Montague Street celebrating the relief of Ladysmith in the 2nd Boer War, 1900.

all nuisances in this line, we think the German brass band the most intolerable, which ought to be put a stop to. One-legged sailors walked the streets shouting in a manner which indicated no diminution in the strength of lungs, and that if they were deficient in legs they were not deficient in wind.

The Rothesay Chronicle, 31 July 1866.

Each year an elderly Chinese juggler, 'Old Malabar', would turn up to assure his audience that 'he would give the same exhibition as he had the honour of giving before George the Fourth', as one witness later recalled.

Guildford Square also became the venue for the six-monthly 'feeing day', when farm hands were hired (see p.266), something that increasingly dismayed politer society. As *The Buteman* reported of the feeing day in May 1857,

What was a few years [ago] looked upon as a curiosity, may now be said to be a public nuisance…. Our market ought not to be in the centre of the town, where most of the engagements between master and servant is completed over the whisky table.

The deals were made outside the Esplanade Hotel, then a noted first-class temperance hotel.

Guildford Square's name commemorates the marriage of the 2nd Marquess of Bute to Maria North, daughter of George North, 3rd Earl of Guildford, and granddaughter of Frederick, 2nd Earl. He had been an unhappy member of the 3rd Earl of Bute's administration, and later Prime Minister himself for some twelve years (1770-82).

MONTAGUE STREET

This, the main shopping street, probably dates from around 1761, a tenement of houses built behind quayhead, and was colloquially know as Laigh ('low') Street. It was named that year after the maiden name of the wife of the 3rd Earl, herself the daughter of Lady Mary Wortley Montagu, famous for her *Letters* and adventurous spirit.

THE CASTLE

Rothesay Castle, a nineteenth century artist's impression of the castle in the Middle Ages. It exaggerates the size of the castle and the buildings around it are a product of fantasy. The castle roofs would have carried Kames quarry slates.

Much of the story of Rothesay's castle is embedded in the history of the struggle for control of the Clyde approaches (p.239ff). The original construction of the castle, which probably consisted of earth banks and timber, was around 1200, but was strengthened with an outer stone wall by 1230, when it was attacked and briefly held by Uspak, a Norse warlord (p.240). It was surrendered to the Norse king Håkon's expedition in 1263. It was only following the Battle of Largs the same year and the consequent decline of Norse power that Bute fell firmly within the orbit of the Scottish Crown as a vital bulwark against sea borne invaders of the Clyde. The stone castle is unique for its early date, its circular ground plan and its 800-year association with one family.

With the passing of the Crown from the Bruce to the Stewart family, Rothesay Castle became an important centre through much of the fourteenth century. In the fifteenth century the castle was a base from which Scottish kings sought to advance their tenuous control over the Western Isles and coastlands. The castle's development culminated in construction of a residential keep, in around 1500, to make the accommodation more acceptable for James IV as a base for his campaigns against the chiefs of the Western Isles. The Earl of Lennox seized the castle in 1544 on behalf of the English King Henry VIII during his War of Rough Wooing, and ravaged the surrounding country.

The building seems to have been neglected for a century until it was occupied by Cromwellian troops from 1650 to 1659. They are said to have demolished part of the defences. In 1685 Archibald, 9th Earl of Argyll rebelled against James VII. His rising proved to be short-lived but he occupied Bute, plundered Rothesay and his forces burnt the gatehouse, the residential part, thus rendering the castle uninhabitable.

During the 1870s the castle was restored by the 3rd Marquess of Bute, who employed the Gothic Revival architect, William Burges. This involved the removal of numerous houses and a smithy which had been built at the foot of the castle wall, the consolidation and also extensive repair of the walls and in 1900 the reconstruction of the first floor of the gatehouse.

THE STRUCTURE

A **The moat** was a wide ditch fed by water from Loch Fad. By the time of its restoration in the 1870s, the moat had largely disappeared under rubble and the encroachment of housing. What you now see are its imagined dimensions.

B **The stone curtain wall** may have been built around 1230, but it was heavily damaged following the Norse assault of 1263. It was heightened for the final time around 1500. The four round towers were added after 1263 when Rothesay became the principal bulwark to the Clyde approaches. The value of such towers was that they allowed the defenders to enfilade, or shoot from the flanks, on any attack on the curtain wall itself. This technology was learnt from the Saracens during the Crusades.

C **The courtyard** would have been filled with wooden structures: stables, a forge and storage for grain and other comestibles.

D **The gatehouse** was a later addition, probably built for James IV, as explained above. The ground floor contains the porter's lodge and prison. The first floor is the restored Great Hall, where James IV and V would have held court.

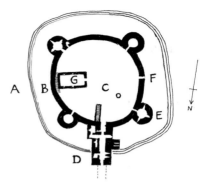

E **The pigeon tower** probably provided the castle's private accommodation before construction of the gatehouse. It was converted into a dovecote in the sixteenth century. Dovecotes were the preserve of the gentry, forbidden to the common man, who might try to get away with a wooden pigeon shack.

F **The postern gate** is thirteenth century, later blocked up.

G **The chapel** was dedicated to the Archangel Michael. Michael's origins lie beyond the Old Testament, in the Zoroastrian idea of the struggle in each of our hearts, as well as universally, between the forces of light and darkness, a powerful idea that persisted into the establishment of Christianity: 'And there was war in heaven: Michael and his angels fought against the dragon; and the dragon fought and his angels, And prevailed not, neither was their place found any more in heaven.' (*Revelation*, 12:7). St Michael as key warrior leading the forces of light is not a bad choice for Rothesay Castle chapel unless you happen to think that political violence in all its forms belongs to the Prince of Darkness. Here perhaps the Faithful prayed, '*signifer S. Michael repraesentet nos in lucem sanctum*': 'Let the Standard Bearer, Holy Michael, bring us into holy light.'

The Old Sheriff Court is now to be residential housing. Built in 1832, to provide a gaol, courthouse, and offices for the burgh and the county of Buteshire, this castellated fortress must have filled those who entered its portals charged with some misdemeanour with utter dread. Even now, stripped of its powers to consign malefactors to purgatorial confinement, its stern tower still has a capacity to intimidate. But its antidote lies at No 9 Castle Street, where the Ionic portico and dormer pediment remind us of the potential for life's grace, elegance and happiness.

The Museum is a delight, a priority for a rainy day. It is a dedicated building provided by the Marquess of Bute in 1927 for the collections of the Buteshire Natural History Society which was formed in 1905 and remains the driving force for study of the island. It contains wondrous exhibits from the island's natural history, pre-history and history.

The Mansion House: the exact time of construction is unknown. A date around 1680 is conventionally given but it may well have been built earlier, then refurbished, as in the case of Ascog House. The house was originally thatched. If you look in at the windows, you will see that the rooms have handsome wooden panelling. If you wonder that a townhouse was fortified at such a late juncture, take a look at the disorders in the middle years of that century (p.246). The house was purchased in 1685 by Sir James Stewart after his own home, the castle, was burnt. In 1710 his son, the 2nd Earl, married Anne, the sister of John, 2nd Duke of Argyll, who wrote of his prospective brother-in-law:

> My Lord Bute is a young man in Scotland who I think the best turned to make a figure in the world.

Lord Bute brought his bride home to the Mansion House. If she ever complained that it was a bit cramped, he must have taken grim satisfaction in pointing out that it was her own grandfather and great uncle who between them had destroyed the more capacious gatehouse in the castle. However, he built her a strait-laced Palladian pile at Mount Stuart, into which they moved in 1719 (p.99). As for Argyll's expectations, they were not fulfilled, for James Stewart died at the tender age of 33 in 1723. The two-storey annex on the right was built in the 1760s to accommodate HM Customs when the building was adopted as Rothesay's Customs House.

Mercat Cross: this replica was erected on its present site in 1939; previously it had stood in the middle of the High Street.

Bute Fabrics Ltd. In 1947 the 5th Marquess set up a craft weaving business, principally for high fashion tweeds. Anyone, however, aware of the travails of the Harris Tweed industry will know that tweed production is highly susceptible to the vagaries of fashion. Most men, unwisely, no longer think of a tweed jacket as an essential appurtenance. By 1977 it was clear that the fashion business was too subject to fluctuation between glut and dearth. Consequently Bute Fabrics abandoned tweed and moved that year into contracting for upholstery fabrics for aircraft, hotels, railway carriage seating and banks internationally. The business remains in Bute family ownership, employing islanders. It occupies an elegant white-harled mill building of the late eighteenth or early nineteenth century, the only cotton mill building still standing though alas, now driven by electricity, not water. Between its original use as a mill, and its adoption by Bute Fabrics it was home to an orphanage (there is a touching grave in the kirkyard for orphans) and to a convent before its present use.

The Zavaroni Story. Walking along Rothesay's sea front it does not take long to notice three cafés all bearing the name Zavaroni. This has been a Rothesay shopfront name for almost 90 years. The first wave of Italian migrants to Scotland was in the 1890s, and one of them, Mansueto Torri, was in Rothesay selling ice cream by 1897. But it is the Zavaronis who are still here and their story is well worth telling.

Cesare Zavaroni ran away from home in Borghetto di Vara, not far from Genoa, at the age of 13, in 1906. He had no wish to be a stonemason like his father. He was joining a growing stream of migrants from that part of Italy. He stowed away on a ship bound for London. Colin Zavaroni takes up his grandfather's story:

> When he arrived he managed to find work at a restaurant, 'The Silver Slipper'. After three or four years, aged 17, he returned home. He had saved 21 guineas, which he exchanged for Italian liras. When he reached his home he was exhausted, but no one was in. His parents found him fast asleep on the bed. He had covered himself with liras, proof of his success. He persuaded his younger brother to join him in Britain.

This time Cesare took his brother direct to Glasgow. Most of the emigrants from the Borghetto di Vara spread out to Port Glasgow, Greenock, Gourock and the Clyde islands where they specialised in ice cream and fish and chips, often out of the same premises. It took some courage for Catholic foreigners to set up shop in a strongly Presbyterian part of the world but they knew they could make a better living than in Borghetto, which lost one fifth of its population between 1901 and 1921. Colin recalls:

> It was during the Glasgow Fair in July 1919 that they went 'doon the watter' to Rothesay. He [Cesare] started at the bottom, chopping kindling for coal fires. He started a fish and chip shop and earned enough

Francesco Biagioni at the door of his West End Café on the corner of Gallowgate and Montague Street with his son.

> to buy a motorbike and sidecar. He opened an ice cream parlour when he moved near to the Ritz on the High Street. In the winter he went to Paisley or Port Glasgow to work there.

Cesare lost no time when it came to essentials. A local girl, Martha Davidson, working in another Italian enterprise (now Hydro-Electric on Montague Street) caught his eye and after a whirlwind courtship they were married, and Colin's father, David, was born in 1920.

All seemed set fair for the future. No one could have seen the cloud on the horizon when Mussolini became Prime Minister of Italy. We tend to forget that at first Mussolini was the wonder not only of Italians but of many European leaders. Eighteen years later, Mussolini declared war on Britain in June 1940, which left Italian émigrés in Britain compromised. Churchill ordered their internment with the instruction, 'Collar the lot.' Within three weeks 700 Italians – those who had been in Italy relatively recently – had been put on board the liner *Arandora Star*, bound for Canada. On 2 July it was sunk by torpedo, with the loss of 445 Italians. One of those who perished was Francesco Biagioni who ran the West End Café on the corner of Gallowgate and Montague Street .

Cesare had not been back to Italy, but as his grandson Colin reports, since all émigrés were required to live away from the coastal areas, he and his wife:

> were allowed to stay in Britain, but compelled to abandon their shop and live in Glasgow where they had to report to the police every day.

David Zavaroni, on the left, served as an army despatch rider. His two colleagues were killed by booby-trap piano wire stretched across a contested road.

My father and one brother were called up, but the remaining four children stayed in Rothesay, looked after by the oldest, who was only fourteen. My grandparents came back in 1945.

Colin's father, David, served as a despatch rider:

My father was demobbed in June 1945 and bought the shop in East Princes Street. He could do it with the money he had saved in the forces. They got sugar on the black market for the ice cream. Each day the chip shop was required to close at midnight. It would re-open ten minutes later. When the police confronted my grandmother, she simply informed him, "It's a new day, Constable" and he departed, baffled.

When the rationing finished and sugar was freely available in 1952, my grandfather put it about that the Zavaronis were making ice cream. He then watched to see how big a queue formed. When he saw it snaked around the corner, he knew he could invest in an ice cream maker. The machine is now 50 years old. In the family's heyday in the 1950s and early sixties, we had many outlets, one in the High Street, another in the Gallowgate, one in Ardbeg, another in Ettrick Bay (but it blew down and was uninsured), and one in Kilchattan Bay. In fact every other café was Zavaroni: at least six. In addition my grandfather had 24 ice cream barrows.

The enterprise remained hugely profitable until the Navy left in 1957, but one may still visit one of the Zavaroni premises and savour a Zavaroni ice cream, still made with equipment purchased in the 1950s.

ROTHESAY HIGH KIRK AND ST MARY'S CHAPEL

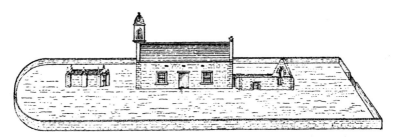

Rothesay Old Kirk, built after the triumph of Presbyterianism over the episcopacy in 1692, and demolished in 1797. The Bute family vault is on the left, St Mary's Chapel on the right.

The present building was erected in 1797, plain rather than distinguished. It replaced the first Presbyterian church here. Next to it, however, stands St Mary's Chapel, a building of considerable significance since it is the last surviving remnant of the original church of St Mary built here. This seems to have been an early fourteenth century structure which for a short while after its completion may have had cathedral status, since two bishops of Sodor (Man and the Isles) were buried here. In 1692, shortly after the triumph of Presbyterianism over the episcopacy, the church was demolished in favour of a Presbyterian design. This in turn was demolished in favour of the present structure.

The chapel is well worth a visit. Its architecture echoes that of the final chancel extension at St Blane's, the lancet windows, the piscina (the basin for washing of communion vessels)

St Mary's Chapel interior.

and the aumbry, or cupboard in the south wall. The tombs are a fascinating enigma. The knight's tomb in the south wall may have been made for Robert II, but he was buried at Scone, while Robert III was buried at Paisley. So we do not know who this effigy represents, except that it was a Stewart of the royal blood. Opposite, the lady's tomb is equally enigmatic. Who is she? Who is her baby? And who are the eight men kneeling before women in the panels beneath? Finally on the floor is a magnificent and very distinctive West Highland-style effigy, probably late fourteenth century. Again, no one knows who he is.

THE HIGH KIRK GRAVEYARD

> Time, like an ever-rolling stream
> Bears all its sons away;
> They fly forgotten, as a dream
> Dies at the break of day.
>
> Isaac Watts

Well, not quite. Those emotionally close to us leave an aura behind them. Beyond that, gravestones allow us to remember the continuities of community and individuals.

So do not dismiss graveyards from your explorations. They often contain remarkable people with astonishing stories. In the second half of the eighteenth century certain grounds were allocated to particular families, for example the McNeils, the Duncans, the McKinlays, the McAlisters, the McKirdys, the McKechnies and the Gillies, all close to the church, not to mention the Bute family vault used until the family became

Catholic. Yet there are also plenty of individuals buried here who demand you should take note:

Robert Thom (1774-1847). Thom's achievements are described on page 301. Bute owes much of its prosperity in the nineteenth century to his engineering work.

John Arnott died in Rothesay in October 1864, at the age of 84 after an eventful life. His grave has not been found but he was undoubtedly buried here. His story

McNeil gravestone, now badly eroded.

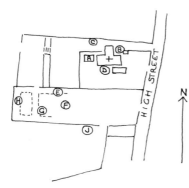

A Bute family vault
B Robert Thom
C James Duncan
D McNeil kindred
E Edward La Trobe Bateman
F Jinty Bell (unmarked, 3 rows above cypresses, on right of Thomas Johnston facing the road)
G Bonaparte and McAlisters of Meikle Kilmory
H Children of the Orphanage, Rothesay
J Bowers & Maxwell

merits retelling. He enlisted in the 42nd Foot (the Black Watch) at the age of 17, in 1799. The 42nd was part of Sir John Moore's expedition into the heart of Spain in 1808, to support a Spanish army to resist Napoleon. Moore's force of 35,000 men nearly reached Madrid before it became clear that no Spanish army would materialise and that the French, far from having only 80,000 men, actually had closer to 300,000. As these were divided into five separate columns, there was not a moment to spare to avoid being cut off from the coast. Moore's men made a midwinter retreat over the mountains to Corunna. Many were lost due to the privations of extreme cold, hunger and exhaustion. French cavalry and *tirailleurs* constantly harried the rearguard. The force reached Corunna so closely pursued that it was unable to embark.

We can ourselves imagine the scene at Corunna thanks to an eye-witness report by a naval officer who had come ashore (which sadly I must abbreviate):

> The soldiers lay scattered about, wearied, and dispirited, ragged in their dress, and many of them sickly, or rather broken down in their appearance, by the fatigues of this celebrated retreat…. The army…. had been marching, fighting, and starving, almost without intermission since the day on which they landed, two months before….
>
> I had but just asked the commanding officer of one of the regiments…. "Whether he thought anything could possibly rouse the men up?" In reply, he said… "You'll see by-and-bye, Sir, if the French there choose to come over."

.... Almost at the instant…a furious cannonading opened from a battery…. At the first discharge from the French battery, the whole body of the British troops, from one end of the position to the other, started to their feet, snatched up their arms, and formed in line with as much regularity and apparent coolness as if they had been exercising on parade in Hyde Park…. I have already noticed the silence which reigned over the field; now, however, there could be heard a loud hum, and occasionally a jolly shout and many a peal of laughter, along a distance of nearly a mile. In the midst of these sounds the peculiar sharp "click-click-click" of fixing bayonets fell distinctly on the ear very ominously…. Their kits….

Bute Museum contains several early Christian gravestones, like this one from Rothesay kirkyard.

being placed on their shoulders, the army, in a few minutes, stood perfectly ready to meet that of the enemy, whose troops, in three immense close columns, by this time were pelting rapidly down the side of the opposite heights.

The 42nd Foot were placed in the centre, where Moore correctly anticipated the brunt of the attack. When they ran out of ammunition the men began to fall back. Moore rode up to them, 'stood up in his stirrups and in a loud voice called to them, "My brave 42nd, if you've fired your ammunition, you've still your bayonets."' They turned about to advance on the enemy for the second time that day. A few seconds later, Moore took a round-shot which ripped his arm off and exposed his lung and ribs. A small party, including Corporal Arnott, carried him off the field in a blanket. Moore survived long enough to know the French had been repulsed and would have to await reinforcements. Throughout the night the rearguard lit large fires on the hilltops and moved across the front of them to give the impression of activity. Down below, in the harbour sailors rowed to-and-fro, ferrying first the wounded and then the whole army onto the ships.

On its return to Britain, the 42nd marched through Edinburgh. Newly promoted sergeant, Arnott naturally needed a wife. He duly wooed and won Margaret McLean in Paisley in December 1810. It was not long before the 42nd were back on active service with Wellington in the Peninsula. Margaret accompanied him throughout the campaign. By her marriage she, too, undertook a daunting duty. Wherever the 42nd was involved in an engagement, Margaret and the other sergeants' wives went onto the battlefield, retrieving the wounded and comforting the dying. John Arnott's final battle was the delaying action at Quatre Bras, the day before Waterloo. The 42nd took very heavy casualties. One of them was Arnott himself. It seems to have been Margaret who carried him from the field. Arnott survived but they never extracted the musket ball embedded in his chest. Margaret outlived him in penury by only two years. Next time you have a glass in your hand toast the memory of this extraordinary couple.

James Duncan (1796-1874). A large bronze recumbent figure rests on a sarcophagus of polished Peterhead granite, itself on a plinth of white granite. James Duncan had made his pile in Valparaiso, but apparently died in London. *The Buteman* penned a nice put-down concerning his tomb:

> As a work of art, it does credit to the sculptor, Mr George A. Ewing of Glasgow…. We cannot say much in its praise, however, as a likeness of Mr Duncan …. Due allowance must be made for the fact that the artist never saw the deceased.

Edward La Trobe Bateman (1815-97) was a minor artist of the Pre-Raphaelite school, a friend of painters like Millais and Rossetti. His interest in the decorative arts is manifest in the elaborately carved cross marking his grave. Perhaps he designed it himself. He moved to a house called the Hermitage in north London, a name he also applied to his home in Bute, just north of Kerrycroy, now discreetly hidden behind rhododendrons. In 1852 he joined the gold rush to Australia. Yet he earned his keep not by panning gold but by drawing pencil sketches of huts and tents which sold quickly at £5 each (over £250 in our terms). He turned his hand to landscape gardening and became a well-known figure in Melbourne. He returned to Britain in the early 1870s to take up a commission to re-design rooms and gardens at Mount Stuart. According to one authority, 'Batemen liked dense planting, and enclosures centred upon picturesque houses with gables and towers, buried in thatch and ivy.' He also re-designed the garden at Ascog Hall for Alexander Stewart, almost certainly including the design of its famous Fernery (p.89).

Stephanie Hortense Marie Mathilde Elisabeth Amélie Bonaparte, died 1 July 1885, aged 48. The temptation is to think she might be part of the imperial family, perhaps a daughter born to the Emperor Napoleon III, but on the wrong side of the blanket. Alas, no evidence seems to exist. In the 1881 census she claims to have been born in Scotland, possibly to French émigré parents. Perhaps she first married a Bonaparte, but she later married Benjamin St John Baptist Joule, older brother of the more famous James, whose scientific enquiries immortalised the name Joule as a unit of energy. Benjamin, however, has his own minor claim to fame as an accomplished organist in Manchester, where he led the Anglican choral revival. Why he and his wife fetched up in Rothesay remains a mystery.

Sir William Maxwell (1841-1923) was a champion of the Co-operative Movement in Scotland. He left school aged 10 and was self-educated. He had already learnt a lesson that most of us take far longer to learn. Aged about nine, he was filled with Presbyterian animus against Catholics and led a group of boys in a raid on a neighbouring Catholic school. His punishment was to spend some weeks attending classes in that very school, 'to study and associate with the hated enemy.' The experience cured him of prejudice for life. In 1862 he decided to educate himself by walking across Europe. Sickness brought his project to an early close but he did spend four months walking the highways and byways of northern Ireland and England, in the company of indigent itinerants and cotton factory men put out of work. During that period he saw what he had to do in life. For the next thirty years he devoted himself to the cause of the Co-operative Movement, to improve the lot of ordinary working people. Maxwell's vision was also internationalist. As late as 1913 he was addressing the International Co-operative Movement, believing it could help 'bring in a time when men would beat their swords into ploughshares and bring peace and hope and comfort to the workers of the world.' Alas, his idealism reckoned without the egos and cynicism of politicians and arms manufacturers.

Maxwell moved to Rothesay in 1904. To its shame, Rothesay gave him a poor reception, distrusting his ideals. In the words of his biographer, 'On learning who he was, no contractor would remove his furniture from the pier to his house.' In addition, many traders in Rothesay shunned his custom. Maxwell understood such hostility to be driven by ignorant prejudice. Recollection of his own childhood bigotry must have stood him in good stead, for he responded with grace and generosity of spirit and won people over. He was delighted to be associated with the Co-operative ventures in Bute. He always kept his distance from the Labour Party. He stuck to the line that his work was about fair dealing for ordinary people and individuals could work out for themselves which political party to vote for. Here, too, is a hero to remember when next you have a glass in your hand.

Emily Bowers was the mother of Henry 'Birdie' Bowers (1883-1912), and it is his story that she (and her daughter Edith, who died in 1964) would have wanted told, for his name is also lovingly recorded on the gravestone. Bowers joined Captain Scott's ill-fated Antarctic Expedition of 1910. He was only 27. He had been born in Renfrewshire and after boarding school in Kent, he decided to be a sailor and trained on HMS *Worcester*, an old man o'war moored on the Thames. He joined the merchant navy, and acquired his master's ticket. Scott described his appearance: 'A very plain pink face carrying an immense beak-like nose (which has of course, gained him the name of "Birdie"), surmounted by close cropped red hair.'

On the expedition he proved his worth with his energy and dedication. Scott's journals repeatedly referred to Bowers as 'a treasure', and added on one occasion, 'his ardour is inspiring.' Early on in the expedition, Bowers had the nightmare of camping in the dark on what turned out to be an ice floe in the process of breaking up. He and two others had been assigned to bring the ponies across the sea ice. Bowers described what it was like, waking in the darkness to the noise of ice cracking:

> We were in the middle of a floating pack of broken-up ice.... Long black tongues of water were everywhere. The floe on which we were had split right under our picketing line.... The two sledges securing the other end of the line were on the next flow and had been pulled right to the edge.... I... rushed out in my socks to save

the two sledges; the two floes were touching farther on and I dragged them to this place and got them on to our floe. At that moment our floe split in two. I then got my *finnesko* [well-insulated Lapp boots] on, remarking that we had been in tight places but this was about the limit.... We packed up camp and harnessed our ponies in remarkably quick time.... Our only hope lay to the south.... We found the ponies would jump the intervals well.... My idea was never to separate, but to get everything on one floe at a time, and then wait until it touched or nearly touched an-other in the right direction, and

Henry 'Birdie' Bowers in the Antarctic.

then jump the ponies over and drag the four sledges across our-selves. In this way we made slow but sure progress.... The ponies behaved as well as my companions and jumped the floes in great style. After getting them on a new floe we simply left them.... till we were over with the sledges and ready to take them on again. Their implicit trust in us was touching to behold. After some hours we saw fast ice ahead, and thank God for it. Meanwhile a further unpleasantness occurred in the arrival of a host of the ter-rible 'killer' whales. These were reaping a harvest of seal in the broken up ice, and cruised among the floes with their immense black fins sticking up, and blowing with a terrific roar.... Killers act in concert.... by pressing up the thin ice from beneath and split-ting it in all directions. It took us over six hours to get close to the fast ice, which proved to be the Barrier... We had only just cleared the Strait in time, though, as all the ice in the centre.... headed off into the middle of the Strait.... Our spirits rose as we neared to the Barrier edge. We rushed up the slope towards safety, and were lit-tle prepared for the scene that met our eyes at the top. All along the Barrier face a broad lane of water from thirty to forty feet wide extended. This was filled with smashed up brash ice which was heaving up and down to the swell.... Killers were cruising there with fiendish activity and the Barrier edge was a sheer cliff of ice on the other side.

Bowers and the others managed to cross when the floe moved against the cliff face, but after all their efforts, they had to abandon the ponies.

Amundsen, of course, beat Scott's team to the South Pole, a profoundly dispiriting experience for them. One by one, the men died on the return journey. Bowers was one of the final three. When the tent was dug out, Scott was found in his sleeping bag, Bowers and Wilson either side of him. In the words of one account, 'Wilson's hands were clasped on his chest like a knight recumbent, 'Birdie' Bower's great nose curved like a scimitar out of his Jaeger helmet. Their gabardine overalls were stiff as armour. With their cross-gartered Burberry leggings, they could have been disentombed Vikings.' The Vikings of Bute one thousand years earlier would have celebrated such heroism in their cups, and so should we.

Let us now praise famous men and our fathers that begat us....
All these were honoured in their generations,
and were the glory of their times.

Ecclesiasticus, 44:1.

ROTHESAY'S NAME

In the English tongue the town was called Rothesay. There have been plenty of theories regarding the origin of this name, mostly deriving from Gaelic and mostly unconvincing. One explanation is that it is a corruption of *roth* (Gaelic for 'wheel' and *suidhe*, 'seat') meaning round seat, hence 'castle'. Another attempt to extort some sense from the name is Righsuidhe, Gaelic for 'the King's seat'. A credible Norse origin is Ruthersea, 'Rother's Isle'. These explanations are all speculative. Gaels once called the town Baille Mhod, the Gaelic for 'town of the court of justice', a name that gets us no nearer the meaning of Rothesay but makes sense since the settlement was a major seat of government in the early Middle Ages. Modern Gaelic renders it: Baille Bhoid, the town of Bute.

Skipper Wood and Craigmore

Distance 5km: 1¼ hours
OS Map 2

BEFORE YOU WALK

As with the excursion around Ascog, this walk is primarily about architecture, in this case the triumph of the professional and middle classes in the second half of the nineteenth century. But, as with the Ascog walk, you must earn your aesthetic delights by walking out to Craigmore, through pleasing beech woodland, 'Bread before cake', as my mother would say.

Start: Walk up the first part of the Serpentine, turning left almost immediately, along Bishop Terrace (see map, p.20), at the end of which, take the path on the left marked 'Woodland Walk to Ardencraig Gardens.'

This path through to Eastlands Road was created by the 3rd Marquess for everyone's delectation. There seems to have been no woodland here before the 1790s. During the Napoleonic war, however, the government, desperate for supplies of timber, offered a subsidy for the planting of trees. At that time this land was the property of the burgh of Rothesay. Rothesay's burghers dragged their feet. The Marquess, closely involved with the London government and therefore fully aware of national concerns, invited the burghers to dinner at Mount Stuart. According to *The Buteman*, after 'a sumptuous repast' arrangements were made to transfer these lands, as well as Skeoch Wood, p.61, to the Bute Estate, and the trees were planted. In 1883 the wood was decimated by high winds. Six years later the newly planted woodland was nearly closed to the public after vandals maliciously snapped a number of saplings.

What you now see was almost entirely planted after 1918, as Skipper Wood was felled in the First World War, like many plantations across Britain. The war used up vast quantities of timber, for barrack huts, for revetments and props for the trenches and so forth. Neither the beeches (p.332) nor the Scots pines would grow naturally here. Beech is more or less at its northern limit, while Scots pines find the climate here on the west coast too maritime. The sycamores (p.334), later along this walk, were probably also initially planted but they will regenerate without encouragement, being resilient against Atlantic rain and wind.

As you pass the back garden of a solid-looking but handsome, almost Germanic Victorian villa with deep eaves, note the Coast Redwoods and Wellingtonias, exotics introduced to Britain in 1843 and 1853 respectively and beyond the house, the ultimate exotics, monkey puzzle trees (p.336) which became hugely popular for large Victorian gardens.

When the ground opens out you are passing the backs of the houses on Crichton Road. Although efforts have been made to improve the grassland here, the ground is inadequately drained, hence the invasion of rushes, slowly returning the soil to its natural state.

On reaching Eastlands Road, you have a choice, apart from continuing the prescribed walk:

(i) **If you wish to visit Ardencraig Gardens (open May-Sept) turn right and take the first left. The gardens are at the far end of the road.**
Ardencraig House was built for a Liverpool merchant in the mid-nineteenth century.

(ii) **If you have little interest in architecture and prefer a fine view, turn right and continue walking up the hill until the road takes a right-angled turn down hill. At this juncture, turn left and walk up the side of the golf course until you reach the summit of Canada Hill, so called because it was the last view folk had of relatives migrating to Canada. Afterwards, simply return to the road but walk straight downhill until you reach the Serpentine into Rothesay.**

Or to continue the walk, turn left down Eastlands Road.
A five minute diversion: If you are eager to admire handsome villa architecture, **turn right** along Ardencraig Road to see, after about six houses on your right, **Tor House**, a villa with a small Italianate tower and gloriously generous eaves, built in 1855. It was designed by Alexander Thomson, and was a forerunner to his villa development at Langside, Glasgow. Retrace your steps to Eastlands Rd. (The name 'Eastlands', of course, indicates the eastern extremities of the royal burgh's lands.)

When Eastlands Road swings to the left, continue straight down, through the pedestrian access to Wellpark Road.
You have entered the land of salubrious middle class villas, built to meet the increasing demand of the professional and middle classes of Glasgow and its hinterland, who would go 'doon the watter' each summer. Wives and children would stay here throughout the summer, while the man of the house would come over every week-end. This was Glasgow's prima holiday land.

On reaching the main road, before turning left back towards Rothesay, cast an eye to the right, where the small round building on the promontory is a sewage screening station, built about 1930 so as to consign our waste matter, nicely dealt with, to the briny.

Turn left for an architectural treat. You will be passing villas which represent the height of Victorian elegance: look out for fine gables, cast-iron work and porches. You will begin to notice one or two architectural catastrophes: poor modern buildings, dreadful replacement windows or additions to what were once fine designs, distressing blemishes to an otherwise wonderful frontage along the shore.

On the right, look out for Bogany Point, the small patch of grass with a shelter on the sea side. Bogany is probably derived from the Gaelic, *both gaothanach*, meaning windy house, something perfectly intelligible given the constant breeze hereabouts. There was once a mineral well here which enjoyed a reputation for its curative properties of cutaneous, glandular and rheumatic complaints, and as a 'painless purgative when taken internally.' However, it was apparently destroyed by the construction of the road and by the small pavilion erected to house it.

The shelter marks the site at which a new battery of two much larger guns was established after the abandonment of Battery Place in the mid-nineteenth century. They stood in a stone embrasure which also enclosed a powder magazine and a bing for the cannon balls. They date from the revival of the volunteer artillery in 1862, and remained here until the end of the century. Volunteers were first deployed at Battery Place (see below), but were disbanded at the end of the Peninsular War. Peace in Europe, it seemed, was set fair for the future. In 1859, however, there was an assassination attempt on Napoleon III. The would-be assassin,

The Volunteer Artillery firing their guns. This photograph is of the battery in Kintyre, c.1890, but the scene at Craigmore must have been virtually identical. These rifled muzzle loading guns fired massive 65-pound shells.

M. Orsini, had been living in Britain. The French press embarked upon a short-lived vituperative and bellicose campaign against Britain for harbouring terrorists and, horror of horrors, officers of the Imperial Court openly insulted Her Britannic Majesty's Ambassador Plenipotentiary. Neither country harboured grievances for which it could conceivably go to war, yet Britain's sense of dignity had been attacked. It ruled 25 per cent of the world's population and possessed more shipping than the rest of the world put together. Yet, as already bloodily demonstrated in the first years of the twenty-first century, mighty nations can behave as if they are more frightened than genuinely vulnerable ones. At any rate, the government decided to prepare the civil population for war and invited young men to enrol in a new volunteer movement. All over the country patriots who felt their great nation had been slighted flocked to arms.

So, mindful of its heroic defence against the first Bonaparte, Rothesay was ready and willing to take on Napoleon III. Besides a volunteer rifle company, it also raised an artillery battery, which was located right here. In place of the now obsolete 18-pounders (see below), two massive guns were installed to cover the approaches to Rothesay Bay and the East Kyle. They were last fired in 1871. In reality, until the last years of the century, when Germany began to present a genuine challenge to Britain, the volunteer battery was, like the rifle volunteers, principally a social club: arranging balls, dinners and dances at which a chap could strut his stuff in

Craigmore Pier during its short-lived salad days.

a uniform that would dazzle the young woman of his fancy. In 1908, with the gathering clouds of possible European conflict, the volunteers here became the Bute Mountain Battery, part of the new Territorial Army.

On your left, (just before Craigmore Pier on the right), stands the first of a series of extraordinarily elegant marine villas, this one named Albany Terrace, designed by John Duncan, in 1882.

On your right, the remnants of **Craigmore Pier**. The pier house is now a tea room with a view. The original pier was fatally made of iron in 1877. Eleven years later, with the iron corroding badly, the pier was sold off. It was revamped using timber piles, and lasted until 1940.

From Lorne Road (just after the bowling green) on your left, The Royal Terrace, also built by Duncan but five years earlier, in 1877, stretches all the way to Leopold Road. These villas mark the climax of patriotic deference, proof of just how successfully the royal family had turned itself into the epitome of middle class virtue.

The lodges are named in succession: (i) Lorne, after the Marquess of Lorne, Victoria's son-in-law, who the following year became Canada's devoted and much loved Governor-General; (ii) Louise, Victoria's least conventional daughter, artistic, liberal and feminist, she was thwarted by the conventions of royalty from fulfilling herself. She married the Marquess of Lorne in 1871, something seen at the time as pleasingly democratic; (iii) Victoria and (iv) Albert need no comment; (v) Greylands is a mystery; (vi) Cambridge House is named after George, Duke of Cambridge, Victoria's cousin, appointed Commander-in-Chief of the army in 1852. He became a dead weight in this role, ousted only at the age of 76, in 1876. For 25 years he opposed essential reforms, most notably the abolition of the purchase of commissions and the conversion of numbered regiments into county-based ones that would attract territorial loyalty; (vii) Prince of Wales Lodge needs no explanation; (viii) Alexandra Tower, named after Alexandra, Princess of Denmark, who married Edward Prince of Wales; (ix) St Margaret's (if it is the original name) refers to the English consort of Malcolm III (d. 1093), who on account of her piety was canonised as St Margaret of Scotland in 1250; (x) Leopold was Victoria's youngest son, a haemophiliac who died aged only 31 in 1884.

After Leopold Road, stands **Elysium Terrace**, designed by John Orkney, 1875, now sadly no longer quite what Elysium should be, since it is seriously blemished by the large picture window in the middle villa. The last villa still has its original and truly magnificent fretted bargeboard gable.

Next, St Brendan's Church tower, the surviving remnant of a church erected in 1889 to serve the local community, now standing uncomfortably in front of a more modern structure. Its most noted incumbent, the Revd. J.M. McWilliam, 1915-28, wrote *The Birds of the Isle of Bute* (see p.319).

Watch out for Nos. 27-19 **Mountstuart Rd**, another magnificent late Victorian terrace (incorporating the Bayview Hotel).

A few doors on, Glenfaulds, built about 1880, displays the new engineering technology: windows with cast iron mullions, enabling more light to enter the rooms, while still suggesting great elegance.

Next door stands **Adelaide House**, which presumably dates from the 1830s. A strait-laced building, loyally but a little unusually named after William IV's consort, who was also strait-laced – a good-hearted German princess. They had married in 1818 when it was clear that he was likely to succeed his older brother George as king. He was 52, she only 25. William had already put away his mistress, the hugely popular comedy actress,

Dora Jordan, who was, in Hazlitt's words, 'the child of nature whose voice was a cordial to the heart.... Her person was large, soft and generous like her soul.' Dora had borne William no fewer than seven children. Poor Adelaide, an innocent abroad, walked into an impossible challenge. Childless herself, she proved kind and sweet to her stepchildren but, being serious by nature where Mrs Jordan had been jolly, never managed to endear herself to the British public, which was churlish towards her and lacking generosity of spirit.

The original Glenburn Hydropathic Hotel, c.1845.

The Glenburn Hotel. The original building here was Scotland's first hydropathic hotel, a centre for 'hydropathy' or more properly hydro-therapy. Rothesay had already acquired a modest reputation as a health resort in the early years of the nineteenth century. An Aberdonian physician, Thomas Morrison, had been compelled to give up his London practice due to asthma. He remembered his old teacher extolling the virtues of Bute for asthma sufferers and duly took refuge in Rothesay in March 1808 where, 'after a residence of four months, he felt his health so much restored, that he resolved to make Bute his chief residence.'

The basic principle behind the hydropathic movements was that the action of water would activate the body's natural ability to recover from malady. The trouble was that the treatment was anything but pleasant. As no less a person than Lord Tennyson commented in 1844, 'Of all the uncomfortable ways of living surely an hydropathical is the worst; no reading by candlelight, no going near a fire, no tea, no coffee, perpetual wet sheet and cold bath, and alternation from hot to cold…' Yet he thought it did him good, as did many others. One of the early British converts to this kind of treatment commended 223 water treatments, of which the first was a real terror: the Cold Dripping Sheet, in which one might be wrapped for an hour or so, before breakfast and, for the tremulous resident unable to resist the forceful blandishments of the establishment's physician, possibly round off the day with an invigorating repetition.

This mortification of the flesh had particular appeal in Scotland and it is difficult to dismiss the notion that the first appearance of hydropathy in 1843, the very year of the Disruption in the Kirk, was not purely accidental. It coincided, too, with the rise of a middle class, which had time on its hands for leisure in the guise of worthy self-improvement, in this case one's health. Hydros banished all the works of the world, the flesh and the devil: no caffeine, no alcohol and definitely no sex. Men of the cloth were offered special terms in order to ensure that hydro residents could be led in the requirements of spiritual improvement, too.

The doyen of the Glenburn was Dr William Paterson. A young man in possession of a father with a highly profitable sugar plantation in Demarara, William was never in want of cash. He studied medicine in Paris and Vienna, and then went to the original fount of hydropathic wisdom, Herr Vinzenz Priessenitz of Graffenberg in Silesia. Aged 31, Paterson took a house, No. 7 West Bay, Rothesay in 1843, and immediately commissioned James Hamilton, son of the more famous David (p.90), to build the Glenburn. Others followed his lead and Glasgow and the Clyde became the centre of the hydropathic craze. In 1858, the tariff for full board and attendance was £3 3s 0d per week, roughly equivalent to £175 today, something of a bargain were it not for the dark threat of the Cold Dripping Sheet. Paterson died in 1875, aged only 63, a modest age in Bute and a poor advertisement for the properties of hydropathy.

The Glenburn, like the Kyles and many other hydros, was severely damaged by fire. Fire damage seems to have been a professional requirement for any self-respecting hydropathy establishment. In the Glenburn's case, fire occurred on 10 July 1891 and was described the following day by Glasgow's *Evening Times* which in addition to reporting that no one had been hurt said:

It is stated that a gentleman named McDowal who was staying in the house, has lost a sum of about £300 which he had in one of the bedrooms that was first to be destroyed.

Three hundred pounds was the equivalent of about £17,000 today. We shall never know what McDowal was up to with so much cash knocking around, but it certainly does not look good.

What you now see is the Glenburn rebuilt by John Crawford, another Glasgow architect, and re-opened in 1894.

In the twentieth century the hydro as a place of water treatment lost its appeal, and the hydropathic establishment went into liquidation in 1936. The Glenburn successfully transformed itself, like a few others, into a regular hotel. Most, like the Kyles Hydro in Port Bannatyne (which had the specific disadvantage of a hiatus while the Navy was in residence), failed to adapt.

Beattie Court marks the beginning of Battery Place (see below). The building was Scotland's first public aquarium, built 1875-7, designed by a local architect, John Russell Thomson. The basement tanks held no less than 100,000 gallons of sea water, and another 40,000 gallons of fresh water. Inevitably, therefore, when interest declined in it as an aquarium, the natural thing to do was convert it into indoor swimming baths. Salt water was pumped in from the sea, chlorinated and heated with gas. It only closed in the 1980s. Today the building is residential.

Rothesay Aquarium, c.1900.

Battery Place. At the end of the eighteenth century this was still undeveloped land. It took its name from the first volunteer artillery battery raised in 1798 to defend Rothesay harbour from Napoleon. In February 1797 leading citizens of Rothesay offered to raise 'a Corps under the appellation of the Royal Rothesay Volunteers.' Three months later they made a further offer,

> Resolved that a Battery at Rothesay of six guns, eighteen pounders, would be of material service for preventing the enemy's ships from either molesting the town and trade that belongs to this port, or from taking Sheltere in the commodious Bay of Rothesay, for the manner of which the Rothesay Volunteers will cheerfully come forward.

Thus a battery of five 18-pounder guns was deployed more or less where Beattie Court stands now, probably along the line where the road runs. The only house here was a small one built for the drill sergeant. The guns were still, apparently, at Battery Place in 1914, but met an ignominious end as bollards on the pier. It seems the volunteers were initially raised as infantry and accoutred accordingly with muskets, 'but engaged to work the guns on the Battery of this place.'

These volunteers were licked into shape by 'a steady corporal' drafted to Rothesay from the Strathspey Fencibles, probably an ex-regular. Volunteers enrolled enthusiastically, since they were thus assured exemption from the militia ballot, exempted from service outwith the island, and above all, free to resign whenever they wished. Compare that with a compulsory five years' service in the militia, with the danger of deployment on the mainland. Lord Bute was not pleased with such skivers, unwilling to serve off the island 'reasons,' as he put it, 'so very disgraceful I am of the opinion the sooner the Company is disbanded the better.' In fact both units were incorporated into the compulsory militia in 1808.

The militia was selected by ballot, from lists prepared jointly by the parish dominie and constable, offering both plenty of scope to pick on those they disliked. Initially a balloted man could pay a penalty and find a substitute. In the case of Bute, as Lord Bute's factor duly reported in 1804:

> not one man who was chosen by Ballot could be brought forward to serve in person, they preferred paying their penalties some Ten and the remainder Fifteen Pounds. In the same manner those Balloted to the Reserve instead of going personally, found Substitutes tho' these cost them Twenty Four Pounds on an average. Except for five

substitutes… all the rest of the substitutes… were procured in other Counties, and chiefly Manufacturing Towns [presumably Paisley, Greenock and Glasgow], where Recruiting for the Army is always found to be most successful.

The militia wore scarlet, a colour that was unpopular in Bute, probably on account of the unforgettable mayhem unleashed on the Highlands by Redcoats following the 1745 Rising, but possibly dating right the way back to the red-coated government troops which harassed the Covenanters in the late seventeenth century. At any rate, Lord Bute, 400 miles away at his seat of Luton Hoo, instructed:

As they do not like in Bute the scarlet colour, drill the men to the Rifle Exercise, and dress in Russia Duck [linen canvas] pantaloons tanned, with dark green jackets permitted by the government…

In addition to the threat of the militia ballot, many men were either pressed or liable under the quota for the Navy (see p. 292).

Battery Lodge 1827, much altered in 1910, is half-timbered, asymmetrical and in the Arts & Crafts style, a desperate effort, it seems, to appear fashionably English.

Glendale is the second notable building with cast-iron mullion windows, but where Glenfaulds is serious, Glendale cannot conceal its frivolity: a tower of jolly bowed windows, with a cheeky crown.

After Glendale there are terraces of smaller, older houses. These were erected after the demise of the volunteer battery. The oldest houses, those nearest the centre of town probably date from the 1830s but the majority are from 1840s or later decades. Despite the modernising damage done to their integrity, they still present a delightful frontage. Behind the houses were courtyards and bleaching greens. In March 1856 a local woman, Catherine Campbell, 'did wickedly and feloniously steal and theftuously away take, four, or thereby, pounds weight of rope.' She got thirty days in the nick.

Look out for the red Provost's Lamp on the pavement. This is one of two or three in the burgh, traditionally erected outside the house of the elected provost. With the massive local government reorganisation in 1974, these lamps became of historic interest only.

WALK

2

Rothesay to Ardbeg via the Westland Road

Distance 7km: 1½ hours
OS Map 2

BEFORE YOU WALK

This is a gentle circuit that takes you over the high ground out of Rothesay northwards to the heights over Ardbeg, then back into town along the seashore. If you are lucky you will find yourself in silence broken only by birdsong on the high ground.

Start at the east end of Argyle Street, about 50 paces west of Gallowgate, almost opposite the end of the Esplanade. Take Chapelhill Road, a very narrow lane running uphill.
You will immediately pass on your left the doorway of the Masonic Lodge, once an important feature of civic life. **On your right:** a car park and the shell of the old West Church, a Free Church, built in 1846 as Rothesay expanded, but long since closed, one of very few churches in Scotland built in the Romanesque style.

As the road runs up to the right, you will pass on your left the now defunct Free Church chapel, built in 1860 for Gaelic speakers following the demise of the Gaelic tongue at the old chapel in the Old Vennel in 1858. (On the tribulations of the Gaelic church see pp.310-312). York Terrace, to the left of the chapel is a delight.

A few paces past the church stop at the steps, marked 'View Indicator', running uphill. On the right of the steps stands the sad empty shell of **Rothesay Academy**. If ever a school building was designed to under-whelm its pupils this surely must be it. Building for anyone should inspire, but for the young especially. Now it is to be converted into flats. There is a back-story to this eyesore. The first Academy building here was opened in 1870. It was august, distinguished and austere. It took children from

Rothesay Academy, 1870-1954

the whole of Buteshire, so those from Arran and the Cumbraes had to board with families in town during the week. A schoolboy prank on a Friday evening in 1954 reduced the Academy building to ash and rubble. *The Buteman* tactfully passed over the names of the three culprits, and so should we. Who has not done frightfully foolish things in their time, and been rescued from disaster more by luck than anything else?

Turn left, but instead of going straight up the steps, turn left again, up the winding path. Whichever route you take, keep going uphill and it will bring you to Chapelhill House. Make your way to the magnificent viewing place on the seaward side of the house.

Chapelhill House, with its castellated tower, was the first home for the Bute Museum. At the time of writing the house also boasts a witty castellated privet hedge.

The house stands on the top of its own hill, the site of a chapel dedicated to St Bride. Judging by its name, St Bride's must originally have been a Celtic foundation here long before the arrival in Bute of the Stewarts. It had been repaired in 1440 but had probably fallen into disuse before the Reformation. By 1830 it was a total ruin and razed in 1860. St Bride was very much a saint for women, believed to be the midwife of the Virgin Mary. It was a good reason to venerate her: '*Bride binn nam bas ban*',

Dulcet Bride of the Fair Hands. Hymns were sung to her on her feast day, now sadly lost. Votive effigies were made in her honour, a straw figure dressed in a woman's garb, placed in a large basket. Did she, midwife of Mary, coalesce with the pre-Christian Bridget of

The ruins of St. Bride's chapel on Chapel Hill.

fertility and fire, the goddess who gave her blessing to smithing, crops, cattle and poetry? And did she also coalesce with Bride, the saintly follower of Patrick, who lived in the late fifth and early sixth centuries? It seems likely. When Gerald of Wales visited the monastery dedicated to her memory at Kildare in the twelfth century, he saw the holy fire tended by the nuns: 'The fire is surrounded by a circular withe [willow] hedge, which men are not allowed to enter.' Was this, too, part of the bundle of belief, myth and ritual that gave meaning to people's lives here?

Turn right up the road passing the 1930s part of the Academy (scheduled for demolition), abandoned in 2007 in favour of a new campus above Townhead, up the High Street. Demolition of all these academy buildings and a return to rough pasture would enhance the general aspect of Rothesay but the ground now being too valuable, it is unlikely to happen.

Continue walking along the road, passing the turn to the burgh dump on the left. Like all refuse dumps, this one is hidden, a discreet avoidance of facing our own wastefulness. We have spent the past half-century believing we can throw things 'away', although 'away' is always somewhere else. With the massive challenges to our environment from climate change and to our pocket from the crisis in capitalism, we may be on the threshold of a thriftier society.

After 1½ km, pass the turning to Gartnakeilly Farm.
Gartnakeilly, means 'the enclosed field by the wood'. Until 1978 it was a

small dairy farm, but that year the European Community quota system rendered it unprofitable, and the farm converted to beef. Today the land, more nutritious than rough upland, is used by hillfarms for overwintering ewes and for lambing.

As you walk along, the power and telephone lines on the roadside have a nostalgic character, yet telephone and electricity here can have been installed not very much more than half a century ago.

As you approach Westland Farm, pause before turning right where marked by the West Island Way sign.
Westland Farm, as its name implies, stands on extreme westerly lands owned by the Royal Burgh of Rothesay, probably since medieval times. It looks nicely protected from the elements, the hill guarding against the north wind, and a doughty band of sycamores providing a windbreak against the prevailing weather coming in from the south and west. In reality it only escapes the full blast of westerlies.

Like Gartnakeilly, Westland Farm abandoned dairy farming. Robert Currie is fourth generation working this farm: 'My grandfather had Ayrshires [cattle], and a milk run in the burgh. My father changed from Ayrshire to Friesian, and then Canadian Holstein. Ten years ago there were 36 dairy enterprises in Bute, now only sixteen.' Today he keeps Texel pedigree sheep. These are crossed with Scottish Mule (a Blue Leicester- Black Face cross) ewes to produce prime lamb for slaughter. The farm no longer makes a viable living. Robert continues because farming is in his blood. Yet he cannot make a living by it, and is compelled to supplement his income with other work.

Turn right and follow the track. The stream beside the track has an orange bed, a sure sign of ferric content in the water, presumably from significant deposits on the higher ground. The line of beeches on the right of the track is the last vestige of a lapsed hedgerow.

Ignore the West Island Way sign after 1 km directing you to the left.
Pass Gortans Farm, and neighbouring buildings. The second, older building, at Gortans, with cabbage trees in front of it, would be immediately recognisable to New Zealanders. Many of the first settlers in New Zealand were Scots, who built in wood dwellings that reflected the mid-nineteenth century stone architecture to which they were used.

Furthermore, the cabbage trees, migrants from New Zealand (see p.337), complete the picture.

Some of the smallholdings on the slopes above Ardbeg were apparently tenancies offered to soldiers returning from the First World War, in an attempt to fulfil the rash promise of Lloyd George of providing 'a land fit for heroes'. Most of the smallholdings across Britain failed, for they were too small to be viable, and sited for the most part on poor soil which could never become prime farmland land. As one can see here, the quality of the ground is not promising and making a living is not easy. As Annie Dougall learnt, eking a living proved tough: 'When I had both cows and sheep I sometimes found myself struggling through a twenty two hour day during calving and lambing.' Today she keeps goats and ducks (eggs available from MacQueens in Bishop Street). It is with some incredulity therefore, that one learns that 'Gortans' is a diminuitive of *gort*, Gaelic for a garden or field of standing corn, suggestive of an easy bounty. If this was ever really so, and it is difficult not to be sceptical, the land must once have been in much better condition. To make a living now, one must find auxiliary work.

Descend, passing a house with a delightfully ramshackle glass lean-to, and then past Rullecheddan hidden on your left. Join the track coming in from your left, and keep descending to the main road. Cross it, and take the path on the left of, but adjacent to, the tenements opposite.
As you make your way to the shore, you will pass on your right a row of classic Scots bungalows, facing Ardbeg's Bowling Club, a thriving local activity established in 1900.

Turn right along Marine Place.

There have been plenty of plans for the greensward, to turn it into a recreational area, to establish a helicopter pad, and perhaps most significantly, in the post war discussion of a ferry at Rhubodach, to site the ferry service here, across to Ardyne Point. The advocate of this route, a burgh councillor, argued it would provide a close link with Dunoon, thereby creating a very much more coherent economic region. It is difficult to fault his logic but it did not happen. The blue shelter, like its several elegant sisters along the burgh shore, was erected in 1914. Marine Drive offers you the pleasures of the shore and its permanent community of oystercatchers, and some wonderful villas on the right of the road.

As you walk back to Rothesay along the main road:

If you admire the monkey puzzle trees, the story of how they came to Britain is told on p.336. Look out for Ardbeg Baptist Church on your right, just before Skeoch Wood, built as an Independent Chapel in 1836. The Gothic gable front, with its eight-leaf wheel window was added in 1883, when constructing a gallery floor inside.

SKEOCH WOOD

This is a lovely wood for a quiet evening stroll. Literally, it means 'hawthorn' wood, but you would have to look carefully to find any. The name must refer to hawthorns which were growing here naturally or possibly a hawthorn nursery, providing the saplings necessary for the eighteenth century hedgerows of much of the island. In any case, the present wood is not natural but a plantation, dating from the Napoleonic war (p.45).

Skeoch Wood became notorious in the decades either side of 1900, for it was used as a camping ground by those who had come by steamer but who could find no room to rent, particularly when the weather was wet. Then the wood would fill with improvident and drenched, or 'drookit',

'The Skeoch Hotel, 1932', a cartoonist's comment, The Buteman, *1932.*

The Bathing Station during its short-lived heyday.

Glaswegians. There is probably no human activity that this wood has not seen: babies conceived or born while others sloughed their mortal coil. The current plantation is not even a century old, for virtually the whole wood was felled to provide timber during the First World War.

The Bathing Station opposite Skeoch Wood. Today we simply have the sad and shabby remains of Rothesay's bathing station, built in 1934 and considered out of date well before 1950, but used briefly as a canteen for the Navy. It badly needs to disappear. Yet the shoreline here had become popular long before, once sea bathing itself had become fashionable in the early years of the nineteenth century. In many parts of Britain men had habitually dipped naked, like the Anglican clergyman Francis Kilvert, who bitterly complained in his incomparable diary that prudish folk considered it somehow indecent:

> At Shanklin one has to adopt the detestable custom of bathing in drawers. If ladies don't like to see men naked why don't they keep away from the sight? Today I had a pair of drawers given me which I could not keep on. The rough waves stripped them off and tore them down my ankles [*sic*]. While thus fettered I was seized and flung down by a heavy sea which retreating suddenly left me lying naked on the

sharp shingle from which I rose streaming with blood. After this I took the wretched and dangerous rag off and of course there were some ladies looking on as I came up out of the water.

Kilvert's Diary, 12 June 1874.

After the 1850s those anxious for propriety were increasingly worried by nakedness. There were still places during the Glasgow Fair, where the polite classes did not yet hold sway and the swimming was 'noticeably primitive in its simplicity, the people enter the water clothed in their native indecency.' However, the prudes steadily advanced. One or two correspondents in the local press over-reached themselves, at least one such exhortation reduced to absurdity by poor proof-reading:

Knitted cotton bathing-drawers, such as are worn universally at continental watering places, and which reach from the waist halfway to the knees cause no inconvenience in swimming and are useful in keeping the lions [*sic*] warm.

By 1890 or thereabouts the beach here was under strict control, the prudes had won:

The ladies bathing place, which is under the charge of a qualified female, is also well equipped. It is separated a short distance from the gentlemen's, and both places are well screened from each other.

It was not only bathers who came here. Had you been here one day in early January 1857 you might have witnessed a life-saving scene on which you could have dined out for weeks. A depressed Rothesay porter decided to drown himself opposite the wood. He waded into the water and stood there contemplating his fate. *The Buteman* takes up his story: 'How long he would have remained in that position is questionable, had not a passer-by who knew the would-be drowner, came [*sic*] forward and finished the farce by handling his gun and threatening ... to shoot him if he would not come out of the water.'

The Red Shed: in the 1850s the fabled Fyfes of Fairlie established a boat-building shed here, where they constructed skiffs and larger craft. Keels of larger vessels were laid on the shore. Walking past, one's nostrils were assailed with the scent of freshly sawn pine. It was removed in 1878, thus making room for the bathers.

The Red Shed, the Fyfe family's boatyard, before it made way for bathing.

You can hardly miss on your right, The Pavilion, opened by the Earl of Dumfries in July 1938, with an evening carnival ball which practically everyone in Rothesay apparently attended. The Pavilion is unrivalled in Scotland:

> International Style Modernism at its best with little if anything of its period to equal it in Scotland... Suave, stylish and *soigné*.
>
> Frank Arneil Walker, *The North Clyde Estuary.*

In fact, one must travel to England's south coast, Bexhill-on-Sea, to see a worthy competitor, the De La Warr Pavilion, built at almost the same time. This style of architecture never took off in Britain, its people far too conservative for anything so daring. It spoke of a brave new future at just the moment when the British were losing self-confidence, looking over their shoulders wistfully at an Empire that was slipping inexorably out of their grasp. Go inside and you will find the interior is worthy of its stunning façade. Seventy years on, the Pavilion remains at the heart of community life for the island, its facilities in constant use. Yet by 2009 it stood in dire need of extensive renovation. Lose it, and Bute would lose the heart of its community life. There is, therefore, a major effort currently to raise the funding to restore a facility so vital to everyone on the island.

Returning to the Esplanade, the statue is of Alexander Bannatyne Stewart, whose brief story may be found on p.88. Just beyond it was Gallowscraig, the place of execution, more or less where the public toilets now stand. The most notorious executions were witchcraft cases (see p.316).

Barone Hill and Craigberoch Farm

Distance 5km: 1½ hours
OS Map 2

Start at St Mary's Chapel on the High Street. Walk up the main road, and after 300 metres take the track to the right marked to Loch Fad and Ashfield Farm, just after the turning to Rothesay Academy.

Pass Ashfield Farm. Ashfield Farm made a very handsome profit in the early 1900s by providing thirty tents accommodating up to 300 men who had come to Bute for the Glasgow Fair. The farmer charged 12s 6d for each tent-space, including straw for bedding. He must have made over £100 clear profit, about £5,000 in today's terms. At the time Ashfield was still an independent farm and exploited the prohibition on camping on the Bute Estate. Put 300 young men in a field and the result is lively. His tents were adorned by the campers with drolleries, for example, 'Hôtel de Drosse', 'The Officers' Mess', 'The Educated Fleas' and 'Jimmy White's Arabs', the ridges of the tents adorned with strings of consumed beer bottles. Yet it was the cacophony of sound that made a particular impact, as *The Buteman* noted in 1904:

> Musical instruments, such as concertinas and banjos, abound in the tents, and the echoes of the loch are awakened every evening, especially when a dance is on.

Walk along the track till it brings you to Lochly and Loch Fad.
Loch Fad lies on the Highland Boundary Fault line, between the schists of the Highlands, and the Old Red Sandstone to the south (see p.226). Today the loch is an angler's mecca. In the nineteenth century and presumably for centuries before, there were plenty of otters here but they had been hunted out by 1900. In 1911 a major effort was made to clear out unwanted fish. Two hundred and thirty explosive charges were dropped in the water to eliminate pike and eels. From 1914 thousands of

young trout from the Quogach trout farm (p.80) were put into the loch. But today the pike are back. Occasionally a lucky fisher takes a large one, for example a 14-pounder in 1970.

Cross the causeway, with the Kirk Loch on your right.

The Kirk Loch was the reservoir for charging the water that drove Rothesay's cotton mills (p.229).

Pause at the road junction.

The road sharp left would take you to Woodend Cottage. This can only be seen from across Loch Fad and the walk along the road through woodland, without a view, is barely worth it. It is, however, worth a mention. Woodend was the home of Edmund Kean (1787-1833), the great Shakespearean actor, whose acting was famously described by Coleridge as 'reading Shakespeare by flashes of lightning'. He had come to Bute in 1821, fallen in love with the island and built this retreat for himself, overlooking Loch Fad. It was, of course, the moment when Walter Scott choreographed George IV's visit to Edinburgh, an event which unleashed Scotland's reinvention of itself. Kean joined the consequent tartan mania, commissioning coat, vest and trews all of the same stuff.

Kean, electrifying on stage, was nevertheless a man whose disordered private life carried the seeds of self-destruction. In 1824 a longstanding affair brought him to court on a charge of adultery. His wife insisted on separation. His career went downhill, while his dissipated and excessive habits led to a progressive breakdown in health. Playing at Covent Garden one evening in March 1833 Kean had to be carried off stage, and he died five weeks later.

The cottage is private but you can walk to the gates if you wish. These have the busts of Shakespeare, Massinger, Garrick and Kean. Philip Massinger is the only one you will be unfamiliar with. He was a Jacobean playwright, and one of Kean's favourite roles was Sir Giles Overreach in Massinger's comedy, *A New Way to Pay Old Debts*.

Ignore the green marker post which directs you to the right along the main road. Take the turning half left that leads you uphill through the spruce plantation. As you emerge from the plantation you will see Barone Hill straight ahead. Turn right up the unmade track just before the metal sheds, and walk up the hill to the stile, just on the left of another small plantation.

You will see a plantation on your right, as you ascend. This is Achamor (Gaelic for 'Large Field') Wood. In the mid nineteenth century the larch trunks grown here were exported as load-bearers in the Clyde shipyards.

Pause on top of the stile.

You will see Greenan (Gaelic for 'sunny') Farm straight ahead, and Eskacraggan Farm to its right, just above the Greenan Loch. Had you been standing here looking at Greenan Farm on Sunday, 19 October, 1710, you would have seen Thomas Henman, his wife and servants all working in the fields. An unremarkable sight, one might think. Yet they had forgotten it was the Sabbath. Once Henman realised his mistake he must have been distraught. This was no casual or laughing matter. Kirk attendance was *de rigueur*. He rushed off to Rothesay to see the minister and offer his excuses for 'his own and his whole familie's mistake'. It was something the minister had to refer to the kirk session. Henman, his wife and servants were each individually interrogated. Fortunately, the elders considered them 'of blameless reputation and honest life and had very much charity' so, to his great relief, Henman got off without a fine and was simply 'exhorted to tenderness and circumspection in their future walk.'

Look across to Eskacraggan. The name may mean 'little crag by the waterfall', but an alternative interpretation, 'the frog-wet ditch', is hard to resist. This was yet another scene of a Sabbath breach, half a century later. This time, however, it was criminal. Elspeth Gellie, from Upper Barone, was spotted leaping the infield dyke intent on snecking turnips, still something of a novelty in Bute. She was already in trouble for 'going to her friends at Drimachloy [*sic*] instead of coming to divine service.' That same evening 'she leaped the dyke a second time and carried off a new parcel [of turnips], that when detected by Mr Blain's servant who lives upon that farm, she endeavoured to corrupt him to connive at her theft.' Elspeth Gellie may have been tempted by the exceptional quality of turnip to be had here. Eskacraggan acquired a reputation for agricultural excellence, and later for its fine Clydesdales. John McMillan produced a prize winning 5 year-old draught mare at the Royal Highland Show in 1950. Tom, his son, still breeds Clydesdales here. John Macmillan also bred fine beef. In 1966 it was his crossbred bullock, 'Standfast', that won the President's medal at the Highland Show in Edinburgh.

Ploughing at Eskacraggan, probably c.1910, just before the arrival of the John McMillan, when his uncle, Thomas Barr, also a Clydesdales enthusiast, still managed the farm.

Once over the stile, follow the drystane dyke on your right to the summit of Barone Hill.

Barone may be pre-Gaelic, a Brittonic word, *barrin*, signifying an enclosure or defensive revetment, a suitable name given that an iron age fort stood here. Yet it could indeed be Gaelic, *barr sroine* meaning 'ridge or bridge of the nose', another comprehensible meaning. There are plenty of hilltops in the Gaidhealtachd with '*sron*' in the name.

Enjoy the view to Inchmarnock, Straad and St Ninian's Bay to the west, Kildavanan to the north, and Loch Ascog to the south east. Looking back, just to the left of Greenan Farm one can see Greenan Mill (currently with windows in red paintwork), where John McMillan's elder son, also John, enjoys international renown for his excellent Clydesdale horses (see p.274).

Descend, keeping the drystane dyke and then the conifer plantation at a distance of about 100m on your right. An indistinct path takes you down to a stile at the muddy bottom of the hill. Cross it and you will find yourself walking up the side of a field. On reaching the gate turn right, down the track.

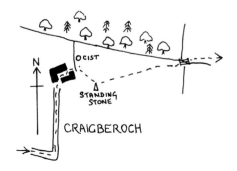

Follow the track when it turns left into the steading of Craigberoch.

This steading, known as an 'inhospitable holding', was abandoned barely 50 years ago. The slates have been stripped from the roof leading to rapid ruination, perhaps to avoid taxation. You should mind how you go. On 18 September 1863 the farmer here, Duncan Currie, was busy binding corn when he punctured his hand, so it was reported in *The Rothesay Chronicle*, on a 'dey-nettle' – a dead nettle. He thought nothing of it, as one wouldn't, but a week or so later his hand and arm began to swell. He died on 1 October. He was only 38 years old. A dead-nettle is such a limp plant it cannot possibly have punctured his hand. The fatal septicaemia must be attributed to something else.

A fresh page was turned when a new tenant took the lease for Craigberoch the following spring. He was welcomed by the arrival of no fewer than forty local ploughing teams to give him a 'darg', a day's labour to get him started. If you are thinking that this kind of behaviour can only belong to a more generous bygone age, Brian and Janet Hill at The Plan will not hesitate to correct you, mindful of the help and support they were given on arriving from Somerset in 1994.

Walk through the steading yard. Just beyond the wall ahead lies a Bronze Age cist (with whin hiding it). Turn right into the next field and you will find the stone which gives Craigberoch ('upright stone') its name.

Three cup marks may just be made out on the west side of the stone. There are hundreds of examples of cup marks and cup-and-ring marks (see p.235), where the cup has an outer ring-like declivity, across western Scotland. Surely they must mean something, but they are tantalisingly inscrutable.

Keep walking east (bottom left if you are facing the cup marks) to the corner of the field where there is a wicket gate, leading down to the road at the bottom of the next field. Leave by the gate, turn left and after 50m turn right along the path.

This path follows one of Thom's famously skilful cuts (p.301), bringing water to the Kirk Dam.

On reaching the Kirk Dam.

In 1926 it was still possible for *The Buteman* to report that 'It is within living memory of many in Rothesay seeing Mr Dymock, the man in charge of the Dam, operating his huge lever, raising or lowering the sluice to regulate the supply of water....' He operated the sluice for a working mill. But even after the mills finally came to a standstill, the sluice still had to be opened and closed until a self-regulating mechanism had been installed (and one's mind goes back to Thom's float-operated sluice, p.302). Dugald Cowan who farmed at Ashfield in the 1950s and '60s held the key to the Kirk Dam sluice until 1968. He let the water down to stop his meadows flooding, but there was also the serious matter of preventing an overflow that might wash the Kirk Dam away, and thus lead to flooding in the town.

Follow the path and it brings you back to St Mary's Chapel, and so back into town. (You may wish to savour the delights of St Mary's Chapel and the graveyard, p.36.)

St Ninian's Bay

Distance 7km: 2½ hours
OS Map 3

BEFORE YOU WALK

This walk is a circuit from Straad to St Ninian's Point, back to Straad and then around to Meikle Kilmory along the shore and back to Straad, via Quogach. This is one of the loveliest walks you can enjoy on Bute. It takes you into the world of Bute's bygone fisherfolk, their lives and their work, and also to one of the most evocative locations on the island, St Ninian's Point.

NB *At the time of writing, one must still walk across a log over a burn at the south end of St Ninian's Bay. If you do not trust your sense of balance, turn back. You will already have enjoyed the cream of the walk. You can always trace the rest of the walk in reverse order.*

Start in Straad, at the top of the lane to the shore, marked to Calum's Cabin. (If you come by car, you can leave it either tucked into the side of the road near Smiddy House and the old phone box, or past Calum's Cabin on the links at the seashore).

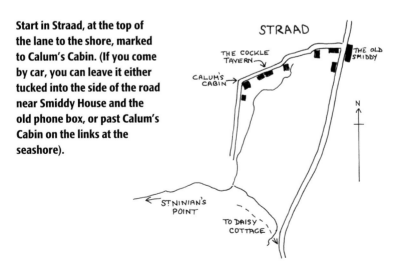

Before walking down to the shore you may like a little background on this small but highly attractive settlement. Straad (from Gaelic for 'street') was simply a 'butt' in the eighteenth century, a leftover parcel of land, part of neither the steadings of Ballycurrie, Nether Ardroscadale nor Ballianlay on its landward sides. Straad was essentially a place for fisher families, for their dwellings and their moorings, with common ground on which to graze a cow and its 'follower', its calf. Apart from them there was a smiddy run by the family Shaw (Shaw cousins ran smiddies in Rothesay and Port Bannatyne), and one or two tradesmen, a cobbler, a joiner and roadmen.

Whatever the kind of vessels they had used earlier, by the second half of the nineteenth century the fishing fleet at Straad was entirely composed of Loch Fyne skiffs, 22 ft long, 7 ft beam, and used by the four principal families: the Hogarths (who stayed at the Point), the McArthurs, the McDougalls, and the Taylors. Annie Gillies (a McArthur) recalled in 1980, 'Straad used to be busy. There were about 750 people here and on Inchmarnock before the First World War.'

Straad was a good location, for the best fishing grounds were on this side of the island. It was only a distance of 4 miles/7km by road to Rothesay, so if the men were not fishing on the east side of Bute, they could put in to Straad and travel overland. If a cart was unavailable to carry the catch, as frequently seems to have been the case, fishermen would walk to Rothesay if the catch was not too great, carrying 2 stone (13kg) boxes on their heads. This walk was at the end of a night's fishing but price depended on getting the fish to market fresh. Try carrying a weight of 13 kg of your head for just 1km and you quickly discover that these men were made of iron. With a larger catch, there was no choice but to sail round to Rothesay. As an old man in 1980, John Hogarth recalled an occasion when he was out fishing with his father. They had taken in a full catch but there was not a breath of wind to take their skiff to Rothesay. So they rowed doggedly around the Kyles to Port Bannatyne, a killer journey, before a light wind took them into Rothesay. On their arrival, exhausted, the buyer offered only £5 for the whole catch. John Hogarth was still disgusted over half a century later but honourably declined to mention the buyer's name since his family was still in Rothesay.

Start walking down the lane to the shore.

Look out for the house on the concave curve of the lane, currently with a bright red front door. For a short while this was very well known as the *Cockle Tavern*. The name conjures up an image of roistering inebriation, but the truth seems to be that it was run on more sober lines, as a place where the fisher folk of Straad could enjoy a little conviviality in the evening. During the Glasgow Fair, custom would be boosted by holidaymakers coming across from Rothesay. Mary Gellan, now retired in Rothesay, remembers:

> My father, Robert Hogarth McDougall, was born here 1889, shortly after the house was built. The *Cockle Tavern* was opened by my grandmother, Mary Hyndman, in the front room in the 1880s, but she was frightened [that when they reached their teens] her sons would take to drink so she closed the door. The tavern was simply one room of the cottage. The beer was kept in a shed at the back of the house.

In about 1980 Annie Gillies, born into the McArthur fisher family, had other recollections from her childhood around 1900:

> They all had a cow and a calf, and hens and a pig and their own fish and a sort of barter system…. Even in my young days my father [Thomas McArthur, see below] used to salt herring and he brought wooden tubs from Tarbert and they would load about 100 herrings and he would exchange these herrings with the farmers round about for corn and potatoes.

She could also remember a crisis over a burial:

> One old lady died in one of the cottages here on the shore. Men carried her to the *Cockle Tavern* in the Straad, taking their spades and mattocks, for the mourners had to bury their own dead in those days. In the tavern an argument sprang up – was the lady to be buried at Croc-an-Raer or at Rothesay? [Straad lies virtually on the old parish boundary] There was a feeling that Croc-an-Raer was the right place but if they went to Rothesay there was another tavern to refresh them. In the end a few of the men went quietly out and buried her in the corner of a nearby wood.

THE COCKLE SHORE

In the early nineteenth century John Blain noted that the bay 'affords an abundance of fine cockles and mussels as to which the peasantry entertain a belief that if any of them are carried off upon horseback the coast will cease to afford any further supplies.' It was an attempt to deter exploitation by outsiders. Their fears were justified. In the 1890s holidaymakers from Glasgow stripped the shore bare and those reminiscing in *The Buteman* in 1924 recalled:

> The hawkers became too free with the cockles, bringing in bagsful for sale at the [Rothesay] pier, and even shipping them to Glasgow.

Yet this is possibly an injustice. In the 1890s a brigantine carrying shell lime was run aground here, having started to take in water. The hot lime shells drenched, or 'slocked', by seawater strained the timbers of the vessel and burnt it out. The lime slowly leached into the water and may have been responsible for destroying the cockles.

Somewhere down here in the mid-nineteenth century there was an old houseboat, perhaps like Peggotty's in *David Copperfield*, a large upturned fishing boat with a door cut in the side. It housed either humans or livestock but by 1924 no one could remember it well enough to describe it.

Burials seem to have enjoyed a favoured place in Annie Gillies' memory, for in her old age she recalled another corpse, this time from Inchmarnock, which received an unexpected burial:

> There was not room in the boat for both the coffin and the eight men who were mourners. So the coffin was taken across first and laid on the beach and the boat returned for the men, but the wind got up and they could not get the boat off the Inch again. The last that was seen of the coffin, it was floating off to a watery grave.

Follow the shoreline to your right, to St Ninian's Point.

One can (and should) walk out along the spit of land unless there is an exceptionally high tide. In the field on your right you pass a couple of small standing stones, both about 1.4m high. For centuries, indeed until very recently, they simply stood as they were, an understated and organic part of the landscape. Grazing livestock were able to rub their flanks against these stones and for countless centuries they did so. Fencing them in may conserve them, but it also reduces their presence here, robbing them of their poetic power.

The fishermen's huts. Just as you approach the first hut, look to your left. At low water one can see the right angle of rocks running from the shore, a rudimentary anchorage. A Bute estate map dated 1781 marks the spot 'here boats lye', but it was also known as 'Stein's Port', Stein apparently being an Arran family name, an indication that Arran folk used to use this anchorage.

One of the two stone cottages still belongs to the family Hogarth. The Hogarth brothers came here in the 1840s from Portencross, opposite Little Cumbrae on the Ayrshire coast, where the small harbour allowed only small boats. The brothers wanted to use bigger vessels, and decided that this headland was suitable. Although there was no harbour here, there was a sheltered anchorage with good holding ground. Besides, it was close to the best fishing grounds at the time, Kilbrannan Sound, and the waters around Inchmarnock up to the Kyles.

Like the other families, the Hogarths kept summer and winter nets. At the end of the season, nets had to be re-barked in hot tannin, thoroughly dried on the net hangers outside, then passed into the loft through a small upper window and stowed on spars, in tightly folded bundles. The loft was jam-packed with gear. (If you look at the south-facing gable end, you can see that the loft window has since been closed with masonry). Below were two rooms, a small one with two built-in beds, and the kitchen, with the usual fireplace and swee, from which to hang the cooking pot or kettle. There were always hams hanging from the roof. Old John Hogarth, interviewed in 1980 when already in his eighties, recalled his great uncle, James, a bachelor who refused to buy any article of clothing, or indeed almost anything else. He made everything himself, including his own oil-skins. If he needed oil for tools, he shot a seal. He made a cart, he built his workshop and thatched its roof. It is nice to know that there was one thing he was quite unable to do, namely to turn the heel when knitting a sock, so he knitted his socks straight. And, according to John Hogarth, he certainly would never admit this failure to a woman. Every man will understand.

The kippering hut. The ruins of the Hogarths' kippering hut, once the family home, stand just beyond. Loch Fyne kippers, such as were prepared here, were reckoned incontestably the best, partly on account of the quality of herring fished, but also on account of their preparation. Each herring would have been split and gutted, washed by hand and immersed for half an hour in a tub of pickle so strong that the herring would float.

The kippering hut at St. Ninian's Point, c.1915. Between the two boats is a cist for storing gear, another by the door of the kippering hut. Note the access to the roof space in the gable end of both dwellings.

It would then be hung, along with twenty or so others, on a one-metre length wooden spit. The spits would be placed on one of the series of rafters rising into the roof, above the kiln. Brown kippers took the best flavour from oak and beech chips, while pale kippers were smoked with oak branches, in the words of one connoisseur, 'It is the heat from the branches which gives them the delicious flavour.'

Beside the kippering hut lies another small anchorage where one can run in a boat. Before the Second World War, Mr McFie would row across to St Ninian's Point from his farm at North Park, Inchmarnock. He would unload his produce: a basket full of eggs, a basket full of butter, and a string of rabbits. The rabbits he would hang around his neck (see p.126), the basket handles would be carried firmly in the crook of each arm. He would then set off on the five-mile walk to sell his produce in Rothesay, his hands gripping his coat lapels to help take the weight of the baskets.

The Chapel of St Ninian. There is so little left of the chapel that is visible, that you may think this site unremarkable. Look out to sea, however, and imagine St Ninian or one of his followers from Whithorn sailing in here to establish a new frontier for Christianity in the late sixth or early seventh century. Where St Blane's church speaks essentially of seclusion from the world, this site proclaims the early seafaring saints, men and women of dauntless courage, who set sail in their flimsy-looking curraghs across the treacherous waters of the Western Isles, as far as Lewis and beyond. We know that these were formidable undertakings. Take, as an example, St Cormac's third oceanic voyage:

> When his ship, blown by the south wind, had driven with full sails in a straight course from the land towards the region of the northern sky, for fourteen summer days and as many nights, such a voyage appeared to be beyond the range of human exploration, and one from which there could be no return.

Adamnan, Life of Columba, c.680.

And, as St Adamnan also observed of such saints,

> Heaven has granted to some to see on occasion in their mind, clearly and surely, the whole of earth and sea and sky.

These were individuals filled with conviction.

The chapel, which can never have been elaborate, measures roughly only 7 x 4 metres, with walls over one metre thick. These were clay-bonded, in the same way, for example, as St Ronan's Convent, Iona. For the name of St Ninian to have survived it must have remained a place of veneration long after the Vikings cut their destructive path through Bute in the early ninth century. Its altar had a cavity for the accommodation of relics. There seem to have been kneeling stones in front of and to the south of the altar, a feature that is unique in Scotland. The chapel stands within a circular cashel, or wall, some 22 metres in diameter, completely removed in some places.

Why was this spot chosen? It is possible that it was specifically sited here to displace a pre-Christian burial site, consisting of long cists, or stone-lined tombs, and graves orientated North-South. One is tempted also to wonder why a site was chosen where it might be cut off at high water. In this respect it is not, of course, alone. Lindisfarne and St Ninian's Isle, Dunrossness, Shetland are also cut off by the tide. Perhaps it symbolised a life lived apart.

Retrace your steps around the bay and follow the track southwards along the shore.

You will pass a couple of houses, the second a fisherman's hut, again with the telltale bricked-in loft window. The third, Daisy Cottage, has a history. Thomas McArthur built Daisy Cottage in 1895, though it seems he actually called it Deas Cottage, after his mother's family. The following year he married a local girl, Catherine Donnelly. In the 1980s their daughter, Annie Gillies, recalled her childhood:

The men used to fish with a long line. The line, a mile long, was wound round a board. It has a thousand hooks, a hook for every fathom. Each hook had to be baited, and that was the women's work. They used to lift mussels for bait. And then shell them.... That was my first job, long before I left school at fourteen.... The men would leave at 2 or 3 o'clock in the morning in their 16-foot sailing boats.... I would look for the boats coming back before I went to school which started at 9.30 [close by, at Ballianlay].... I would take a fish up to the teacher, Miss Hogarth [Agnes Hogarth was from St Ninian's Point].

If the wind was right in the summer, boats from all over, from Campbeltown and Tarbet, would land their catches here. I would hear the carts at four or five in the morning. The fish would be in Rothesay in an hour, and then straight on the boat for Greenock or the Broomielaw... From autumn to May they just pulled the boats up onto the grass. My father died in 1953 when you could still get a pail of fish, whiting, haddock, cod and flounders – in the Bay about half a mile from the shore. Now you might sit out all day and not catch a fish. There's nothing left.

Annie's great nephew, Colin McArthur, recalls:

My great grandfather was Thomas McArthur, and this was the family home, but in 1896 my great grandfather lost his boat in Loch Torridon and could only re-start as a fisherman by selling his house and leasing it back for 99 years from the Marquess of Bute. [Thomas only died here in 1953, aged 85.] My great aunt [Annie] was here until 1995, when the lease ran out. My wife and I were able to buy the house back from the Marquess.

Paradise, one might say, regained. Colin McArthur's *Mo Mhairi* is one of only three full-time fishing boats in Rothesay harbour, taking up prawns, and the life is a hard one.

I am fourth generation here. The McArthurs came from Islay. John Hogarth and my grandfather, John McArthur, fished together in a boat they jointly owned, the *Pioneer*, for scallops and herring, and later for king and queen scallops with *Sheine Glen*. My grandfather worked on the 6th Marquess's boat *King Duck*. He used to crew yachts going down to the Solent. His brothers also crewed yachts – my Great

Uncle Robbie was lost off a yacht [off Portsmouth, 1935]. The other, Tommy, went to distance trawling out of Hull. My father, Ian, and my uncle Ronald worked up to the mid-1970s, fishing on both sides of the island. They bought another boat in 1978, *Mo Mhairi*, second-hand from Tarbert, and restarted fishing. It is a clinker built boat, oak frame and larch strakes. I took it over. I go out at first light. But the rising fuel costs are crippling. I used to sell prawns by auction at Largs. There would be a shortage early in the week and therefore high prices, but the price would drop towards the end of the week. There are two other full time boats in Rothesay harbour – and two part time boats.

Shortly after passing Daisy Cottage, cross the log over the burn and turn left at the style. (If you do not trust your balance, turn back.) Follow the path up to the road and turn left again. Although this road is relatively quiet, please walk with care on the right hand side of the road.

Immediately opposite stands Meikle Kilmory, farm and castle. All that remains of the castle is a small tower, now only 2 metres high, attached to the farm outhouses. It once consisted of several towers and buildings. These cannot ever have been up to much, for the walls have no mortar. The castle was the fortified house of the Jamieson family, in their time a famous Bute farming family. The Jamiesons were chamberlains of Bute during the years 1436-1672. Indeed, one of them, John Jamieson, Provost of Rothesay, died in the notorious massacre of Clan Lamont by Clan Campbell in June 1646. At some point a branch of the MacNeils laid claim to 'the Coroner's Castle' at Meikle Kilmory. A red sandstone tombstone, now sadly flaked from frost damage, in St Mary's Kirkyard, Rothesay (see p.00), testifies to the MacNeil association with Kilmory, but it probably only dates from the late seventeenth century.

This was the farm of one of Bute's finest farmers, Mary McAlister (1856-1941), the only woman president of the Bute Agricultural Society, elected to that honour in 1922. Since Kilmory was once 'the chapel of Mary', it was appropriate that Mrs McAlister shared the Virgin's name. She herself was one of the MacKays, farmers at Bruchag (near Kilchattan). In marrying a McAlister, she married into Bute's best known farming family, one that has been in Bute at least since the eighteenth century. The McAlisters had many medals to their name for livestock, both Ayrshire cattle and Clydesdale horses and also for root crops through the mid-1800s. James McAlister, Mary's husband, had come across to Meikle Kilmory from Mid-Ascog, the principal McAlister farm. James worked hard to improve his livestock. In December 1907 he accidentally drowned. He was aged only 56. Now widowed, Mary nurtured both her family and the Ayrshire herd. She had brought into the world seven sons and four daughters. It is impossible to dismiss the thought that her nurturing skills with her family fed seamlessly into her livestock rearing too. She proceeded to produce the most famous Ayrshire prizewinners of her day in Scotland, at a succession of agricultural shows. In 1920

Mary McAlister with White Rose, one of her champion Ayrshires.

she entered her Ayrshire pedigree cow Lady Bute III for the Kilmarnock Show, the most important show at the time for this breed. Lady Bute III won effortlessly, evincing the rare encomium:

> In body, size and colour she pleases the taste of the most fastidious, and carries a good vessel with fine teats.

In November 1968 the farm was very nearly destroyed by fire. Three haysheds and the silage pit were gutted but by a stroke of good fortune the wind was unusually in the east, so the steading itself did not catch light. Even so, farm hands and the fire brigade were here for 24 hours extinguishing the conflagration.

Continue walking along the road for almost 1 kilometre.
You will see on your left the remains of the Quogach trout farm, established in 1914. Within its first four years it supplied Loch Fad with 85,000 fish, but it did not last long before closing.

After another ½ km or so, turn left down the track past Quogach Farm, on your right.

John Thomson (Ettrick Smiddy, p.207) remembers taking his first job at this farm, aged fourteen:

> I started on 9 September 1935. I had to be there at 5.30am and got home at 6.30pm, six days a week. On Sunday I had to go in the morning to feed the cows and back at night. For that I received 7 shillings a week [in today's money, about £12], a miserable reward. The farmer family there was Gillies. They were all single [a widow and adult children: two sons and two daughters. The Gillies family had been farming Quogach since about 1820, longer on the same Bute Estate farm than any other tenant. The family finally left in 1950]. I did whatever I was told, lifting the turnips, mucking out the byres, baling the straw. I thought nothing of it. Summers were so hot it was often insufferable. I helped with the harvest. The corn was cut with a binder, drawn by three horses. The corn fed up the machine on canvas belts, it was cut and sheaved and dropped out. We gathered the sheaves into stooks to dry. If the corn was laid flat by heavy rain, we had to cut it by hand with a scythe.

Farmers drove their workers far harder than we would think reasonable today.

A few steps beyond Quogach steading, look up to your right.

You will see a handsome mansion, Stewarthall, built in about 1764. It was built by James Stewart, the ex-minister of Kingarth. He had got into hot water in 1746 (p.309), since he had Jacobite sympathies and little respect for the London government. Thereafter it seems he was a marked man. The authorities eventually found a pretext to eject him from his living. It was some months before he physically left the parish, with the intention of staying in Edinburgh. He apparently left by sea, presumably from Scoulag. All the parish turned out to wish him well. He may have been eccentric but they had enjoyed a minister who had scant deference for the authorities. As his boat was casting off, 'it so happened that the sea advanced and retreated in an unusual manner.' It was a tidal wave triggered by the great earthquake that destroyed Lisbon on 1 November 1755. For some the destruction of Lisbon shook the foundations of their faith, for it called into question the essential goodness of Creation. It also unleashed a major philosophical enquiry by the greatest thinkers of the day into the nature of evil. The good folk of Kingarth had no such philosophical qualms. They knew exactly what the erratic sea signified: divine disapproval of those who had displaced their much-loved minister, a man prepared to cock a snook at the high heidyins.

Since then the house has hosted a wide variety of residents. In 1808 Dr Thomas Morrison, an asthma sufferer, having discovered the benefits of Bute's benign climate, took a 25 year lease on the house. Other tenants have included a publican, a pigman, a pensioner, a ploughman and a provost, and a century ago there were children from Govan and Glasgow boarding here.

Continue, passing Ballycurrie Farm on your left.
A family of the prolific McFies farmed here in the mid-nineteenth century. It was recounted by William Martin, chronicler of *The Farmers of Bute*, that James McFie 'succeeded his father, but not having taken unto himself a wife to rub the corners off him, his peculiarities were many and he did not reign long in his tenancy.' Rub the corners off him? Every woman will know what he means, while every man will be baffled.

Turn left on reaching the road to return to Straad.

PART 2

Kingarth and southern Bute

Kingarth is the name of the parish covering most of the island south of Rothesay. Only recently has it begun to mean a specific place. This section is laid out sequentially by location from the north-eastern corner of the parish, from Ascog southwards and back up the west side, but finishing with a walk from the Kingarth War Memorial back into Rothesay.

The Parish of Kingarth is the earliest documented part of Bute because of the monastery of St Blane. No one is certain about the meaning of the name Kingarth (*Ceann Gàradh*). It may mean the 'enclosed headland', a reference perhaps to the cashel of St Blane's, or 'rough headland', or 'thicket headland'. My money is on the first definition, but take your pick.

There have been people here, close by Little Kilchattan, since Mesolithic times and more or less continually since then, except perhaps during the ninth century AD, the time of the Viking raids. It was at around this time that Kingarth became a parish, from which a parish to its north, Rothesay, was later created.

Until the eighteenth century, Kingarth seems to have lacked a coherent centre, apart from the kirk, located first at St Blane's near the southern tip of the island then a little more centrally at Langalchorad, a couple of hundred metres from the Kingarth Hotel, still the site of the graveyard. The parish would have been composed of scattered fermtouns, of which the principal ones have survived as steadings following the agricultural revolution from 1750 onwards. Many others, like Kelspoke, Branser and Kingavin, simply disappeared.

The Norman chancel arch, St Blane's, Kingarth.

Around Ascog

Distance 4½km: 1½ hours
OS Map 2

BEFORE YOU WALK

Ascog, possibly Norse for 'boat-mound', is easily accessible by bus or bicycle, but if you come by car there are two limited parking sites on the left side of the road (opposite the Chandlers Hotel), just beyond Millbank. Ascog is a casket of modest architectural delights, but to build up an appetite for what is on offer, the walk takes you in a short circuit onto the hills behind, before walking back along the shore.

Start at the walker's signpost by Millbank.

Looking back, below the main road on the seashore where the burn debouches, lies 'Millhole', where a mill used to be until about 1870, very close to the shore. The present villa in the dell on the north side of the burn, a house with handsome fretted bargeboards and arched attic windows, stands on the old bleaching green.

ASCOG MILL.

The mill at Millhole, Ascog (the horseman is near the start of the walk).

Take the track to the top of the hill, marked 'Footpath to Loch Ascog'.

Before Loch Ascog became a reservoir, it flowed down the glen on your right to the sea. The burn must have had an excellent flow, since it powered three mills, for grinding corn, fulling cloth and carding wool.

Follow the signs, past the old silted-up curling pond near the top of the hill.
The curling pond must have frozen routinely when it was formed. That it
no longer does so is indicative of climate change.

Cross the field ahead, keeping close to the fence on your right.
This farmland was transformed at the end of the eighteenth century. (For
the story of how Bute's agriculture was dragged out of the Middle Ages,
only 200 years ago, see p.258).

Pass Ascog Farm on your left.
Ascog Farm is one of the few not owned by the Bute Estate. For much of
the nineteenth century it was farmed by McLeans from Argyllshire. In his
old age the chronicler of Bute farming, William Martin, recalled: 'Lachlan
and Hugh [McLean] were finely built men and outstanding holders of the
plough in their day. Hugh farmed here and retailed sweet milk for a long
time. He was fond of a smart pony and turnout and often won in harness
class at the show.'

**Turn right up the track to get a view of the western end of Loch Ascog. The
rest of the loch lies behind the hillside (for more on Loch Ascog, see p.169). On
reaching the tarmac road, turn left, and turn left again at the first opportunity,
down an unmetalled track. On your right you will pass an elegant one-storey
stone dwelling belonging to Balmory Hall, once housing for the stables and
stable hands. Continue down the path. The second house on the right was for
the gardener. On your left you will soon see Balmory Hall.**
Balmory Hall, or Balmory House as it was originally known, was built in
1860-61, a true temple to Victorian mercantile prowess, full of self-con-
fident bombast. At the time it was described as 'a typical example of the
modern Italian villa style of villa architecture…. One of the characteristic features of the style of architecture exhibited is the heavy denticulated
cornice' under the eaves. The house was built by a Glasgow magnate,
Thomas Croil, a West India spice merchant with interests in Trinidad. It
was Croil's father, William, who had established the family's mercantile
ascendancy, jointly owning a very early steamship, the *Industry*, built by
the Fyfes at Fairlie in 1814 and trading out of Greenock. Thomas Croil
died aged only 58 in 1874, of 'General Paralysis, Congestion of Brain and
Lungs for 7 or 8 years', so he did not enjoy his mansion for long, before
falling ill. After his death, the house was occupied for some time by the

Residents of the Salvation Army's first home for married couples, Balmory House, c.1930. But where are the men?

3rd Marquess, after the destruction of the first Mount Stuart and during the rebuilding.

Balmory House then passed into the hands of a Robert Laidlaw, senior partner of an iron works which had supplied the City of Moscow with all the piping for its public services. In 1927, following his death, his son gave the house to the Salvation Army, to be its first 'Eventide Home' in Scotland to accommodate married couples. Two previous homes had been single-sex establishments. One might wonder at this, but the vast majority of elderly requiring care are either already single or find they need help once widowed. Catherine, granddaughter of the Army's founder, William Booth, attended the opening ceremony and asked the assembled dignitaries to think about stumping up funds to convert the stables into holiday accommodation for slum children from Glasgow. Catherine was back in 1933 to see how things were going. The local civic and religious dignitaries turned out too:

> During the afternoon, tea was served at daintily-appointed tables on the lawn and in the house itself... The occasion was favoured with

beautiful weather conditions, and the admirable arrangements for the function, made by Major J. C. Wilson and her capable staff, reflected credit on all concerned.

The Salvation Army closed the house in the 1990s but, because by then it was so run down, had difficulty selling it. Enter Beryl and Tony Harrison in search of an awesome challenge, to create a home and also to provide the ultimate B&B. They bought the house in 1999 and embarked upon the massive task of dragging it back to its former glory, something they triumphantly achieved mainly through their own labours, undaunted by the extensive dry rot that ambushed them at the back of the building. Fortunately few original features had been removed since the house was built. Those that had, for example the iron ballisters on the staircase, could be replaced, the iron foundry's original mould having miraculously survived.

Continue down, passing more dwellings on either side of the track.
These were clearly for farm hands, gardeners and domestic staff for the houses established here. Just before reaching the main road on your left are the remains of the stables and coach house of Ascog Hall.

On reaching the main road and before turning left, cast an eye to your right, into the grounds of South Park, another sumptuous high Victorian villa, this one built by the family Thom. Then turn left, back towards Rothesay, and almost immediately turn into Ascog Hall, Garden and Fernery.
Ascog Hall was built in 1844 by the Revd. James Monteith of Dalkeith, who had joined the Free Church following the Disruption in 1843 and become first minister of Ascog Church (see below). With its hatted towers, it plays up to Walter Scott's romantically invented idea of Scotland. The estate was acquired in 1856 by Robertson Buchanan Stewart, a Brandane whose diligence had made him Glasgow's foremost draper. His Glasgow shop rounded the corner of Buchanan and Argyle streets, stretching as far as Mitchell Street, his drapes a good deal further. In the fullness of time Ascog Hall came to his son, Alexander Bannatyne Stewart.

You will have seen A. B. Stewart before, for his statue stands at the west end of the Rothesay Esplanade's Putting Green, his head providing handy parking for the port's gulls. The young Alexander became a partner in his father's business, yet while he continued his father's work with great competence, his passion was elsewhere. He was a budding aesthete, so he spent some of the brass his father had accumulated on building (and fill-ing) a large picture gallery at Rawcliffe, his home at Langside, Glasgow. Yet he was also big in Bute. He soon became the principal mover and shaker on the island, appointed Convenor of the County:

> His erect, smart, and well-dressed figure as he walked along the street – a choice specimen of some flower seldom wanting from the buttonhole of his coat – betokened the prompt and active man of business, but he was at the same time distinguished by his affability and generosity.

His generosity on the island became a bye-word: the hospital, the parish church and many Bute charities had much to thank him for and all in a very short space of time, for he died aged only 43, in 1880.

The Garden and Fernery (a must): At Ascog Hall Alexander Stewart gave free reign to his passion for horticulture, creating a distinguished collection of orchids. He commissioned Edward La Trobe Bateman (1816-97, p.41) to landscape the garden. However, in the admiring words of *The Gardener's Chronicle*, 'The principal attraction is a most beauti-ful fernery.' This, too, was almost certainly Bateman's work. For during his sojourn in Australia, Bateman had become a great fern enthusiast. 'A cool temperate rainforest grove' was intended as the core to his design for Melbourne University's extensive gardens. To his chagrin his design for housing the grove remained stillborn, and he sought solace by living in a tree fern gully in the Dandenong Ranges in precisely the sort of scenery subsequently created in Ascog's fernery.

The fernery was skilfully restored in 1996, using an illustration and written description, so that the ferns you now see are in the style of the original planting.

As for the ferns themselves, we should admire them, for they emerged roughly 400 million years ago, and are the oldest surviving tree form. Ferns reproduce through spores. Each one sends out a small shoot that grows into a rudimentary plant. This organism contains male and female cells, which fuse to form an embryo fern. But this can only happen in highly propitious damp circumstances. Bute, needless to say, has the per-fect climate. Seed-bearing plants first appeared around 360 million years ago, forty million years after ferns. In the words of the botanist Colin Tudge, 'Spores are like children setting out on a wild adventure with nothing but high spirits and a bag of toffees.' Unlike spores, seeds go forth equipped with carbohydrates, protein and fat for an arduous adventure. Conifers, among the oldest surviving seed-bearing tree forms, appeared about 300 million years ago. To put this into perspective with the animal world, the first dinosaurs appeared 150 million years ago, and ourselves, *Homo sapiens sapiens*, only around 100,000 years ago. So stand in awe of these tree ferns, the true Ancients of the Earth. Against all the odds, their bags of toffees and their high spirits got them through.

Continue northwards along the road, passing the Railway Convalescent Home.
Once the home of a sister of the Marquess and known as Ascog Mansion, this property was purchased by the Railwayman's Convalescent Home in 1924. The charity had nine convalescent homes in all, but this one uniquely was not single sex, spouses were allowed in too. Perhaps it inspired the Sally Army at Balmory House three years later.

On your right you will pass a dilapidated boathouse, possibly dating from the mid-nineteenth century. Behind it is an abandoned narrow inlet in the rock, modified by Robert Thom in 1832 for the import of coal and limestone. It looks as if the red sandstone blocks of the boathouse may have been purloined from the abandoned saltpan (see below).

Ascog Church. This site took the fancy of a man called David Bell, who was not an Ascog resident but lived in Craigmore. He thought it was an ideal location for a church. Architecturally, one can see why. When the minister of Kingarth's support for his project began to cool, he pressed ahead and turned to the minister in Rothesay, a policy, one might say, of divide and rule. The church was the last commission for the architect, David Hamilton, completed in the last year of his life, 1843, probably by his son, James. You will see his handywork again, a couple of hundred metres on. Hamilton was Scotland's leading architect and the doyen of Glasgow architecture. You may have seen his work before. He designed Glasgow's Royal Exchange, now home to the city's vibrantly innovative Museum of Modern Art. When in 1857 a new concert hall was erected in Glasgow, decorative medallion heads included George Frederick Handel for music, Joshua Reynolds for art and David Hamilton for architecture.

You might be thinking, since it was built in 1843, that this church was erected specifically to provide for the congregation displaced by the Disruption that year, but no. It had been commissioned without any

obvious purpose except that the headland cried out for a suitable sce-
nic building and possibly to save local people the need to trudge either
to Kingarth or Rothesay for Sabbath worship. It was a building nearing
completion when the Disruption unexpectedly gave it a more vigorous
purpose, as a meeting place for the democratically-minded who had resolved to establish a Free Church in Bute. It became the very first Free
Church building in Scotland. Sadly now empty, it still exudes an air of
elegant simplicity.

On the south wall, a stone between two yews marks the burial place
of Montague Stanley (1809-44), an actor and landscape painter, whose
career began at the tender age of seven in the role of Ariel in *The Tempest*.
He subsequently played in Dublin, Edinburgh and London. Although entirely untrained, he also became a regular exhibitor at the Royal Scottish
Academy, of which he became an honorary member. His landscapes were
romantic, but almost all were lost in a fire. With his health failing due to
TB, Stanley moved to Ascog in January 1844, hoping to benefit from its
climate, but he died that May, aged only 35. A man of deep faith, he presumably faced death with perfect equanimity.

The Salt Pan. Adjacent to the church, facing onto the edge of the bay,
stand the ruins of a drying kiln for salt panning. It is of indeterminate
date, but there is a strong case for 1763. The flues ran horizontally in the
bowed end, with a chimney at the opposite end. However, there is no
record of it ever being put into production.

The place remains an intriguing mystery. Two reasons were given by
a local historian a century ago for its failure, the first being that the vessel
bringing two saltpans from the mainland foundered. Surely, however, if
the project were viable, replacement saltpans would have been ordered.
The second reason offered was that the local coal seam, upon which the
kiln was predicated, proved insufficient. That would date the building
to 1763 when there was an unsuccessful attempt to revive mining of the
Ascog coal seam (there was another attempt in 1926). Yet there is a more
compelling reason to plump for the year 1763. Scottish salt had never
been of good quality. Since the sixteenth century, if not earlier, 'Bay' salt
from the Biscay coast was greatly preferred, particularly for curing herring. At moments of military conflict when supplies were interrupted,
the Scottish salt industry revived. When Spain was drawn into the Seven
Years' War in 1761, on the side of France against Britain, Bay salt would

have been unavailable. There would have been a sudden demand for Scottish salt, as there was again later, during the Napoleonic wars. The Seven Years' War ended in 1763, when the market for Scottish salt collapsed overnight.

As you enter the bay note on your left the Old Manse. It was built around 1860, presumably because Ascog Hall, the first manse, was the private property of the first incumbent, James Monteith.

Turn left up the drive immediately after the Old Manse. At the top of the drive stand three buildings, from right to left:
Meikle Ascog was built by Robert Thom (p. 301) in 1840 as a home, having purchased the whole estate including Ascog House nine years previously.

The miniscule stair tower to its left is a piece of Edwardian whimsy.

Ascog House, the *pièce de résistance*, appears to have been originally an L-shaped tower house of the early seventeenth century. It was extensively modified towards the end of the century (one of the altered east dormers is dated 1678), with floor levels altered and windows moved, and a stair tower added, topped with a gable watch-chamber.

It is difficult to be sure what is original and how much was changed around 1678. It is similar to and contemporary with Rothesay's Mansion House, making one suspect the same builder's hand. The house was built by the Stewarts of Ascog, a cadet branch of the principal Bute family. Yet its most colourful owner must have been Archibald MacArthur, an Edinburgh lawyer of the second half of the eighteenth century, who adopted the surname Stewart on inheriting the house. *Kay's Original Portraits* tells us he was:

> a gentleman somewhat eccentric in several particulars. He generally wore white clothes…. and had a peculiar manner of throwing his legs over each other in walking, which was owing probably to his great corpulency…. a bachelor not of the most continent of habits, he is said to have been exceedingly parsimonious in his domestic

Archibald McArthur Stewart, who loved pigs.

arrangements.... He had a great attachment to swine, and kept a litter of pigs in his bedroom.

If he ever came here with his pigs, he must have been in acute need of more generous windows. Backing out, mentally, from the porcine noisome-ness within, one can see that the landscaped garden belongs to a quite different era, reputedly the work of Edward La Trobe Bateman and dating probably from around 1890.

Both Meikle Ascog and Ascog house are now let as holiday homes by the Landmark Trust.

Ascog Bank, the epitome of elegance at the apex of the bay was built by David Hamilton, possibly for Robert Thom, around 1833. Only thirty years separate the symmetry of Ascog Bank from the asymmetry of the Old Manse, yet one can see what a revolution has taken place in architectural fashion.

As you leave the bay's sandy strand on your right, on your left once stood a Victorian villa, Anne's Lodge.

You must excuse this excursion into a building one can no longer see, for it had three claims to fame. A successful cotton merchant and provost of Glasgow, Robert Bartholomew, built his holiday home here, naming it after his wife's nickname, Annie, her full given name being Susan

Anne's Lodge, seen from across the bay.

Jane Cunninghame Graham. Bartholomew was a keen gardener and friend of the curator of the Glasgow Botanic Garden, who passed to him a gift of seeds from the director at Kew. Thus it was here that *Rhododendron edgeworthii*, a species with 'delightfully pink-flushed petals' first flowered in the open air in Britain in 1863. Joseph Hooker had brought its seeds back to Britain in 1849, among the awesome array of rhododendrons he had found in Sikkim, Assam and Nepal. His father, Sir William, the director of Kew, managed to grow it but only under glass in 1851.

Susan Henn seems as much at home with a golf club as a jib sheet.

Bartholomew, however, triumphantly enticed it out of its shyness with the clemency of Bute.

Widowed early, it was perhaps natural that Robert Bartholomew should nickname his infant daughter Annie, though she too was a Susan. More to the point, she was a Cunninghame Graham on her mother's side, and thus naturally imbued with a thirst for adventure. On her marriage to William Henn RN, she became a passionate yachtswoman, making history as the first woman to compete in the America's Cup, in 1886. It was not the sort of thing nice ladies were supposed to do, but as the *New York Times* reported:

> The…. participation in the races by Mrs Henn has largely added, no doubt, to the feminine interest taken in the contests…. It is gratifying to feel that the recipient of this interest and attention had justified it by her brave sharing of her husband's voyage and contests and her devotion to *Galatea* [their yacht]. If there was any regret felt among the thousands who on Tuesday witnessed the finish that the fleet-winged cutter had not vanquished her rival, it was when pretty Mrs Henn, in her sailor costume and jaunty crimson Tam O'Shanter, stood saucily, with her arms akimbo, on the deck of *Galatea* as she swept through the long line formed by hundreds of excursion steamers.'

When she died, in 1911, aged only 58, she bequeathed Anne's Lodge to her cousin, that romantic hero, Robert Bontine Cunninghame Graham (1852-1936).

This is Anne's (or rather, St Anne's, for it was canonised at some point) Lodge's greatest claim to fame. Samuel Johnson famously observed that 'every man thinks meanly of himself for not having been a soldier', yet take it from an ex-soldier, if we men should think meanly of ourselves, it should be for not having lived a life like that of Cunninghame Graham. His was filled with romantic adventure. As the young 'Don Roberto', he rode with the gauchos of Argentina, but he was also imbued with political passion. For having started his career as a Liberal, he became a founder, alongside Keir Hardie, of the Scottish Labour Party and then, disgruntled with Labour, of the Scottish National Party, with Hugh MacDiarmid and the Duke of Montrose. Although born into the landed class, he had a passionate concern for so-

Robert Bontine Cunninghame Graham (1852-1936) in convict's attire, found guilty of unlawful assembly in Trafalgar Square. As an MP he delighted in being controversial. He condemned imperialism, racial prejudice, corporal and capital punishment and child labour. He was an advocate of the eight-hour working day, free education and home rule for both Ireland and Scotland, and the general nationalisation of industry. Only on the latter has he proved not sure-footed.

cial justice. None of this prevented him from becoming a prolific writer too. Endearingly, but fatally for political success, his heart often ruled his head. Whether his politics appeal to you or not, Cunninghame Graham was a dauntlessly free spirit and it is impossible not to feel envious of that quality.

After 200 metres on the left stands Chandler's Hotel. Built in 1900, this was originally a Catholic school for girls aged 8-15, but during the summer vacation part of the building was used by Glasgow Corporation for an August 'Fresh Air Fortnight', for poor children, a scheme that lasted into the 1970s.

As you round the final corner to Millbank, from where you started, you may care to know that when the road was laid here, the labourers 'dug treasure to the amount, it was said, of many hundred pieces of silver pence.' It is unclear what precisely happened. One version suggests that the discovery was made as the light was fading and the overseer, clearly a complete innocent abroad, instructed that the hoard be covered over, to be recovered the next day. Needless to say, he was disappointed in human nature the following morning. The alternative version, given by John Blain, is that as soon as the hoard was revealed:

> upward of a dozen [workmen] immediately seized on the precious store – some carrying off handfuls which they disposed of as they thought fit. Purchases were made of them very freely at sixpence apiece. They were chiefly Edward I of England, a small quantity only of Alexander of Scotland.

Blain was the driving force behind construction of this road in 1814, when he finally overcame the objections of local proprietors, so his version is likely to be the correct one. As for the coinage, it was reckoned to date from about 1334. It is thought that this hoard must have been cash, either dropped or hidden, by a member of the English garrison fleeing Rothesay castle after the battle of Barone Hill (see p.342).

End of walk.

Kerrycroy

Kerrycroy (in Gaelic, *ceathramh-cruaidh*, 'the parcel of land in the hillside declivity') is such a delight that it merits a 10-minute halt. It was created as a small port when Scoulag ferry port was enclosed within the Mount Stuart estate in 1804. It served the route to Largs. At one time cattle were ferried across from Kintyre to Scalpsie Bay, driven across to Kerrycroy and ferried to Largs. This lasted barely a generation before steamer traffic rendered the port obsolete.

This delightful model village proclaims its split personality: there are Scots houses, built to house estate workers, probably just after construction of the quay, around 1810, and English Arts & Crafts vernacular houses built in the 1880s by the 3rd Marquess for his English wife, Gwendolen, so that she could have something comfortingly English to look at. Somehow each style says something about the Scottish and English character: the Scots, straightforward, strait-laced and unpretentious, the English more elaborate, wealthier and softer. The central house served as an inn for ferry passengers. Today the scene is politely trim. Coming here on her way to Mount Stuart in 1840 (thus, well before the English housing), the novelist Catherine Sinclair spoke of the working village:

> a very pretty, prosperous village, tastefully festooned in all directions with fishing-nets, and with graceful lines of salted haddocks and whitings basking in the sun.

A local man, J. Burnett Lawson, remembered in his dotage in 1923, what Kerrycroy had been like in his youth,

> a happy smiling hamlet of small uniform one-storey houses, with small gothic windows.... The houses were white washed, had little flower pots in front and large culinary gardens behind. The centre house was two-storied and for a number of years was the village

inn…. Though the houses were small the people thrived in them, as well they might, for cows, pigs and poultry were in the village in sufficiency, and from well-tended gardens, there was extracted potatoes and vegetables in abundance so that plain wholesome food, rich in all the vitamins, found its way to the table in every home.

In the 1880s the central house ceased to be an inn and was adapted as a schoolhouse, but this too had closed by 1920.

Mount Stuart and its Family

THE HOUSE

The original house was completed in 1719. The 2nd Earl commissioned it from Alexander McGill, a leading builder of country houses in Scotland, on the advice of his Edinburgh lawyer who wrote:

> If [McGill] give you ane plane of your house and lykwayce of the grounds for gardens and other policies with any schem of the cost, my friend and I thinks, ye can give no less than ten guineas and tua or thrie guinies for his charges in coming and goeing soe long ane journey. I hope he will please you exactlie for he knows his business verie well.

In 1718 McGill's design for a chaste classical building was put into effect, its timbers imported from Norway. (The closest surviving similar house is the House of Gray in Dundee, recently rescued from dilapidation.) The walls were faced with white lime harling, edged at the corners with pink sandstone. When it was first built, it must have looked smart. By 1840, however, in the words of Catherine Sinclair, 'the external aspect is very like a dilapidated barrack, [and here she gives herself away] greatly requiring a few touches of the trowel... to metamorphose the very plain front into a more tasteful exterior.' One must bear in mind that she was visiting just as the classical style was going out of fashion and she clearly had no awareness of the maxim 'less is more', that spare quality that so characterises British architecture compared with its more florid continental counterparts, be it in classicism, the Gothic Revival or indeed Arts & Crafts. Nor did she live long enough to see its replacement.

Opposite: The original Mount Stuart House celebrates the coming of age of the 3rd Marquess in 1869.

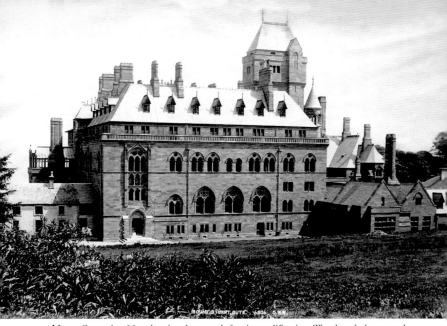

Mount Stuart in 1889, showing the tower before its modification. The chapel, the covered porch and the gallery on the 4th floor have yet to be added.

The new house. In December 1877 the house was destroyed by fire, but mercifully not before almost all its contents were saved. Despite his passion for medievalism and the gothic, the 3rd Marquess had been fond of the old house and he must have been thankful that his one significant addition, the installation of the gem of a chapel by William Burges in one wing, was saved. He must have considered using Burges again, since it was Burges he had commissioned to design Cardiff Castle and Castell Coch.

However, he liked to vary his choice of architect. He was sufficiently versed in both the Gothic Revival and in medieval scholarship to recognise the up-and-coming Robert Rowand Anderson (1834-1921) as the man he needed. In due course Anderson became Scotland's leading architect. Like all great architects, Anderson believed that the beauty of his designs would lie in their functional and structural efficiency, not in their decoration. Lord Bute had no wish to rush this great project and construction did not start until 1880. He himself knew a thing or two about good architecture and pored over Anderson's plans, examining everything minutely. Unlike many country seats simply done to order, here one can sense the owner's own passionate belief in the project, a triumphant

symbiosis between architect and client. It is Lord Bute's own close in-
volvement in every detail which, surely, makes Mount Stuart a truly great
building.

Look at the Italian Gothic flat wall planes of Mount Stuart, wonderfully
free of fiddly décor, and the Venetian windows of the principal floor. The
elegant eaves and gallery were an afterthought, based on work Anderson
had done elsewhere. In contrast with so many disappointing Gothic
Revival buildings, Mount Stuart is a shining example of successful asymmetry, after the symmetry of the classical tradition. One may walk around
the exterior taking delight in every last detail, each the product of careful
thought.

Lord Bute commissioned the finest craftsmen of the day to furnish
the interior, in stone, timber, glass and decorative paintwork. Of these,
the most noteworthy was the young Robert Weir Schultz (1860-1951), a
leading exemplar of the Arts & Crafts movement and a noted Byzantinist
(see p.111).

THE GARDENS

The entry ticket includes a map of the garden, but it may be useful to have a
short background.

The pleasure grounds, or policies, surrounding Mount Stuart House
have been the object of assiduous planting ever since the house was constructed. The policies were laid out at first to be productive, orchards and
vegetable gardens surrounding and on the landward side of the house.
Yet the seaward side of the house, with its magnificent view, demanded
a layout in keeping with the ideas of the landscaped garden which had
taken root so rapidly in England in direct contrast, one might even say
antagonism, to the highly formalised layouts which characterised the
great gardens of Europe, essentially staged settings on which the aristocracy could pose and look cool. In England, and by extension Scotland,
the new idea was to re-create 'nature'. To our eye the result is still formalised, but to those who had once minced along formal paths past pocket
handkerchief-sized lawns, with fountains, statuary and flowerbeds that
imitated soldiers on the parade ground, such gardens were a visual revolution. One of the early champions of the new style was William Kent
who, in the words of one admirer, 'leaped the fence and found that all
nature was a garden.'

Large trees, both natives and exotics, became highly desirable. The first planting here reflects this: natives such as beech, alder, elm, and hornbeam. It was probably in the 1740s that the young 3rd Earl planted sessile oak, ash and lime. He also planted exotics, some old established introductions, like the sweet chestnut and sycamore, and more recent ones, for example the holm and cork oaks, and the tulip tree.

Straight wide avenues were laid as walks through woodland, both in grid pattern and diagonals, the whole described according to the fashion of the day as 'Wilderness'. One traveller, sailing past in 1797, noted 'an avenue is opened from the front of the house through the Trees the whole way to the Shore which makes it look very pretty.' Limes were a popular tree for lining an avenue on account of their compact shape, compared with the spread of oak or beech. The intersection of these avenues is marked by a column, surmounted by a statue of Princess Augusta, the mother of George III, for whom Lord Bute had the highest regard (p.106). He had it erected at Luton Park on her death in 1772, and it was brought here in the 1870s. You will find an inscription from Virgil's *Aeneid*, pledging not to forget her: 'As long as I have my memory and my spirit controls my body.' Another structure to enhance the delights of strolling here is the Folly, probably built around 1800.

Much of the lower policies down near the shore are beech woodland. This seems to be deliberate. Beech trees have shallow roots and so can still flourish even though the red sandstone is frequently little more than 12 inches beneath the soil surface.

SCOULAG PORT

This ferry port is still visible at low water, with Old Red Sandstone blocks at the head of the cove, and the footings of an old boathouse. (It is opposite the Edwardian dwelling near the seashore, marked on the Mount Stuart map as a green inlet through the rock). In 1680 Donald McFie was given the monopoly as ferrier on the Largs route, 'provydeing always that he keep meet drink and bedding for strangers and particularly that he want not meile for ther entertainment quhile thay are lying att the ferry.' It was expected for ferriers to provide board and lodging ashore. Perhaps he failed in these requirements, for he was replaced in 1683. The trouble with running what, effectively, was an inn was that it attracted local topers. In 1751 the kirk sessions record that 'several peopel continue drinking in the fferrie house upon the Lord's day not only betwixt sermons but sometimes also during the afternoon sermon.' It must have been here that the Welsh traveller, Thomas Pennant landed in 1772. In 1804 the 1st Marquess enclosed Scoulag port to enlarge his policies and created Kerrycroy Port on the new north boundary.

Scoulag Kirk is a classic Presbyterian mid-eighteenth century church. Following the enclosure of Scoulag within the Mount Stuart policies, the church became, in John Blain's words, 'a very genteel and convenient chapel of the [Bute] family.' It is usually locked but still contains many original features such as the oak pulpit, the laird's loft of panelled wood with an entablature above. It may have been here that the Reverend James Stewart got himself into trouble with the Presbytery in 1746 (p.309), and Alexander Carlyle preached (p.114).

NINETEENTH CENTURY ADDITIONS

The Wee Garden was started in 1823 by Maria North, wife of the 2nd Marquess. On the opposite side of the Forty Five Avenue (feet between trees, not the '45 Rebellion), lies the Bowling Green, laid out in the 1720s for the 2nd Earl, but noteworthy for the fine steps leading down to it, designed by Robert Weir Schultz in 1897 (see p.111).

The Pinetum contains exotic conifer discoveries of the nineteenth century, principally from north east America, by such daring collectors as David Douglas and his successors. Most notable are the Douglas fir, the Western Red Cedar, Western Hemlock and Wellingtonia, and from the Himalayas the Deodar Cedar. But there are plenty others besides.

The Rock Garden. This was designed in 1896 by Thomas Mawson (1861-1933), well enough known to have acquired the epithet 'landscape architect of the Empire'. At the time when the 3rd Marquess commissioned him, however, he was still a young man with promise, working on private gardens principally in the Lake District where he was based. Although the Rock Garden has been replanted at least twice, the skill of the original design remains evident. Mawson wrote one of the gardening best-sellers of his day, *The Art and Craft of Garden Making* (1900).

The **Via Dolorosa** and **Racers Burn**. Mawson was also asked to make something of the Racers Burn that ran down to the shore south of the house. He installed a number of small cascades, best seen from the bridge on the principal drive. These were intended to replicate the stations on the Via Dolorosa in Jerusalem but remained unfinished owing to the failing health of the Marquess.

TWENTIETH CENTURY ADDITIONS

The Kitchen Garden. Kitchen gardens were an essential accessory to any large mansion and the first one was, naturally, close to the house. The present garden, on the site of one laid out in the late nineteenth century, has been designed decoratively, with plenty of space yet to be used, around a central pavilion purchased in 1988.

General restoration. Most of the gardens have enjoyed careful restoration since the 1950s.

The Stuarts and Crichton-Stuarts up to 1900

The following lists family members who made a notable contribution to development of the island and of Mount Stuart. The Stuarts are descended from John Stewart, the natural son of Robert II who, in 1385, was appointed the hereditary Sheriff of Bute, Arran and Cumbrae. The spelling of Stewart was changed around 1600, to conform with French and English ideas of how the name should be spelt.

The 1st Earl. Sir James Stuart (1651-1710) had a chequered career on account of the overthrow of James VII. Although he represented Buteshire in the Scottish Parliament, he refused to take the oath of allegiance to William III. King James, after all, was a distant cousin, moreover his home had recently been destroyed by the anti-Stuart faction, p.30. He was compelled to vacate his parliamentary seat in 1693. With the accession of Queen Anne, his Stuart loyalty was rewarded, not only with reinstatement to the Scottish parliament but also ennoblement. His title was quite a mouthful: '1st Earl of Bute, viscount of Kingarth, Lord Mount Stuart, Cumra, and Inchmarnock.' He absented himself when the Union was debated and carried in the Scottish parliament in 1706.

The 2nd Earl. His son, James (1690-1723), succeeded him in 1710 and built the original Mount Stuart in the classical tradition of the period. He sat in the Westminster Parliament in the Tory interest as a representative peer for Scotland.

The 3rd Earl. His son, John (1713-92), was brought up in London and sent to Eton College, assuming the title at the age of ten on the death of his father in 1723. He was brought up as a firm Hanoverian by his two Campbell uncles, the 2nd Duke of Argyll and Archibald, Earl of Ilay. He spent his holidays at the Ilay seat at Whitton (now engulfed in Greater London). It was here, in his uncle's renowned arboretum and library, that the 3rd Earl acquired his love of botany and horticulture. After studying in Leiden, he settled at Mount Stuart in 1732, staying there until 1736. That year he married Mary Wortley Montagu, a wealthy heiress, a match bitterly but unsuccessfully opposed by her mother, the famous writer and adventurer. Her father gave her away, ill-temperedly withholding her dowry. The marriage proved happy and eventually endowed the penniless earl with the wealth he badly needed to advance his prospects. Over the next six years Lord Bute proved his qualities, his once disapproving mother-in-law re-writing history: 'the character I always believed belonged to him from the first of our acquaintance, and the opinion I had of his honesty (which is the most essential quality) made me so easily consent to the match.' And another six years later, she wrote: 'What I think extraordinary is my daughter's continuing so many years agreeable to Lord Bute; … that he was as much in love with his wife as before he married her.' Doubtless she realised her daughter was no beauty but she was, in the words of Horace Walpole, 'one of the best and most sensible women in the world'. And, clearly, Lord Bute was an amiable man.

After his failure to be re-elected to Parliament in 1741, Lord Bute retired for five years to Mount Stuart. It is probably to this that we owe the creation of the magnificent and extensive gardens. It was indeed during this time that he became yet more obsessed with botany. He left for London in 1746, and seems not to have returned to Bute again. Attending the Egham races on a rainy day in 1747, he was asked by Frederick, Prince of Wales, to look after his son, the future George III, in the royal tent. This was clearly a great success, for Prince Frederick and his wife, Augusta, soon asked him to be tutor to the young Prince George.

In the meantime Lord Bute had acquired an international reputation as an expert in botany, and patron of botanists. So widespread was his fame that in 1753 Carl Linnaeus, the great botanical cataloguer, was asked to name the North American *Stewartia* shrub after 'a

Lord of Iland Bute in Scotland, an ingenious gentleman who knows Dr Linneus' Methods extremely well.' Indeed, we owe Britain's distinguished contribution to botanical study in great measure to him, for he encouraged, advised and actively helped the widowed Princess Augusta to create her botanical garden at Kew. He moved to Kew Green to be close to her and her project, which caused scurrilous and almost certainly false innuendoes to be made about their relationship. They shared a passion for botany, not for each other.

Lord Bute enjoyed such trust with the young George III on his accession in 1760 that he was asked to form an administration, once the government which the king had inherited collapsed in 1762. Yet his premiership was short-lived and unhappy and he resigned fifteen months later. He never returned to Mount Stuart, but settled in Hampshire. However, he used the extensive wealth of his wife to advance botanical and scientific study, particularly in Scotland. Indeed, he was the outstanding noble patron of scholarship in the second half of the eighteenth century. He lies in the family vault in Rothesay kirkyard (p.38). As for his development of Bute, he must be credited with initiating the revolution that transformed the productivity of the island (pp.258-262), and inspiring his descendants to follow suit. We are all in his debt.

The 1st Marquess. John (1744-1814) was born at Mount Stuart. Like his father, he was brought up in the South, and educated at Harrow and Winchester. Like his father, too, he made a shrewd dynastic marriage, to a wealthy heiress, Charlotte Jane Windsor, who inherited a substantial slice of Glamorgan, including a little known market town and port by the name of Cardiff. His political career and support of William Pitt in 1794 led to his elevation as 1st Marquess of Bute, having briefly been 4th Earl.

However, it was during his father's lifetime, as Lord Mountstuart, that he was particularly zealous in advancing the agricultural revolution his father had started. Alongside his diligence, he also had a major care for the well-being of ordinary people in Bute, by no means a common characteristic of the landed aristocracy at that time.

The 2nd Marquess. John Crichton-Stuart (1793-1848) was his grandson, since the son of the 1st Marquess predeceased him. It was through his mother, the daughter of Patrick Macdowal Crichton,

6th Earl of Dumfries, that he acquired the name, titles and estates of his mother's family. Like his grandfather and great grandfather, Lord Bute was a passionate improver. Unlike them, however, he devoted his time almost exclusively to attending to his estates in Bute, Ayr, Wigtown and Glamorgan, not to mention his other properties in Newcastle upon Tyne and Luton Hoo. It must have been confusing, having so many places to think about. He is best known for investing most of the family fortune into the development of the Cardiff docks and the Rhondda Valley. In 1801 Cardiff had been twenty-fifth in size among Welsh towns. By 1870, some 22 years after the 2nd Marquess's death, his project had rendered it the largest. Back in Bute his reputation rested on his commitment to his tenantry and his practical interest in their agriculture, so much so that the extent of arable land was trebled during his period of tenure.

The 3rd Marquess. John Patrick Crichton-Stuart (1847-1900) was born at Mount Stuart. Orphaned as a child, he acquired a love for medievalism and the ritual of the Catholic Church. Packed off to a preparatory school, his first school report warned that he had 'a liking for the Romish priesthood and ceremonial' and that his attitude to religion would not prove to the taste of the British public.

Thus, even as a child, Lord Bute belonged mentally to Rome. Before going to Oxford he made a tour of the East, including Palestine. We can sense his rare piety from a letter he wrote from Christ Church, Oxford, during Holy Week in 1867. He had very reluctantly just promised not to convert to Catholicism until he reached his majority, and felt he had betrayed his Saviour: 'Instead of feeling these holy days, the thought of the suffering of Christ simply haunts me like a nightmare.' He longed to be a member of a colourful, artistic and emotional church rather than the straitlaced kirk of his upbringing. The news of his conversion to Catholicism caused the people of Bute to gasp in horror. In the words of *The Rothesay Chronicle*, 9 January, 1869,

> The announcement respecting Lord Bute's conversion to the Roman Catholic faith, which was made a fortnight ago.... fell like a thunderbolt on this island....we must join with our fellow islanders in deploring his Lordship's abandonment of the faith of his fathers.

The 3rd Marquess in his robes of office as Provost of Rothesay.

JOHN 3ᴿᴰ MARQUESS OF BUTE. K.T.

The faith of his fathers? Lord Bute's forebears had built St Mary's in Rothesay in the fourteenth century and more distantly granted St Blane's to Cluny. At the time of his conversion there were about 500 Catholics on the island, some Highlanders, others Irish. One catches the mood of this remarkable young man from a letter written in 1870:

> Last Sunday I was at Largs, on the mainland opposite, and heard an early Mass in a very poor cottage – said in the kitchen on a small chest of drawers. The house was crowded with the congregation, standing on the stairs, in the passages, and all the rooms. They were wonderfully devout. Out of the East I never saw such a sight.

Lord Bute was not only given to piety but to great learning, about the medieval and eastern churches. Brandane Presbyterian prejudice was silenced by his intelligent philanthropy on the island. One retired farmer described Lord Bute as 'one of the most generous landlords in the country.' He restored Rothesay castle, St Blane's and Wester

Kames, employing the skills of William Burges for the castle, and Robert Weir Schultz for the latter two projects. Further afield he was well known as an enlightened sponsor, scholar and patron of archaeology, architecture and medieval studies. He was twice mayor of Cardiff, and provost of Rothesay, both duties carried out to acclaim. He was president of the University College, Cardiff and rector of St Andrews University. At Glasgow University he funded the Bute Hall, built to the designs of George Gilbert and John Oldrid Scott. He collaborated with William Burges in rebuilding Cardiff Castle and creating Castell Coch, both landmarks of the Gothic Revival. Indeed, his architectural work with Burges in Cardiff was a prelude to the rebuilding of Mount Stuart.

The family in the twentieth century and beyond

Since the death of the 3rd Marquess in 1900 his descendants have continued imaginatively to curate Mount Stuart and the wider Bute Estate covering much of the island, and to support and foster the island community. To these ends the 4th Marquess donated the Meadows in Rothesay to the community (for shinty and other activities) and the Bute Museum building (for the study of the island's natural and human history), while the 5th Marquess donated Rothesay Castle (so painstakingly restored by his grandfather) to the nation. He also established a factory in 1947, 'to help to give employment to ex-servicemen and women in the Isle of Bute', now known as Bute Fabrics. Still run as a family business, it remains a principal employer on the island. The 6th Marquess (1933-93) carried out extensive restoration at Mount Stuart, completing projects unfinished by the 3rd Marquess, an undertaking unmatched elsewhere in Scotland. He also provided financial and practical support to save the Winter Garden and Victorian toilets, the first buildings that greet visitors to Rothesay. As a natural progression of the work of his father, the 7th Marquess, Johnny Bute, opened Mount Stuart to the public in 1995, and in 2001 also commissioned the award-winning Visitor Centre (designed by Munkenbeck + Marshall). He and his immediate family seek to follow the work of their forebears: to cherish and advance the interests of Bute and its inhabitants.

Schultz's design for Scoulag Lodge, drawn by William Curtis Green.

Scoulag Lodge
(on the road to the Kingarth Hotel)

This house is a little gem, built in 1897. It is the work of a highly gifted architect, Robert Weir Schultz (1860-1951). Schultz, born in Port
Glasgow, had come to the notice of the 3rd Marquess because of their
mutual interest in Byzantine church architecture. Schultz carried out a
number of commissions for him, and had he been willing to become a
Catholic, he might have been invited to design Westminster Cathedral,
which was to be constructed in the Byzantine style. Here, however, he
was asked to build a small lodge. The site is extremely awkward because
of the narrow angle of two roads, but Schultz was determined to dem-
onstrate that small, as well as grand, houses merited and benefited from
careful design. As Schultz himself wrote: 'there is always a workable, reasonable, commonsense solution to every problem, and here I would say
that it consists in adhering, as near as may be, to the general influence of
the type of the district and not using materials that will jar.' The result is
a minor masterpiece, which embodies the other great passion of Schultz,
the Arts & Crafts Movement. The heraldic arms displayed are those of
Windsor, Stuart and Crichton (the Glamorgan, Bute and Dumfries estates). In keeping with the Scots vernacular, the exterior is rough harled,
and the roof slated from the Kames quarry (where else?). The guttering
is of lead, characteristic of the best of Arts & Crafts building. It comes as
no surprise that Schultz was also the architect of the reconstruction of
Wester Kames.

Kingarth

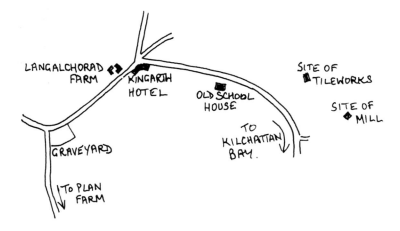

The **Kingarth Hotel** was built as a farmhouse in 1786, long after Langalchorad – its actual location – became the acknowledged centre of the parish. Today 'Kingarth' seldom means the whole south end of Bute. It is used only to refer to the settlement at Langalchorad, comprising the Hotel and the graveyard and the four or five houses nearby. It is now Bute's country pub, well known to all islanders for its conviviality. Adjoining the hotel is the smiddy, now incorporated into the hotel.

Ian Fisher (p.123) remembers one of the last smiths, Jimmy Begg, here in the 1920s, 'who lived in the broken down cottage beside the school…. He had a clay pipe…. He'd draw on the anvil with his clay pipe [to show a client how he would do a job]…. He did all the repairs to ploughs and other bits of machinery… There were no tractors then.'

Kingarth School, 1923/24. William Esplin, the parish dominie stands on the left of the back row. Ian Fisher stands one row forward, fifth from the left, his sister Jenny and brother Robert, seventh and eighth respectively. This photograph must have been taken shortly after Ian had been leathered by Mr Esplin. One can see how unequal a contest it must have been.

The School House was still standing in 2009. In 1915 there were 80 children attending school in Kingarth. Over the twentieth century the numbers slowly attenuated, and the secondary school closed in favour of attendance in Rothesay. Finally, the primary school closed. Ian Fisher remembers attending school here in 1920:

> Boys ran about all summer, barefoot, short trousers and grey jerseys, till they left school anyway. We got out of our boots as soon as we got out of school. We were at the village infants' school till the age of eleven, when we went to Rothesay. The schoolmaster we had here in Kingarth, he was a real devil. He used the belt on your hand. If you took your hand away he used his fists on you. I had a fight with another boy once, and the schoolmaster took me to the cloakroom. He leathered me all around that cloakroom.

The dominie was William Esplin, who had nearly succeeded in getting the names on the war memorial stripped of their ranks (p.166). When he left Kingarth in 1929, he was dined and toasted: 'As a teacher who could look back for a period of fifty years, Mr Esplin had maintained the high traditions of the country dominies of Scotland, and had left indelible marks on the character of generations of children who had passed through his hands.' Perhaps we should be thinking of the marks on Ian Fisher's buttocks, still tingling with indelible indignation 85 years later.

Kingarth Graveyard. Like the other old kirkyards of Bute, this one has real atmosphere and merits a visit. It was here that the 'Mid Kirk' was completed in 1680 following the untimely collapse of St Blane's, further south (p.147) at the end of 1675. The new site was chosen to make Sabbath attendance easier for the majority of parishioners who lived mainly in the fertile farmlands in and north of the narrow neck of land between Kilchattan and Stravannan Bay. The kirk was designed to seat 250 persons. The elders did not forget the need for discipline and 'it was also appointed that the space betwixt the north door and the aisle be for a pillar of public repentance.'

It was either here or at the North Kirk (Scoulag Kirk) that that most genial of clerics, Alexander Carlyle, came with his friend, William Robertson, one Sunday in August 1766, 'where I lecturd [an exposition of Scriptural text] and Dr Robertson preacht.' Both were champions of the moderate wing of the Kirk and leading lights in the Scottish Enlightenment. They deserve a brief mention. Carlyle periodically got into hot water for his broad-mindedness. He wrote a wonderfully entertaining autobiographical journal which includes a vivid eye-witness account of the Jacobite army's entry into Edinburgh in 1745 and the subsequent battle of Prestonpans. Robertson also made his name as a moderate when he argued that since human knowledge of the Word is always imperfect, tolerance must of necessity be a fundamental religious principle. He went on to defend David Hume and other radicals from the wrath of the Kirk. But he also became Scotland's most celebrated historian of his day, his *History of Scotland* running to four editions and a French translation within six years of first publication in 1758. The Earl of Bute, one of Robertson's most enthusiastic supporters, helped secure his election as principal of Edinburgh University in 1762, an election described as 'the single most important step in institutionalising Enlightenment values in Edinburgh'.

Robertson and Carlyle had come to Bute on a jaunt with a large group of friends. Where they stayed is unclear, but it seems it was not in Rothesay itself:

> [We] passed our time very agreeably. Alexr. M'Millan was one of the best Landlords for a Large Company, for he was loud and joyful, and made the Wine flow like Bacchus himself. We past the Mornings.... in Riding about the Island which we found very Beautifull, tho' but little cultivated.....

It seems from Carlyle's journal that after Sunday service, they were entertained at Mount Stuart, where

> Our Conversation at Table was Liberal and Lively.... The wine was excellent, and flowed Freely. There was the best Cyprus [probably the dessert wine] I ever saw, which had lain there since Ld Bute had left the island in 1745 – The Claret was of the Same Age, and excellent.

In fact, it seems that the party drank their way through Lord Bute's wine cellar, consuming all his best claret. Belatedly Robertson began to have misgivings that they were abusing Mount Stuart hospitality, but it was far too late to stop. As he told Carlyle, 'Let us end as we began.' And so they did.

As for the 1680 church building, it fell into acute disrepair like its predecessor and was replaced in 1826, after it had been ruinous for some time. This building, too, eventually succumbed to the weather. A storm in January 1968 ripped the slates off the roof. Then, along came two Rothesay slaters who snecked all the roof lead, 375lbs in all. The kirk site, however, remains obvious from the open ground in the north-west corner of the kirkyard.

The kirkyard contains some remarkable graves, which testify both to the enduring kindred names of the island, particularly around the site of the old kirk, but also to the astonishing array of incomers, not merely from other parts of Britain, but further afield. The best thing is to wander around enjoying them. There are plenty of McFies, variously spelt. They are thought to have come from Colonsay in the early eighteenth century (but the McFies of Inchmarnock seem to have arrived in the seventeenth). In Kingarth some were wrights, presumably working at the Kingarth smiddy; others farmed at Gallachan and Quochag.

Stones of particular interest include:

A   **The Ardnahoe Seven:** 'the Seven Sufferers who Perished in the fire at Ardnahoe Farm, 8 July 1887' (their story is on p.153).

B   **Louis Conod,** 'a Swiss by birth, faithful servant to the Marquess of Bute who whilst bathing in the sea was unfortunately drouned, 12 July 1808.'

C   **John Sanders** had been ordained into the parish of Kingarth in 1878. In 1918 he suffered the unbearable blow of losing his son, Frank. He died in 1926, aged 74, after suffering ill health for some years. It seems, judging by the harsh words thrown at him (p. 166), that there had been a clash of egos between two of the 'top dogs' of the parish, himself and William Esplin, the dominie.

D   **The family MacKay.** Margaret McAlister knew a thing or two about bereavement. Born into the famous farming family at Mid-Ascog in 1859, she married Archibald MacKay of another well-known Bute farming family. Archibald had a well-founded reputation for a fine dairy herd at Bruchag Farm. He and the farmer at Meikle Kilchattan provided the south end of the island with milk and butter on alternate days. He was also an ace at breeding Clydesdales. He and Margaret lost their fourteen-year old son, Archibald, in 1901. Twelve years later Margaret was widowed, and a couple of years after that her 15-year old daughter Elizabeth died. Then the war claimed her eldest boy, John (see p.163). Like so many Brandane farmers, Margaret was possessed of dogged courage, ability and energy. She ran the farm with great flair after Archibald's death, until her eldest son, Robert, returned to take over in 1928. She died aged 90, in 1949.

E   **Archibald Ferguson** was a distinguished pipe-major in the Argyll & Sutherland Highlanders. He was born, appropriately, at Piperhall (just ½ km east of the Kingarth War Memorial) in 1871. His body was found floating in the Forth & Clyde Canal on 27 March 1907, not far from his barracks at Maryhill, Glasgow. He had been missing for a fortnight. Whether he jumped, fell or was pushed remains a mystery. He was buried here with full honours, four regimental pipers played his corpse into the kirkyard to *'Land o' the Leal'*, and after his interment the regimental lament, *'Lochaber No More.'* His brother, Donald, was also a piper, born in 1882. He migrated to British Columbia, married and begat five children. He died during military service in February 1918, his name inscribed on the Kingarth memorial.

F   **The family Fisher.** See p. 123.

Kilchattan Bay

In 1800 Kilchattan Bay was no more than a fishing settlement. The few fisher families lived in but-and-ben cottages, of which two or three survive and are easy to spot. Several of these cottages were still thatched in the early years of the twentieth century. The families probably grazed their cow on the hill behind and also on the links along the shore of the bay. The other significant building would

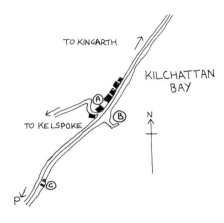

have been the corn mill, sited on the stream running into the northwest side of the bay. The first mill was licensed in 1474 and there was still a corn mill here in the mid-nineteenth century, now converted into a cottage. Under the feudal system of thirlage, tenant farmers were obliged to have their corn ground in the sheriff of Bute's mill here and pay a levy in kind, sometimes surreptitiously increased by dishonest millers. Thirlage occasioned massive resentment.

Sometime in the second half of the eighteenth century the 3rd Earl had 'built a draw-kiln for burning lime, which was sold to tenants at prime cost' Its **successor** (A), probably built around 1820, is still standing (just on the right hand side of and behind Kiln Villa). The limestone was quarried from the land below Kelspoke (it is now a long narrow reservoir on the hillside). Lime of particularly high quality was extracted by burning the limestone, with two uses in mind: as an essential ingredient for rendering Bute's acid soil fertile and as a building material, for mortar, harling and plaster. The economic potential of the kiln was considerable, for while limestone was scarce in Scotland, the country's mainly acid soil badly needed liming. Limited supply, high quality and huge demand ensured the lime produced here fetched a good price. It was particularly advantageous since the kiln was sited right beside the sea, rendering the transport of lime easy, compared with the then crippling cost of land transport. Demand rocketed from the late eighteenth century, since the agricultural revolution (p.258) led to demand not only for fertiliser but also for the construction of new steadings. The kiln only ceased production in about 1890.

Kilchattan's fine **stone quay** (B), more or less opposite the kiln, was built in 1822, presumably to export lime to destinations not only in the Clyde but also along Scotland's western seaboard. Lime is extremely volatile and would ignite if it came into contact with water. Great care would have been taken with its shipment to keep it dry. Because land routes were so atrocious, lime was shifted by boat even to destinations close at hand, Rothesay and Port Bannatyne, from where it was distributed by horse-drawn cart.

Low water at the stone quay, Kilchattan Bay, c.1900, with fishing vessels grounded. The boys in the foreground look like summer visitors.

Bute, The Old Pier, Kilchattan Bay.

The quay had other important uses, at first for the export of agricultural produce, but later for the delivery of coal and dross, and the export of bricks and tiles from a factory here. Between 1850 and 1880 it was also used for steamer traffic, although Ordnance Survey could still report in the early 1860s that 'the only traffic to it [the Bay] is an occasional lugger with coals, manure and lime for farming operations,' the coal, of course, imported, the lime exported. Ian Fisher remembered the coal boats:

> In my young days [1920s] two wooden sail boats brought the coal, the *Jess Ian* owned by John Hogarth, and the other boat called *The Vineyard*, owned by very religious people called Macmillan who said a prayer of thanksgiving each time they returned.

The *Jess Ian* may have had sail but it was also a 'puffer', driven by a coal-fired engine. It could carry 100 tons of coal and used to supply the gasworks in Rothesay, but also frequently took turnips to Greenock.

Behind the houses the slopes are covered in deciduous woodland, principally ash. We know the trees were here by the 1860s, for Ordnance Survey reported that 'the inhabitants were principally employed in fishing and woodcutting.' In fact there was a coherent fishing community here until the 1930s.

A tile works (now gone, marked on map, p.112) was established further north in 1849. Initially it also produced bricks (the nearby Mill Cottages were built with these bricks) but they proved too porous for Bute's damp climate. It was not a promising start and by 1855 the tileries and brickworks lay idle. Help was, however, at hand. In 1833 a civil engineer by the name of Josiah Parkes had been attempting to drain a moss in Lancashire for the local farmer when he made the startling discovery that deep drains (4 feet minimum), rather than the customary shallower drains, would remove excess water from soils. Ten years later he became consulting engineer to the newly formed Royal Agricultural Society of England and was thus able to propound his views in print. The removal of the stagnant water below rendered the topsoil porous and friable. It was the Great Leap Forward for nineteenth century agriculture. By the 1850s the government was beginning to provide subsidies to encourage farmers to lay deep drains. This unleashed a massive demand for drainage tiles, just when the Kilchattan Tileries had closed.

In 1866 a dynamic new manager took over the tenancy. He built a second kiln, designed his own steam-powered machine where his

The puffer Roman loading with early Kingarth potatoes, Kilchattan Bay in 1923.

predecessor had made tiles by hand. For the next thirty years or so, the kilns produced 1¼ million tiles annually, of which 250,000 were laid yearly in Bute. Such was the demand that carters in north Bute would set off shortly after midnight to be sure of a place in the queue that would have formed by dawn. The rest of the tiles left Kilchattan Bay by the stone quay, to enable the drainage of farmland all the way up the west coast, as far as Stornaway. Carts offloaded the tiles to the quayside, and uploaded with dross just landed from Ardrossan with which to fire the kilns. With virtual saturation of the market and exhaustion of the clay seam in c.1910, the business suddenly collapsed. But by then, Britain led the world in agricultural technique. Kilchattan can claim a place in that achievement. The last batch of tiles went out in 1915.

Potatoes. The other major export from the quay was early potatoes, for which Kilchattan Bay enjoyed a reputation across Lowland Scotland. They were often the first in the Glasgow marketplace, but potatoes were also exported through the summer. In August 1902, *The Buteman* reported what, in fact, was hardly news at all, since it happened yearly, 'Carts laden with fine tawties have been passing freely through the village for

Kilchattan Steamer Pier in its heyday.

some time…. And the steamers are kept busy clearing them from the quay.' Ian Fisher remembers both the sowing and 'howking' of potatoes:

> There was a big business in early potatoes. They would be put into barrels so that they would not bruise. There were three principal farmers here growing early potatoes…. They were mostly for Glasgow, but some were sold locally. Sowing potatoes was a back-breaking job, the farmer made sure of that, he kept you going. There were whole families did it, particularly girls and boys who had left school and not yet found work. You had to plant them at the right distance apart. There was a special plough for making the drills and then covering the potatoes over after they were planted. The Irish came over for digging the potato crop. They stayed in the farmer's barn, and cooked outside on a brazier. You used three pronged forks, called graipes, the prongs having blunt ends which could not pierce the potatoes. The baskets were filled and tipped into the farm cart. (For a vivid description by a tattie howker in 1905, see p.280.)

A wooden steamer pier (c) was built in 1880, marking the real development of Kilchattan. All that is now left is the stone approach, the old pier buildings converted to domestic housing. The wooden pier beyond was closed in 1955 and dismantled the following year. It had provided a regular service across to Fairlie. One could, in fact, get from Kilchattan Bay to

Glasgow in one hour 20 minutes.

As with Rothesay, an important new seasonal business grew up of receiving summer visitors from the Clyde and beyond. In its heyday, it is said that some six coaches would await the arrival of the steamers. Kilchattan Bay families would vacate the main rooms of their dwelling for the summer holiday month and move into one room. It is said that one family, having slaughtered its pig in April, retreated to the pig-sty when their house was let.

Most of the houses south of the stone quay and quite a few north of it, were built in the late nineteenth century, to accommodate holiday makers. Many were built by Glasgow families rich enough to build for letting and most were built after the establishment of a wooden pier for steamers in 1880. In the 1930s Kilchattan Bay had thirteen shops.

The family Fisher. Kilchattan Bay as a thriving community was short-lived. In their lifetime Willie Fisher and his son Ian saw its rise and fall. Willie was born in 1879 and grew up in a small dwelling with a thatched roof on the shore side, near the stone quay. In about 1889 the family moved to the Gatehouse, a thatched cottage on the Plan Road, half way between Kingarth graveyard and Largizean. Willie looked after the

Gatehouse, the thatched but-and-ben where Willie Fisher once lived, on the Plan Road, between Langalchorad (Kingarth) and Largizean.

golf course and bowling green there, paid 6d an hour (about £1.35 in to-day's terms). He started work with the General Post Office in 1898, deliver-ing mail on foot through the southern part of the parish, Kerrytonlia, the Butts, and on foot across to Ardscalpsie. In 1907 he married Christina Black from Kilchattan Butts, up the hill towards Mount Stuart. By the time their son Ian was born in 1912, they were staying in the Bay at Daisy Bank, a tenement that still carries the name. Ian recalled his childhood in the following words:

William Fisher in his Post Office kit with his wife, Christina, and his bike.

We were all born in the kitchen. At Daisy Bank we had one room and a kitchen, like a but-and-ben. There was no electricity, no gas, just an open fire, and the toilet fifty yards up beyond the house. It was shared by four tenants. When there was a bug going about, you took a shovel with you. Good for growing leeks.

I was the third child. My mother was born at Kilchattan Butts. My great grandfather used to look after the beavers [unsuccessfully in-troduced by Lord Bute] up in the wood there. We used to make a Sunday visit, my mother pushing the pram up the hill, the rest of us followers, chickens after a hen to see granny and grandpa.

It was hard. We were as poor as church mice. My father left the house at 5.30am to get on his bicycle to Rothesay with the mail col-lected from Kilchattan Bay and Kingarth. In winter he had to light the acetylene lamp on his bike. It was sometimes hard to get going. My poor mother had to get up to get the fire cracking so as to boil an egg. It was up to us to find kinders sticks and wood to keep the fire going till the water was boiling. We mostly used coal once the fire was going. The fire was a big open place with a swee, an arm and chain with a hook from which to hang the kettle, that swung over the fire.

The [incoming] letters had to be sorted in Rothesay into pigeon holes so that they could be delivered in the right order. [He set out from Rothesay at about 8am, delivering southwards]. In the summer there was a second delivery at 5pm at Kilchattan Bay. He also worked with McFie of the Post Office delivering carts of coal to different farms for eight shillings a week.

My father did a lot of gardening during the middle of the day, and once I was old enough, he took me to help him. There was one house especially, the Tileries, Kingarth [where the drainage tiles were made]. We used to get our tea there. They kept a daily maid there. She would give us a lovely set table, not like at home but with a cloth I was frightened of spilling something on, with scrambled eggs, cheese and home baking. She would call for us to come in for our tea and I'd feel like pushing my dad in that door, I was so hungry.

We used to go up the hill (Suidhe Chatain) and poach Lord Bute's trees. My father was a good poacher. He cut trees as low to the ground as he could, and blackened the stumps and spread a fallen branch or two over so that the gamekeeper would not see. He would cut the trunk into lengths and roll them down the hill to the house. He also used to catch rabbits. He set wire snares, and also poached with a ferret and nets. The nets would be pinned to the ground, top and bottom over every hole save one. The ferret would go down that one. You would hear a rumble inside the tunnels, they'd come straight out into the net. You had to be quick, to kill the rabbit and re-set the net for the next one. Sometimes the ferret would catch a rabbit under ground. You had to listen and then dig with a small spade to dig them out. You could clap the ferret on the head and he would let go of the rabbit. Occasionally it was impossible to get the ferret out, if it had settled in with a dead rabbit, so we blocked all the holes with whin and came back next morning and whistle like a rabbit screaming and out he'd come. The gamekeeper knew what my father got up to. One day he said to him in the Kingarth Inn, "I don't mind you taking a rabbit for the pot but not too often. But, by God, if I catch you it'll be a different story."

When Willie retired in 1939, his weekly pay packet from the Post Office was £2 14s 6d, roughly £86 in today's money, no more than today's state pension.

Ian discovered early that life was hard:

> I sometimes stayed with my grandfather and grandmother. I was responsible for pumping the water, and fetching it to the house. They lived up at Kilchattan Butts, there were five crofts up there. He had a croft of eight acres of land. He kept a cow for their own milk and a follower, a calf to bring on, hens and pigs. It was self-supporting style for food. He was friendly with the schoolmaster. He used to get me out of school to help with the potatoes, but it did not save me from trouble for the lessons I had missed.
>
> I left school at 14 years of age. My first job was for a rabbit catcher who was paid so much a pair by the Bute Estate. We worked with traps and snares over a certain area, mostly the southern end (Garrochty), for seven shillings a week [about £12 in today's money] plus a pair of rabbits. It was a 6-day week. They gave the catcher so many cartridges for the stony parts, where snares could not be set.
>
> Then I had a job as a baker, and I got ten shillings a week, and I got broken biscuits. The baker [who next employed me] had been an elder of the church in Kilchattan Bay. I was at his beck and call morning noon and night. I had to go out to the baker's at 4 o'clock in the morning and at 9 o'clock I went out to do the deliveries in the country. The baker's daughter and I went out on a couple of bicycles with large baskets on the front. I carried the bread, she the fancy goods. Then he got better off and bought a horse van and I would take off through the country in that.
>
> After a year or two the bakery failed, because the Co-op came out

A Bute rabbit catcher, c.1890, looking much as Ian Fisher's rabbit catcher must have looked.

*Ian Fisher
with his wife
Mary, 1970s.*

with a van from Rothesay and sold cheaper bread with a dividend. I was lucky. I got a job with the United Co-operative Baking Society. The pay was good. You had to wait for someone to kick the bucket before you could get his place.

I used to go to church every Sunday, at Kingarth. My father was church officer but he gave it up. I used to ring the bell on Sunday and open and shut the church. Sunday was the only day I could lie in but I had to get up at seven in the morning to get the church stove going. There were ten windows and I kept a potted plant in each window. There was not electricity or water there. As a child I would fetch a glass of water for the minister from the burn that ran past the church door.

When war broke out Ian joined up and served in Norway, North Africa and Italy. After the war he worked as a drystane dyker.

I was 15 years drystane dyking. My immediate boss was the head forester. One day I was sent to the Bute factor's house and told to take the gardener's post. I pleaded to go back to dyking, which I loved [on how it is done, see p.276].

Few people went abroad until the two world wars. A few travelled with the Navy or on merchantmen. Yet by 1950 most men under the age of 60 had been to a foreign theatre of war, while hardly any women had travelled. That only changed with cheap air travel.

KILCHATTAN BAY'S DECLINE

The parish minister Cameron Somerville wrote in 1962:

> One feels more and more how disastrous to character, to independence of spirit and opinion, and to a proper place in local society, have been the passing of individual crafts and the disappearance of individual ownership. In this parish which once held so many skilled and important people – tileworkers, foremen, fishermen owning boats, owners and skippers of smacks and lighters, the miller, baker, butcher, cobbler and smith…. It gives unpleasant thoughts of an unbalanced economy, centralised and vulnerable, instead of a dispersed independence.

Somerville may yet be proved prescient. Ian Fisher remembered in 2008 how the village had been before 1939:

> The village down here [when it had no fewer than 13 shops] was a thriving village. You could get anything you wanted in the village. There were big families but now they are all gone. I watched the village as it was thriving and now it is dead before me. I feel very sad about that.

When so many of these things had gone, the final deathblow came with closure of Kilchattan's church and school, the two mainstays of the community.

Kilchattan Bay – Kelspoke Castle – Dunagoil – St Blane's – Kilchattan Bay

Distance 14km: up to 4-5 hours
depending on how long you allow for breaks to savour the two principal sites
OS Map 4

BEFORE YOU WALK

The principal theme of this walk is the Iron Age and Early Christian settlement of Bute, as exemplified at Dunagoil and St Blane's. The walk provides a succession of magnificent sea views. Instead of walking on the high ground, via Kelspoke, you can follow the shoreline, if you prefer. This is quicker, more interesting geologically, since there are a number of lava dykes running into the sea but a good deal less rewarding in panoramic views and in agricultural history. If that is your option you should obtain a copy of Hill & Buist, *Reading the Landscape of Bute: A Geological Field Guide*, available from the Museum. The principal prize along the shoreline is to be found at low water almost immediately, at the foot of the southern corner of the small car park at the very far south end of the Bay (where the bus turns). This is Columnar Sandstone, Old Red Sandstone which metamorphosed under intense heat from adjacent hot magma and took columnar form on cooling. This rock is unique in Britain for the perfect quality of its columns, so it is worth a detour when you have time to spare.

Start at the old stone quay in Kilchattan Bay.
If you wish to read about the stone quay now, see p. 119.

Turn around, cross the road.
Before setting off up the track on the left of Kiln Villa, look to the right of it and you can get a glimpse of an early nineteenth century limekiln (p.118).

Follow the uphill track on the left side of Kiln Villa, and around the hairpin to the left (south eastwards). Once you have passed through the gate, follow the green signposts to Kelspoke, up the hill. At the second post turn left and walk along the hillside, following the green signposts.

After 500m you will begin to notice up to your right the traces of plough-ing two or more centuries ago, known as 'ridge and furrow' or 'runrig'. Even on relatively level ground, care would be taken to plough down the slope to ensure optimum drainage. Each ridge or 'strip' traditionally rep-resented one allocated plot of ground. But all the tenants would follow the same rotation and therefore the same crop. It is difficult to be sure when this land was last ploughed.

Because the old Scots plough was so heavy, it required a yoke of up to twelve oxen (p.259). Because it was so difficult, it made sense to minimise how often the plough had to be turned, hence the long strip. In theory each strip was one 'furrow long' or fur-long (220 yards) in length, but there were inevitably variations. The general intention was to plough a distance until the oxen required a breather, and then to turn the plough. The plough threw earth to the right, and the ploughman would start at the centre and work his way clockwise outwards. There were two virtues to this procedure. First, the ridge ran along the centre of a strip and the furrows marked a clear border between one strip and another. More importantly this method allowed the water to run off.

How runrig is created.

Ploughing was a task that demanded skill and a patient temperament, as a thirteenth century English text states:

> The art of the ploughman consists in knowing how to draw a straight furrow with yoked oxen without striking, pricking or ill-treating them. Ploughmen should be neither melancholy nor irritable but gay and joyful and encourage the oxen with melody and song.

So it was not just about being good with a plough. You needed a mel-lifluous voice, too. By the mid-seventeenth century it seems that draught horses were used in Bute rather than oxen. Whether or not they also enjoyed the song of the ploughman, they certainly responded to steadiness and calm.

The observant John Blain, writing around 1816, noted 'In many places evidences of cultivation appear where not a furrow has been turned over for more than a century past' The strips here probably predate the agricultural revolution when Lord Bute introduced sheep farming in this part of the island. As Peter May, Lord Bute's factor (p.261), reported in 1780, '…one part of the island towards the southeast projects like a peninsula, and is let at £200 a year for a sheep park. It contains 800 acres.' The land is unlikely to have reverted to arable once it had been let go.

Just as you reach the small reservoir on your right, you will see a small fragment of red sandstone wall on your left.
This is Kelspoke 'Castle'. Frustratingly there seems to be no record of what was here. All the evidence on the ground, however, suggests a steading, which presumably fell into disuse when the arable land was abandoned.

The view from here across to Great Cumbrae and the mainland is spectacular. Great Cumbrae deserves a visit if you have not already made it. Geologically, it is composed of Old Red Sandstone. Millport, just visible at the south end of the island, was created by the 3rd Earl of Bute in about 1760, out of the fishing hamlet there. It was part of Lord Bute's policy to develop Millport as a base for the Revenue men, and so construction of The Garrison was begun. It was out of Millport that the cutter, *Royal George*, patrolled the Clyde approaches in an effort to suppress smuggling (on smuggling see p.296).

Between 1799 and 1831, the Cumbraes enjoyed the ministry of James Adam. He would lead his congregation in prayer saying, 'O Lord, bless and be gracious to the Greater and Lesser Cumbrays, and in thy mercy do not forget the adjacent islands of Great Britain and Ireland.' Or so, at any rate, Walter Scott would have us believe, having heard about the eccentric minister of 'two miserable islands in the mouth of the Clyde' (a phrase that should cause outrage in Millport), from a pair of dinner guests at Abbotsford in September 1827. Standing here, who could possibly challenge the Adam perspective or fail to deplore Scott's putdown?

Adam was a man o'pairts. As someone 'of a shy and retiring disposition', one is not surprised to learn that he had been a bookseller in Glasgow before beginning his ministry here. He had a reputation for great medical skill. More remarkably, it was also said that he could handle a day's shearing as well and better than most farmhands and famously proved it against all comers when challenged to compete one day on an Ayrshire farm. He never married and on his death divided his savings between relief for the poor children of the parish and a student bursary for Glasgow University.

Quite a few of those who prayed with James Adam each Sunday were not fisher folk, but weavers producing muslin for the Glasgow and Paisley markets. Muslin originated at least a thousand years earlier in Mosul, hence the name. How astonished the early weavers would have been to learn that a thousand years later, their manufacturing skills would finally travel via India to such distant northern climes. The few who had ever heard of Europe probably shared the view of the tenth century globe-trotter, al-Mas'udi, who was dismissive of Europeans beyond the Mediterranean fringe: 'Those of them who are farthest to the north are the most subject to stupidity, grossness and brutishness.' How prejudiced, one might think, until one recalls how often today, over a thousand years later, Westerners judge the Islamic world in similarly crassly ill-informed terms.

Proceed, keeping to the left of the reservoir. Pass through the gate, and continue straight ahead over the shoulder of hill, passing the crag about 50m to your left. When you see it, head in the direction of the southern tip of Little Cumbrae. Resist the temptation to move right into the gully (that comes later). As you begin to descend you will reach a gate.

From here you get a good view of Little Cumbrae, which guards the Clyde estuary. Geologically unlike Great Cumbrae, it is a series of terraces, or traps, of lava. A castle was built on the east side of the island, probably in the early fourteenth century, to protect the Fairlie Roads, the sea approach to Largs. What one can see from here, however, are the remains of Scotland's second oldest lighthouse on top of the island, built in the 1757, a century after the one built on the Isle of May in the Firth of Forth. The ten metre-high tower was lit by a coal brazier, which can hardly have been useful except on the clearest of nights. Fitted with candles in 1785, it remained inadequate.

A radical improvement was achieved by a Fife-born metal worker, Thomas Smith. He had become fascinated by lamps and lighting while working in Edinburgh's emerging New Town. He began experimenting with reflectors and on the basis of his experiments was appointed first engineer to the Northern Lighthouse Board in 1787. His compressed oil gas lamps revolutionised many Scottish lighthouses. In 1793 a lamp 'fitted with prisms for strengthening it in its seaward arc... and... visible at a distance of fifteen miles' was installed in a new 35 metre-high lighthouse. This structure was built by a nineteen year-old stripling who happened to be his stepson and apprentice, by the name of Robert Stevenson, grandfather of the more famous R.L. That lighthouse, too, has since been replaced by a light on Little Cumbrae's west shore.

In 1831 the island had a population of 17, by 1975 two, and today nil.

Go through the gate, go half left through the bracken (there is a green signpost, in summer largely obscured by the bracken). Take great care where you put your feet as you approach and cross the tumbled down stone dyke. Follow the path downhill and cross the gully, down to sea level.
On your left as you descend is Hawk's Neb, an Old Red Sandstone crag, beautifully eroded over the millennia.

Turn right and follow the West Island Way signs to Glencallum Bay.
Rubh'an Eun ('bird headland') Lighthouse is a good place from which to look out for porpoises. The channel here between Bute and Little Cumbrae is over 100 metres deep, testimony to the formidable scouring power of the glacier that passed this way.

Follow the path around the edge of Glencallum Bay.
As you enter Glencallum Bay the eastern hillside is composed of tiers of lava on top of Old Red Sandstone. The lava flowed down the glen along a fault line in the sandstone.

As you cross the burn the remains of the old ferry house, probably the Branser Inn, lie in bracken about 100 metres inland, visible in winter but overgrown in the summer. The ferry ran across to Ardrossan, taking livestock that had been sold at the fair, held above St Blane's (see below). It is also said that this was a favoured bay for smugglers.

Continue following the path, over the shoulder of the next headland and after 500m, over the saddle on your right. Follow the path (you will see the white-topped sign post to the left of the small loch, Loch na Leighe).
Loch na Leighe is Gaelic for 'Healing Lake', but the origin of the name

is a mystery. It sits in a basin scooped out by ice. To its west St Blane's Hill is a massive lava sill. Its summit is 'Tertiary', the result of an eruption occurring perhaps some 25 million years ago, an intrusion from the principal volcanic eruption in Arran. If you wish to learn more, you need Hill & Buist's geological guide.

The land here is all part of The Plan Farm – a name which is something of an enigma, but possibly derived from the Latin *planum* meaning 'level ground'. It was once known as North Garrochty Farm, but now includes the lands of Kelspoke, South Garrochty and Dunagoil further north too.

The Plan is a livestock farm. Blackface sheep have probably roamed Bute's hill country for the best part of the past thousand years. They have certainly been at The Plan since the late eighteenth century. Like other breeds, over the centuries the Blackface has progressively been bred larger, today probably over twice what it was in 1400. The Blackface has always been highly regarded because of its hardiness.

In 1994, however, the livestock picture changed with the arrival of Brian and Janet Hill. Brian brought a beef herd with him, a new venture, and Janet rears sheep. Both have a mission: to produce the ideal creature for this climate, in hardiness, quality of carcase and of taste. Janet inherited over 1,000 Blackface ewes. While keeping a small quorum of pure bred Blackface ewes, she has experimented crossing the rest of the flock. Having successfully crossed with Lleyn, a hardy Welsh animal used to living out through the winter, she is trying to breed a lamb that does not need to be clipped before slaughter. She is trying to get back to what sheep were like centuries ago before their wool productivity was 'improved'. To this end the Lleyn is being crossed with a sheep that sounds more like a detergent, the 'Easy Care' breed, which sheds naturally.

Meanwhile, back in 1994 Brian brought 30 Limousin cattle to The Plan. He needed a good beef animal, but one which also produces plenty of milk to rear strong and healthy calves. He began crossing them with a South Devon bull. To get more size he crossed a third way with Swiss Simmental. However, in his own words, 'More recently we have wanted to produce a hardy foraging cow, reduce dependency on silage and be able to sell a hardy productive heifer into the breeding market.' He therefore crossed Luing bulls (the 60 year-old breed hails from an island of that name, near Oban) with South Devon. The females will be hardy and maximise the out-wintering potential of The Plan and will eventually reduce the bracken infestation. The Luing x Devon males provide an un-usual cross for distinctive flavoured beef (if you are interested in tasting it, pick up a leaflet at the car park at the end of The Plan Road).

Take care to follow the signposts up the east side of The Plan, eventually off the track and up a steep path to the left marked 'West Island Way', leading you into the church precinct of St Blane. Step over the old turf-covered stone perimeter wall on your left as soon as you are able.

This is where you have an option, depending on how energetic you are feeling, whether to go first to Dunagoil and return to St Blane's, or whether to make a separate visit to Dunagoil on another occasion.

If your resolve weakens and you decide to skip Dunagoil now, turn to p.140, but you must see it before leaving Bute. It is an imperative. If your resolve holds, ignore St Blane's for a moment and cleaving to your left make your way around the wire perimeter fence to the gate leading down to the road.

To Dunagoil: when you reach the car park, take the road on your left (south) leading to The Garrochty. Pass the sign 'Garrochty Farm – Private Road'. Passing over the culvert, look to your right to see the columnar lava on the sill across the field. At the farm entrance (marked by a wedge of trees on the right side of the track), turn right through the wicket gate and proceed to the far end of the field.

The Garrochty (Gaelic for 'rough field house), is a Victorian man-sion built by Sir William McEwan in 1898. McEwan was the most distinguished brain surgeon of his day, and president of the BMA. It was, coincidentally, in his professional heyday that the perforated Bronze Age skull (p. 235) was found. One hopes he felt a warm professional bond with his Bronze Age surgeon predecessor. McEwan's father had been a master mariner who ferried Dr Chalmers and his colleagues around the Western Isles during the great Disruption of the Kirk, 1843.

Follow the path just below the ridge running towards Dunagoil.

As you emerge close to the sea there is on your left an old concrete and stone boatshed. On the far side is a small inlet, tucked inside Cradh Rubha ('vexation point') where the puffer offloaded the winter's coal for nearby dwellings each year until the 1950s. The name suggests it required a calm sea to get in by oar. The second, almost adjacent inlet, called Port Dubh ('black port'), is a small anchorage where boats must have come in during Iron Age and Viking times. This or Cradh Rubha was possibly the site for a ferry for men and horses established around 1680. John Fraser was appointed ferrier, charged to provide:

> a sufficient boat well furnished with mast, sayle, four oares and uther sufficient furniture and to furnish to passengers comeing and goeing to Arran and from thence meett and drink, fyre and bedding....

The ferry does not seem to have been greatly used, and it was abandoned sometime in the eighteenth century.

Dunagoil

(Warning: take care to keep back from cliffs in high or blustery winds.)

INTRODUCTION

Dunagoil must be one of the more important Late Bronze Age or Early Iron Age sites in Scotland, in use for over one thousand years, certainly until about AD 1200 and possibly beyond. Its name, 'Fort of the Foreigner', immediately suggests that it refers to the 'Gall', the Gaelic description for Norsemen. But the name may refer to previous foreigners here. Dunagoil's appeal is not merely that the site is spectacular, although only small traces of walls remain, but that one can easily make rewarding sense of what is visible without any knowledge of archaeology. Given the size, complexity and position of the site, it may have been the principal strategic base for control of the Clyde approaches, but that must be speculative.

Dunagoil is composed of the strongpoint, or citadel, and a 'bailey', a defendable open area into which livestock, for example, could be herded in case of attack. The fort is, in essence, entirely geological, with twin ridges of a basalt sill. One forms the citadel and the other surrounds the inland side of a small corrie, thus making it nigh perfect as the 'bailey'. If you wish to meander beyond the fort itself, its northern cliffs boast a cave, and Little Dunagoil stands on a volcanic vent 200m northwest of the fort, with traces of a couple of Norse longhouses at its foot. Dunagoil cannot possibly have functioned in isolation, even though that is precisely how one thinks of it during a siege. In reality it must have enjoyed a very close interrelationship with the hinterland, particularly St Blane's. Prehistoric and Norse activity is evident on both sites. Grain would have been grown where possible. Livestock would probably have been folded at St Blane's except in times of danger, when it would be driven into the Dunagoil bailey.

Saddle querns, a brooch and a ring-headed pin found at the site provide compelling evidence that this was at least an Early Iron Age fort, if not Late Bronze Age, dating from anything between 300-150 BC. Rotary querns became universal in this part of Scotland in the second century BC. Metalwork fragments indicate if not a trade, as least the traffic of skills and design from as far afield as La Tène in Switzerland.

Little Dunagoil was probably part of the defensive complex. If one bears in mind that the now improved farmland on its landward sides must have been very boggy and difficult to cross, Little Dunagoil could only have been attacked from the beach, or by coming within range of missiles from the heights of Dunagoil.

THE SITE

The description takes you in sequence to the essentials (sketch map overleaf).

Cross A and enter the Citadel by B

This seems to be the lower gate, from the bailey up to the fort.

Ascend to C, where one can still detect the rubble-filled gateway, and thus into the keep.

Dunagoil is famous as a 'vitrified' fort. Vitrification occurs when the stones are fused by intense heat. This occured as a deliberate act of destruction. The remaining scraps of the vitrified wall are mainly right on top of the citadel (D and E). Imagine the great pall of smoke created by burning the walls. It would have been seen for miles around, sending a message of triumph to allies of the victors and a message of despair to those, probably in the other hillforts in Bute, that the game was up.

Before leaving the high ground of the citadel, admire Dunagoil Bay to the north. If you had been standing here early on the morning of 10 February 1900, you could have been forgiven for momentarily assuming you were witness to an eccentric art installation. For the shoreline, which the previous evening had looked much as it does now, had turned a pulsating, vivid hue. A ship had run aground, its hold had sundered and discharged a cargo of 2025 tons of Valencia oranges. In the staid words of *The Buteman*: 'The shore presented a curious appearance, there being at some parts a depth of several inches of oranges.' Word soon spread. The coastguards claimed that they made all those who removed the fruit pay for it but do not for a second believe this, for:

> … there was a constant stream of visitors from Rothesay, Kilchattan Bay and other parts of the island, picking up the fruit, many laden

with sacks and other receptacles. Some went to the length of carrying the fruit away in polo carts, while various farmers had cart-loads stored away in their barns.

In fact the farmers proved unable to shift such gargantuan quantities, nor could their families cope. Farm children doubtless began to beg for mercy. Delight in the exotic has its limits after eating the fifty-fifth orange of the week. As they began to rot, farmers fed them to their dairy herd, so that for a while Kingarth parish milk, it was noted, had a distinctly citrus tang.

Return to A.

This is the site of a wall across the eastern flank of the bailey. You can walk around the eastern ridge, and you may note traces of the man-made defences at (F), (G) and (H).

On the northwest side, at the foot of the cliffs outside the defences may be found a cave, (J). This is 20m deep, with a midden or prehistoric rubbish heap near the entrance. Slabs of sandstone on the ground were brought here, presumably to form a hearth. The cave's use seems to predate the fort, with Neolithic material and possibly even Mesolithic remains.

Cross to Little Dunagoil.

This is a much smaller fort, a volcanic eruption, with remains of a rampart, as marked on the sketch map. Excavations indicate use over a similar time span, with Early Iron Age artefacts found. The 1990s survey concluded that the north-eastern extremity (K) was probably a livestock compound. A rampart seems to have enclosed the whole hill and two Norse longhouses (M, N). The two longhouses, 14m long and 7m wide, were occupied in the twelfth and thirteenth centuries AD. They are the only two so far located between the Isle of Man and South Uist. We are left wondering when they were abandoned. Could it have been when Norway renounced its claim on Man and the southern isles, after the Battle of Largs, 1263 (p.241)?

Return to St Blane's.

St Blane's

SITE INTRODUCTION

The explanatory notice as you enter from the direction of the road may tell you as much as you wish to know about the archaeology of the site.

There is a profound tranquillity here connected with its sense of seclusion, intimacy and sanctuary. You may wish to imagine those who have used this place over the centuries and through silence have sought to refresh the inner life, an unfashionable idea in our materialistic times. I have put some of the story of St Blane's at the end on p.143, partly on account of its length but also to help spark your imagination as you savour this most remarkable of places.

SITE GUIDE

Outlying structures along the cliff-foot: the dwellings of St Blane's disciples may have been bee-hive shaped huts, possibly with stone footings, but mounted with wood, wattle and thatch. In this area you will find a well and also a basin for washing feet. According to his biographer, Adamnan, on the arrival of pilgrims St Columba would instruct his monks: 'Prepare the guest house quickly, and draw water for the visitors' feet.' Ceremonial washing after the rigours of the journey was the first imperative of hospitality, applied by all the religious houses of the time.

The church: The building which now exists contains elements of the parish church, dating from around 1135, but not the earlier monastery. The builder of these oldest surviving parts may have been Norse, perhaps Olaf the Red, father-in-law of Somerled (p.240). As a chronicler shortly after his death commented: 'He (Olaf) gave to the churches of the islands lands and privileges, and was with respect to divine worship devout and fervent.' Olaf died in 1143. Bute fell into the hands of the Stewart family sometime in the closing years of the twelfth century, and was gifted to Paisley Priory in 1204. It is difficult to believe that there were not further significant alterations at that time, and one is tempted to think that the Romanesque arch must have been Norman rather than Norse. The building was certainly added to in the fourteenth century. What survives was heavily restored in the 1870s, as were the graveyards.

The graveyards: The shape of the graveyards seems to have been modified during restoration work. In the upper graveyard lies a Viking-style tomb, characteristically hogback in shape, and dating to the tenth-eleventh centuries, presumably connected with the two longhouses at Little Dunagoil, and also perhaps with the rebuilding of the monastery after its presumed destruction in Norse raids in the late eighth century. One grave dated to the ninth century bears a primitive cross. Others date from the period 1200-1500.

There seems to have been a longstanding tradition that the upper graveyard was for the burial of men, and the lower for women. Segregation of the sexes in death is unusual, but there are a few cases at monastic sites in Ireland, and most famously at the medieval St Ronan's on Iona. Closer at hand, on Inchmarnock there seems to have been a burial place beside the church set aside for women. Moreover, among the living many Celtic abbeys divided into two separate complexes, one for each sex.

"ST BLANE'S" BUTE
GENERAL VIEW FROM THE S.W.

Key:
A *cashel, the wall separating the church precinct from the rest of the monastery*
B *vallum, the wall separating the monastery from the secular world beyond*
C *upper graveyard*
D *lower graveyard*
E *Celtic chapel*
F *probable site of manse/presbytery*
G *well*
H *cauldron, its purpose and origin unknown*

The Clunaic monks who were apparently sent here in the Middle Ages (see below) may also have deprecated the burial of women adjoining their foundations. Before you reach for your gender-equality manual, this was not misogyny (though they may have been infected by that too). The annual customary concourse of women to mark anniversaries by graveside devotions had a way of distracting celibate monks from their own divine avocations. So Cluny and one or two other religious foundations ensured that female graves were at a distance from their own churches. This may have been the case here.

Gravestone at St. Blane's.

Needless to say, this eccentricity did not go down well with the Reformed Church's local Presbytery at Dunoon, which in 1661 rebuked the local elders for: 'ther tolerating ye people in a superstitious custome, viz., of burying yr men and women in two diverse churchyards', and required that 'men and women shall be promiscouslie buryed in ye upper kirkzard [*sic*].' This must have left Kingarth's elders spluttering with indignation. Were they not busy enough attempting to thwart this same principle of promiscuity among the living, without getting too prissy about the sleeping arrangements for the dead?

The cashel: the round 'cashel', or wall, to the immediate church precinct, is a feature characteristic of Celtic religious foundations at this time. Its significance, however, extends well beyond Britain and Ireland. With the first conversions of Vikings in the mid-ninth century, Christianised Norsemen began to colonise Iceland, from about AD 860. Pre-Christian Viking graveyards were rectangular in layout, but the earliest Christian graveyards of Iceland and Greenland imitated the circular cashels of Ireland and Britain. The cashel of St Blane is a good example maintained (probably rebuilt) in modern times.

The Vikings here must have belonged to the first generation not only to embrace Christianity but also to marry Gaelic women, for it is in this very period that Gaelic texts start to refer to those of Gaelic-speaking Norse-Gaelic stock as Gall-Gaels, or 'foreign Gaels', rather than simply as pagans. (Many of the sea kings (see p.239) who dominated Scotland's western seaboard in the early Middle Ages were Gall-Gaels.) One might view all of this as unremarkable, so here is something to make one gasp. Two-thirds of today's Icelandic women have mitochondrial DNA (MtDNA, female specific DNA) closer to British and Irish MtDNA than to any other population group in the world. Thus, some of their forebears may even have sailed from Bute with their Norse husbands. (By contrast, to this day the DNA of Icelandic men shows an overwhelming connection with Norway.) DNA is going to give us many more surprises as geneticists increasingly master what it can tell us.

The cauldron. The date and purpose of this enormous drystone enclosure remains a mystery, though it is suspected of being a pre-Christian feature.

THE STORY OF ST BLANE'S

(i) *The Celtic church of Ceann-Garadh (Kingarth)*

You may wish to refer to p.237 for a broader background on saints Catan and Blane. Stories of Blane's life and ministry are so garbled that you should treat the following with a historian's scepticism. Blane was a native of Bute, sent by his Uncle Catan to be properly grounded in the faith at Bangor Abbey in Ireland. Seven years later, in about AD 600, he returned allegedly in a boat without oars, a fact which smacks of either the miraculous or the improvident. As you will have guessed, Blane was possessed of powers we can all envy, so he could afford to be a little bit casual when it came to the oars. Here is another example of what he could do: 'His light having gone out one night, he brought fire from his long finger-ends, as when flint is struck with steel.' No need for lucifers, then.

As a bishop, Blane is said to have gone to Rome where he received the papal blessing and then walked home through Anglia. At one city 'he performed the extraordinary miracle of restoring a blind wicked boy [English, naturally] to life in three stages: first with his eyes; then with his sins; and lastly in the state of grace.' It is the latter phrase that wipes the sceptical smirk off one's face. We live in an age when grace, however you care to interpret that word, is in woefully short supply. At the start of the twenty-first century we seem less anchored and more hectic than our predecessors: hyperactive without quite knowing why. Little wonder, then, that Grace is currently such a fashionable name: in our heart of hearts, most of us yearn for grace – and that quality of stillness so powerful here – in our daily lives.

Blane, according to the fourteenth century chronicler, John Fordun, was buried here in about 630. If so, his grave remains unmarked and we should remain doubtful that it is here at all, for Fordun was almost as distant in time from Blane as we are from Fordun.

We know the identity of only a few of Blane's successors. By their titles we can infer that first there was a bishopric of Kingarth, then an abbey in the eighth century. In keeping with widespread Celtic practice, it seems likely that leadership of the monastery was kindred-based. At Iona, nine of Columba's successor abbots were of his noble family. Kingarth may have had a similar pattern, for one of these Bute bishops was Blane's kinsman Ronan 'the kingly', who died at Kingarth in 737. Ronan deserves momentary notice, for it may be he who undertook missionary endeavour along the western seaboard of Scotland as far as the Isle of Rona, north of Lewis. It is impossible to be certain since there seems to have been more than one St Ronan. Buteman or not, Ronan's story points to the readiness of the early Celtic saints to undertake immensely dangerous sea-voyages in their work.

In 790 Viking raiders apparently burnt the monastery of St Blane's, but presumably it was Norse converts who rebuilt it, about 930.

(ii) *The medieval church.* The triumph of Rome over the Celtic church was inevitable with the growing supremacy of a feudally-ordered culture that pushed northwards from Anglia. Walter Fitzalan, the High Steward, founded a Clunaic monastery at Paisley, c.1163, sending to Wenlock (his old Shropshire stamping ground) for monks with whom to populate the foundation. Paisley prospered, indeed it was one of the richest houses of Scotland, partly because it enjoyed royal and Stewart patronage. But its success also reflected the power of the mother abbey of Cluny, in deepest Burgundy.

In its heyday, Cluny was arguably the most powerful institution in Europe, immensely influential with the Vatican (it produced several early medieval popes) to which it was solely accountable. It possessed over 1,400 dependencies across Western Christendom. Paisley was an outlying one of these, one of only three Clunaic foundations in Scotland. Cluny's political clout was such that it has been blamed for goading the Vatican into proclaiming Crusade against the infidel. True or false, Pope Urban II, who made that fateful call to arms, had previously been Prior Superior at Cluny. Cluny Abbey was the largest building of its day. It exuded power. It lay in the Rhône valley, the principal route between the Mediterranean and northern Europe, and so was also well placed for trade. It had everything going for it except that fundamental monastic requirement, humility.

After Walter's death in 1178 his son, Alan, gifted the custody of Kingarth with all its revenues (at the time the parish covered the whole island) as a grange to Paisley Priory, just before he died in 1204. Given St Blane's sacred history, this must have been a significant symbolic gift. Kingarth curiously does not appear in the records of Paisley Abbey (elevated from priory to abbey in 1219), as one might expect, so it is just possible that the gift was never implemented. But given that it was, Kingarth entered into the wider embrace of Cluny and so represented the very tip of one of Cluny's far-reaching tentacles.

One or two monks from Paisley would have been posted here as grangers, to maintain the church lands, bring in their yield and to serve the local community. They would have fulfilled the daily office and maintained the silence for which Cluny was famous (its monks developed a sophisticated form of sign language). Perhaps they also read the teachings of St Gregory, a man greatly revered by the whole Clunaic network. In the words of a modern admirer:

> The reading of his [Gregory's] work communicates a feeling of peace... On every page one finds alternately suffering and experience, but also their reconciliation, their synthesis in charity.

Monks, however, are as human as the rest of us, and Cluny's great wealth drew its members less to charity than to lives of luxury, a shortcoming that seems to have been emulated at Paisley. It had not always been like this. In its early years after its foundation in 940, Cluny had been known for its ascetic discipline:

> When you wish to sleep they wake you; when you wish to eat they make you fast. The night is passed in praying in the church, the day in working and there is no repose but in the refectory: and what is to be found there? Rotten eggs, beans with their pods on, and liquor fit for oxen.

How easily, one might say, the Faithful traduce the teachings of the Founder. Cluny's later gluttonous lifestyle, making up perhaps for all those years of self-denial, was the target of biting sarcasm from that great early medieval ascetic, Bernard of Clairvaux:

> Who could say, to speak of nothing else, in how many ways eggs are cooked and worked up? With what care they are turned in and out, made hard or soft, or chopped fine, now fired, now roasted, now stuffed?

So, if St Gregory's suffering and experience sticks in your craw, go for St Bernard and speculate how the monks here liked their eggs.

(iii) *The post-Reformation parish church*

Rome took responsibility for the souls of its adherents, as long as they obeyed the teachings of the Church. The Reformed Church, which displaced it in 1560, made its followers individually liable for their own salvation, demanding personal belief and personal responsibility. Inevitably, human frailty became more of an issue. One gets a flavour from a resolution of Kingarth's elders in 1641:

> That ane act be mad against prophaners of the Sabbath by fighting or drinking etc., as also against absents from the Churgh on Sabbath day, against cursers or sverers in lyk maner.

The elders did not, of course, succeed then any more than the local constabulary succeeds now. Humans are wont to misbehave: fighting, drinking, blaspheming and, not least, indulging in sexual misconduct. One particularly striking example of the latter that same year – but possibly not a particularly unusual one – involved both fornication and incest. Let us pass over the names of the guilty twosome but recall that they were required:

> to stand bare headed and bare legged in sackcloth at the Kirk dore from the 1 bell to the third and efterwards in the pillar during the tyme of Divine service, and that for the space of tuell [twelve] Sabbaths.

Today, for the famous at any rate, the gutter press has replaced the kirk door. Yet, as Rothesay's minister observed in the 1890s: 'No modern Society journal could have afforded so choice a weekly budget of Sabbath entertainment as the Covenanting Kirk of Scotland.'

The elders also did their best to stamp out superstition, though it was probably the Enlightenment and scientific progress that succeeded where the Church had failed. Just a few hundred yards away, at Garrochty Farm, 'Lachlan McKirdy.... confessed that he and Alester McKaw did use the charme of the riddle... for getting of silver that was stolne from him.' It seems that the riddle, an agricultural sieve, was turned or swung to indicate the direction of the lost object. The frequency with which parishioners in the seventeenth century were charged with 'turning the riddle' suggests that as a method of finding lost objects it must have worked really quite well.

In 1650 the Kingarth elders detained Finwell Hyndman, because she would take herself off, no one knew where, and was supposedly with the fairies. She even brought a little fairy home to nurse. We are inclined to think of fairies as fey saccharine creatures like Tinkerbell. As far as the seventeenth century was concerned, fairies were malign sprites intent on evil. We do not know Finwell Hyndman's fate. She was probably a poor and single woman of a certain age, given to eccentricity. Her supposed offence was well within the territory of witchcraft, a serious matter for which the extreme penalty was death (p.316).

However, busy as the elders were keeping the morals of the parish in good repair, they were culpably negligent regarding the fabric of the church. The roof blew off one night in December 1675. What remained of the building was deemed beyond repair. The new church was built more centrally for the parish at Langalchorad, a couple of hundred yards from the Kingarth Hotel. That, too, has gone, but the kirkyard remains (p.116).

Leave by the north entrance to St Blane's, pausing as you pass beyond the vallum wall.

The hump of a corn-drying kiln just outside the vallum wall can still be made out on your right, between the stone socket for a cross and the gateway. Sherds of pottery were found at the foot of the wall, similar to sherds found at the longhouses at Little Dunagoil, which date back to the twelfth century. As for the socket stone, this was for the mercat cross. A fair, St Blane's, took place here annually on Lammas Day, 1 August, but seems to have fallen into disuse by the mid-eighteenth century. Livestock was driven south from Argyllshire for sale here, before being ferried from Glen Callum Bay to Ardrossan.

Follow the signs which take you over a couple of fields. Once you are on the track, watch out on your right as you begin to go uphill for the remains on the ground of the settlement of Kingaven (you will see a wooden marker post).

Kingaven (in Gaelic *ceann abhainn*, or 'river head') seems to have been a small fermtoun abandoned in the eighteenth century, perhaps as a result of the agricultural revolution when sheep were put onto this end of the island. There were four buildings inside an enclosure, presumably for cattle, defined by a now ruined dyke. Just beyond the dyke on the north side is the ruin of a corn-drying kiln, one of the best preserved in Bute. It lies a little way up the hillside, barely 15 paces from the track, and not more than 35 paces from the Kingaven wooden marker post. Its roof has fallen in but one can still clearly distinguish its key-hole shape. It is the only part of the settlement worth exploring.

Resume your route over the hill.

The magnificent view ahead is of Stravannan Bay.

Cross the stile and turn right down the hill. Cross the bridge at the bottom. Follow the marked route uphill, over the south shoulder of Suidhe Chatain (Catan's Seat).

As you pass over the shoulder, you get a view of the 'waves' of lava sills, running northwest-southeast axis, separated by faults, the valleys in between. From west to east these are (i) the Garrochty-Dunagoil sill; (ii) the Torr Mor sill, which lies along the west side of Glencallum; (iii) Suidhe Chatain and the line of lava flows down to Rubh'an Eun (the lighthouse), and volcanic vents on the very east edge at Creag a'Mhara and Hawk's Neb.

Follow the signs down the far side of Suidhe Chatain, back to Kilchattan Bay.

Stravannan Bay and Ardnahoe

Distance 9km: 2½-3 hours
OS Map 4

BEFORE YOU WALK

This walk takes you from the Kingarth Hotel out to Stravannan Bay, along the coast to Ardnahoe and then back to Kingarth via the main road. There is a relatively frequent bus service to Kingarth during school term-time, so there is no need to drive or cycle here in order to walk. The wait for a return bus can be turned into a pleasure with refreshment at the Kingarth Hotel. (Consult the bus timetable. Buses will always pick you up at the corner). The predominant theme of this walk is the farming world, its delights and sorrows.

Start at Kingarth Hotel and take the road up to the graveyard and turn left on the single-track road to The Plan and St Blane's. After 300 metres turn left on the track marked to Kilchattan Bay. Almost immediately on your right you will find the Kingarth standing stones to the right in a small clearing in the conifer plantation.

Only three stones are left, one of them propped by a metal strut. There were still seven stones here in the late eighteenth century. The circle is probably Early Bronze Age, c.1500 BC, but the unusual conglomerate quality (p.227) of two of these standing stones gives them, even disregarding the metal strut, a feeling of transience and disintegration rather than permanence and solidity, in stark contrast with that at St Colmac. Indeed, it seems remarkable that even three stones have survived. On seeing what their cousins had done here, the builders of St Colmac's stone circle (p.206) must have returned home muttering 'jerry-built' sniffily to themselves.

As you return to the road, you will see a landing strip on the ground opposite, (usually with an orange windsock). Turn left and follow the road, but after 300m turn right along the marked path.

If you look southwards you will see Largizean (Gaelic for 'Daisy Field' Farm, which you pass on the road down to St Blane's), sheltering in the lee of the volcanic basalt trap (p.227). In the second half of the nineteenth century it was occupied by Archibald Martin and his wife, Jeanie Duncan (from Scoulag). They had quite a reputation:

> Night or day they never counted it trouble to entertain, even the gangrel [vagrant] body would not be turned away with an unkind word but, on the contrary, get shelter and a bite of something. Doubtless some there would be who reckoned this as foolishness and a waste of time and money but in it they had great pleasure and satisfaction throughout their long lives, and left behind them in the hearts of their many relatives and friends fragrant memories of kindness and geniality.

William Martin, *The Farmers of Bute* (1951)

To the right of Largizean you will see the imposing features of Dunstrone, which had a fort on its summit, a satellite, presumably, of Dunagoil. It is, of course, another volcanic basalt trap.

You will pass the edge of the airstrip with its bench, the most unassuming air terminal you are ever likely to clap eyes on. Afterwards, you skirt the golf course. This will take you to the shoreline. On reaching the shore, turn right, northwards, and continue to walk around the perimeter of Stravannan Bay. (You can, if you wish to shorten this walk, turn back inland at the signposted track on the edge of Stravannan Bay, which will take you to Langalbuinoch Farm, from where you can turn right, back to Kingarth). Follow the coastline beyond Stravannan Bay. Keep to the shoreline. On your right you will see a large cave at the foot of the cliffs. Resist the temptation to investigate. If you venture inland you will find yourself crossing a bog. Generally speaking streams are easiest to cross close to the shore where they tend to be wider but shallower, and one can find stepping stones to cross with if necessary.

The shoreline is composed of outcrops of conglomerate rock. Note the sharply inclined upthrust of these rocks, which have clearly been worn away and broken down. It may well have been from hereabouts that the stones for the Kingarth stone circle were hewn.

As you enter Gallachan Bay you will see Ardnahoe Farm on the raised beach on the far side of the bay. You will eventually be taking the track up to it.

Looking back across the Sound to Arran, if it is not shrouded in cloud you will see the silhouette of Goat Fell and the Sleeping Warrior. Between the two, but closer, stands Mullach Buidhe, the Yellow Summit. The Sleeping Warrior, lying on his back, sounds suspiciously like a piece of nineteenth century whimsy. In Gaelic the features carry older names: the helmet peak, nose and chin of the warrior are known as Cir Mhor, the Great Comb, and one can see immediately how like a cock's comb it is. The warrior's chest was known in Gaelic as Caisteal Abhail, which probably means 'death castle'. The warrior's arms are supposedly clasped across his chest. The visible 'arm' is a ridge running down from Caisteal Abhail, known as Ceum na-cailleach, the Old Woman's Steps.

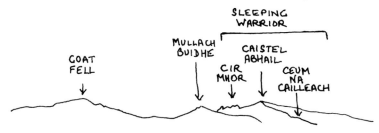

Skyline of Arran's Sleeping Warrior, as seen from Stravannan.

Then there is the expanse of sea, across to Arran. It was here that Patrick Walker, crossing to Bute in late summer, 1797, was given by a crew member:

> an account of their mode of fishing the basking Shark or Sail fish as they call them. They are generally taken in August or July and principally between Arran and Bute; they yield a good deal of Oil…. And are generally from 20 to 35 feet long; their Dorsal Fins very large and always above the water when the fish floats on the Surface, which it generally does in sunny weather. It is in this situation that they fall prey to the Fishers; a four-oared boat goes out to him, when two men drive each harpoon into him as near the gills as they can; it is often some time before he seems to feel the pain; at other times he is very sensible, and then it is that the fishing is attended with danger, for he immediately tosses up his Tail and goes to the bottom: boats have been

frequently upset and cut down by this flounce of his tail which is very strong. After he is harpooned, he attempts to get clear by rolling at the bottom of the sea and then runs out a prodigious length of line (sometimes 200 fathoms) till he is quite exhausted: he is then hoisted up to the boats side, his head is fixed to a beam at the bow of the boat, and his tail to another in the stern, and in this manner is carried to the shore and his liver taken out and melted. The boat I was in had taken one last summer, it was 30 feet in length and yielded a quantity of Oil for which the Boatmen got £24 Sterling [about £1,400 today], besides a quantity they retained for their own use. They also got from the Trustees [of the Board of Fisheries] a premium of £7 [about £390 today].

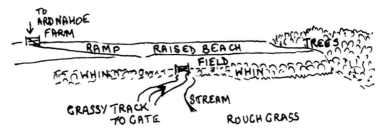

Keep to the shore perimeter. The closer you are to the shore, the easier the going. When you have passed an old delapidated drystane dyke (on dykes, see p.276) on the shore, you cross several streams. Watch out for a gate on your right, but do not take it (it runs up to Gallachan Farm). Once, looking to your right, you have clearly passed the edge of the woodland and scrub on the rising ground, cross the next stream a few paces later and follow a track on your right taking you up through a gate to a field. You should see a ramp-like track running up the side of the 'raised beach' on the far side of the field, from right (bottom) to left (top). Before crossing this field, however, if you wish to inspect the caves after which the farm takes its name, turn left and follow the edge of the field and go through the gate. You will find caves at the foot of the conglomerate cliff.

The caves have so far yielded no archaeological detritus, something of a surprise. After the collapse of the church at St Blane's in December 1675, the parishioners sometimes came here for Sabbath morning prayer, until the new site at Langalchorad was decided upon. Presumably they took shelter in the larger cave in inclement weather.

Retrace your steps to cross the field and take the ramp-track up to Ardnahoe Farm.

Writing in about 1816, John Blain describes Ardnahoe as 'one of the most beautiful farms in the island – well managed and productive of every article desired by the farmer.' Indeed, in 1844 the Bute Farmers' Society awarded first prize for the best stackyard to Mrs Hall, doyenne of the farm, 'whose stacks are remarkably well formed, stand fair, are well headed, neatly thatched, secured with particularly small, tight, well-made straw ropes…' You cannot say fairer than that.

The Halls were succeeded by the family Martin in the 1870s. John Martin married no less than three times but died in 1885, leaving his widow with five young children to rear. Two years later, on the night of 7 July 1887, the straw shed and barn caught fire and burnt down. There were nine labourers asleep in the upper storey of the barn. Two men, John Fraill and William Docherty, survived to tell the tale:

> [Docherty] was awakened by hearing the crackling of the straw, as it was being consumed by the flames. He at once roused up the others, and told them to make haste or they would be burned to death. One of the women said to him – "O, for heaven's sake, save me," and clutched on his arm, while one of the men took his other arm. He dragged them towards the top of the ladder. The heat was intense, and the smoke was apparently overpowering the poor creatures hanging on to him, as he said he felt their grip gradually relax, till they dropped down, and as he felt himself being scorched, he quickly slipped down the ladder into the burning pit beneath, and dashed to the door…. He observed that John Fraill had made his way out of the window. Both of them were naked…. Docherty says that after he made his escape from the burning barn, the screams of those he had left behind were something terrific…. He was burned about the back, the head and the arms.

When Docherty was interviewed that very morning by *The Buteman*, he was already at work thinning turnips. Six itinerant tatty-howkers (p. 280) and a casual labourer perished in the conflagration: 'It has been impossible to ascertain the names of the poor creatures who so suddenly met such a terrible death, as they were all strangers in the district.' So their next of kin would never have learnt of their fate. You can pay your respects when you reach the Kingarth graveyard (p. 116), for their remains were buried there.

Six months later, one of Mrs Martin's two daughters caught an illness and died. 'Thus,' in the words of her son William, 'in two and a half years she had seen nine coffins go down the road and her cup of sorrow was filled to overflowing, but like Job of old, she refused to be beaten.' She made old bones, dying aged 85 in 1929. The family Martin is still here.

Pass through the farmyard, turning right. Having passed the farm buildings on your left, a detour is in order, to Ardnahoe Fort, since it commands such magnificent views. Cross the stile where the farm track turns right towards the main road. Follow the blue flashes which take you along the left edge of the field till you reach the next stile, cross it and follow the edge of the field until you reach the next stile, turn right to the next stile, keep left to the promontory, with disturbed ground covered in whin.

Ardnahoe (G. *Ard na h-uamh*) means 'the height above the cave'. Even if they have left no evidence of their presence it is hard to believe that the people who built this fort did not also use the caves beneath.

Retrace your steps and follow the track up to the main road. Turn right and walk back towards Kingarth. You will pass steadings on your right:

Gallachan. (from Gaelic, probably for 'meadow field'.) Back in the 1870s the farmer here was Thomas McFie. In William Martin's words,

> Tommy, because of his fondness for a good time and his dislike of work, had to vacate the holding in due course, later finding employment on farms at fencing and like jobs where the passing of time did not push him too fast.

Kerrymenoch. (from Gaelic for either the 'middle' or 'monk's' quarter). This farm too, was worked by a Martin, but his sole relationship with Martin of Ardnahoe was as brother-in-law: they both married sisters. Unlike his neighbour, Tommy McFie, John Martin was reserved, diffident but hardworking: '[his] milk was regularly churned and sold with the butter on the Craigmore shore on alternate days with Ardnahoe.'

Stravannan or **Nether Stravannan** (from the Gaelic, probably for 'smooth-stoned stream or valley'). Fire is one of the great fears on any farm. On the Feeing Day in May 1915 everyone had gone off early to Guildford Square (p.266), except for James Little, aged 75 and feeling it, and his grandchildren, a girl aged 14 and two boys aged five and three. Somehow the children managed to set fire to the cart shed, which contained hay. Adjacent was the stable, containing two horses. Little managed to drag the two Clydesdales out, but the cart shed, stable, and barn were lost.

Shortly after Stravannan the road dips down into 'the smooth-stoned valley'.
In the words of John Blain, 'going on our route, with agreeable fields on each side, we reach the dell or glen of Stravannan…. This glen appears to be a proper situation in which to plant trees.' As one can see, trees were indeed duly planted.

Pass other old steadings on your right, Langalbuinoch and Quochag. Both names are a tease as to their meaning. Langalbuinoch seems to be a conjuction of a Norse prefix 'Langill' a valley stream (we know gill or gully in English place-name usage) and Gaelic *buannachd*, 'profitable'. Langal is a prefix for several steadings on the slopes down to the Kingarth isthmus, and might have simply meant 'well-watered slopes'. As for Quochag, it

Hugh Duncan in hat and morning coat, with his dairymaid at Langalchorad, possibly c.1870. Neither, probably, had been photographed before.

might be *caochag*, Gaelic for a puff-ball or empty shell, hardly helpful, or perhaps 'windy', more probable.

Just after the turn southwards to St Blane's, the Kingarth graveyard on your right merits a visit (see p.116),

Opposite the Kingarth Hotel stands Langalchorad Farm.
Here is another Langal prefix, and the suffix supposedly means 'livestock fold', but it is difficult to be sure.

Just over a century ago, Langalchorad enjoyed renown for its fine prize winning Ayrshire cattle. Hugh Duncan, whose cattle they were,

> maintained throughout his lifetime the old time dignity of being always attired in cut-away tailcoat and square-topped hat, even when he was to be seen among his early potatoes, touching them up for the early market in which he strove to be first.
>
> William Martin, *The Farmers of Bute* (1951)

In June 1875 his potatoes were indeed the first in all Scotland to reach the Glasgow market.

A return bus to Rothesay may be picked up on the corner, by the Kingarth Hotel.

Scalpsie Bay

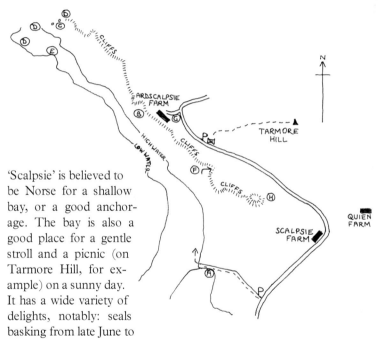

'Scalpsie' is believed to be Norse for a shallow bay, or a good anchorage. The bay is also a good place for a gentle stroll and a picnic (on Tarmore Hill, for example) on a sunny day. It has a wide variety of delights, notably: seals basking from late June to late August; the biggest geological puzzle of Bute; highly visible prehistoric and industrial archaeology; traces of Second World War defences; and stunning views. There is a small car park on the road, just before Scalpsie Farm, and a larger one on the eminence just below Tarmore Hill.

Features to look out for, and to visit:

Scalpsie or Ambrismore Mill (A). This was located just before the beach, where the burn meets the informal track from the road. The mill was in operation as early as the mid-fifteenth century, but was abandoned by 1840. The disturbed ground covered with whin, or gorse, on the far bank indicates its location. In 1780 there were no fewer than seven buildings here. The stones are now all gone, some doubtless covered in topsoil, but others probably recycled for housing or drystane dykes nearby.

Air defences. At low water a few upright posts are visible. They are set in concrete and were apparently built to prevent enemy aircraft landing on the beach. Similar posts seem to have been placed at Ettrick and Kilchattan bays. They cannot have been intended to prevent an invasion, for no meaningful invasion could have taken place without a German supply base, requiring the partial occupation of Ireland. The posts only make sense as a means to thwart the picking up or landing of enemy agents. However, whatever their original purpose, they came in handy for practice landings for D Day, when coils of barbed wire were stretched across Scalpsie and Kilchattan Bays, to frustrate luckless troops as they waded ashore, hoping not to rip their battle dress on the wire.

The sea. Scalpsie Bay had a reputation with fishermen as a spawning ground for herring. There seems to have been an expectation about the Bay which was only occasionally fulfilled. One day in December 1870, 'an enormous take of herring at Scalpsie Bay, Bute', was recorded. 'The trawler-net broke with the weight of herrings, after upwards of 1,000 crans had been secured, which realised about £700.' Yet on other occasions fishermen could also easily be frustrated. A couple of skiffs from Maidens, just south of Culzean Castle, came down the West Kyle into the Bay. They found thousands of gulls and 'herring could be seen quite plainly in the form of a big triangle.' Typical of the unpredictable nature of fishing, the tide was, in the words of one of the fishermen, 'thrawn', or perverse, and the strength of the current broke the bridle of the net and they came away empty handed.

The Haystack (B). This extraordinary composite stone stack remains a tease. It lies a few metres north of the Highland Boundary Fault Line, yet it seems to be an old sea stack formed of Old Red Sandstone or later Permian sandstone. It sits on a raised beach. If it was formed by flashfloods, its composition is derived from rocks south of the Highland Boundary Fault line. Is it the sole survivor of a major deposit along the cliffs? If its age could be determined it could be fitted into the sequence of events already established but its age, like its location, remains an enigma.

The seals. If they are around you will see the seals as you make your way to Ardscalpsie Point, on the western extremity of the bay. You are more likely to see grey than common seals (on seals see p. oo). There is a viewing point on the cliff just below the Tarmore Hill car park.

The limekilns (C). Two crude limekilns may be found close to the lava dyke (D) running from the raised beach out to Ardscalpsie Point. It is here that 'cornstone' was burnt in order to derive the lime. There is an outcrop of cornstone (E), or Carboniferous limestone, visible at low water in the slight recess in the bay, just north east of Ardscalpsie Point. The crudeness of the kilns makes one appreciate the relative sophistication of the one at Kilchattan Bay. Cornstone is a sedimentary rock formed in a semi-arid environment (i.e. as Laurentia made its way from the southern to the northern hemisphere) with the evaporation of water containing lime in solution. The first person to propagate the term was the father of English geology, William Smith, whose geological map of England in 1815, was ground-breaking in its achievement and proved astonishingly accurate. He called the limestone he found in Wiltshire, 'Cornbrash' ('brash' being a local quarrying term adding to it the fact, well-known to local farmers, that corn grew very well on it).

Make your way back along the shoreline, but cut in to the cliff where there are several appropriate points (F) where one may scramble up to the road. On reaching the road turn left.

Thom's Cut (G). The best example, perhaps, of Thom's Cuts (p.301) runs along the left or outer side of the road (indeed, you will have crossed it to get to the road). If you walk as far as the turn to Ardscalpsie Farm, you will also see one of Thom's culverts.

Retrace your steps to the carpark. Just east (right) of it you will find the path leading to the top of Tarmore Hill.

Tarmore Hill. You may enjoy the view with the help of the direction-finder plinth, but beware. The current metal plate has been wrongly orientated about 6 degrees east of north, perhaps the result of some confusion between magnetic and Grid North, so it is out of proper alignment. You can identify landmarks by holding your right arm straight out and aligning the left knuckle of your clenched fist on the landmark, count off two knuckles (nearly 6 degrees) to the right and look down at the direction finder to establish what you are looking at.

Inchmarnock. The 'island of St Marnoc' bears modest traces of an early Christian heritage. It has been farmed for many centuries, probably for millennia. In the early nineteenth century its shores were highly valued for its:

> 'inexhaustible banks of coral, which is now very much used by the tenants of the Marquess of Bute, and by other farmers in that island. It is carried in boats to the distance of 20 or 30 miles, and still reckoned a cheap manure: an unequivocal proof of its intrinsic value.'

There is still one functioning farm, Midpark, where a century ago there were three. It is said that folk with an alcohol problem and also scolds were dumped on Inchmarnock in order to return them to their senses, but this may have only happened once or twice, and as a practice may simply be myth. By 1943 there were only two functioning farms, but 20 persons actually lived on the island. Their only connection with the outside world was by small boat across to St Ninian's Bay one mile away, while horses and cattle swam across at low water.

The island was requisitioned, virtually overnight, for commando training. As one can imagine, this was hardly popular. As *The Buteman* reported:

> For one family [McFie] this is the first break of an uninterrupted tenancy for about 390 years. One of the farmers has been looking around for another farm, and when shown one in a fairly well-populated area, he is alleged to have said that it seemed all right, but that it was in a rather out of the way sort of place.

Sadly, once the continuity was broken the McFies did not return.

Descend back to the main road, turn left towards Scalpsie Farm and after ½km, turn right though a gateway, follow the track till it peters out in the field. Dun Scalpsie is straight ahead, on the heights overlooking the bay.

Dun Scalpsie (H). This Iron Age fort (c. 100 BC) commands a view across to Dunstrone and Dunagoil. When Dunagoil was stormed and fired, the inhabitants of Dun Scalpsie would have seen the great pall of smoke and known that they were defeated. Whatever was done to Dun Scalpsie at the time, it was probably nothing compared with the damage wrought by the Local Defence Volunteers during the Second World War. They apparently replaced the old stone fortifications with sandbags, to defend the Bay against a possible but surely highly improbable German landing.

Dun Scalpsie is a good vantage point for appraising the volcanic landscape of the south end of Bute.

Make your way down to the left till you reach the drystane dyke at the bottom, when you can double back along the track at the foot of the cliff to the beach.
Scalpsie and Quien Farms on the far side of the road have been a single farming unit since about 1850 when Dugald McKillop farmed here. McKillop started his working life as an apprentice, barely in his teens, at Ettrick Smiddy around 1815, but then went for farming, first working on Nether Ardroscadale farm, just north of Straad, and going on to become a breeder known throughout western Scotland. According to the local farming practice, McKillop, often abbreviated to 'McGilp', was more usually known as 'Scalpsie'. He was known as 'a character', often chided by his wife, to whom his stock reply to her hectoring was 'It's Arran shores for me, Mary.' He never put his threat into practice and they both lived to a ripe age. He died in 1890. On the far side of the road, past Quien Farm lies Quien Loch, on the west bank of which is a crannog (see p.236). It cannot be approached unless you are willing to get wet. It was connected with the adjoining shore by a 2 metre wide causeway edged with oak posts and laid with small flagstones. These were still visible a century ago, but the water is a metre deeper now.

WALK

8

The Moor Road from Kingarth War Memorial to Rothesay

Distance 7½km: 2½ hours
OS Map 4, then Map 2

BEFORE YOU WALK

Every day most of us pass a war memorial somewhere. We seldom give it a moment's thought. On Remembrance Sunday we are easily distracted from the true nightmare of human conflict by a beautiful ceremony with uniforms, bugles or the pipes. Unless we have a forbear who fell in war, it is extraordinarily difficult to relate to the reality of conflict. Here, through the story of one or two of those who fell in the carnage, one can engage in a more personal act of remembrance.

Start: Take the bus from Guildford Square bound for Kilchattan Bay, ask the driver to put you down at the Kingarth War Memorial (it is about 4 minutes' drive after Mount Stuart, on your right).

The War Memorial

Standing alone near the centre of this rural parish, there is something about this war memorial that is particularly moving. It is partly its simplicity. Because it relates to so small a community, we can relate to it too.

Consider the 32 dead from the parish in the 1914-18 war and another 11 dead in the 1939-45 conflict. The numbers would have been greater had not so many houses in Kilchattan Bay been holiday homes. Yet the Great War cut a swathe through a narrow cohort of young men who had grown up in the parish, principally young workers on the Bute Estate: for example, Hector McLeod, a widow's son, who lived in the grounds of Mount Stuart and Duncan Lamont, the mole catcher's son at Piperhall. Then there was Robert Bell, who bore the stigma of illegitimacy. His mother had been a luckless servant girl in Albert Place, Kilchattan Bay. The father most probably had come by steamer, charmed the girl and then disappeared. Robert was brought up by his grandmother Jeanie at

Duncan Lamont   *Robert Bell*   *James Gordon*

Millhouse, Kilchattan. He died on the same day as James Gordon, whose father was Lord Bute's head gamekeeper.

Robert and James must have known each other well in their school-days. They had both volunteered and been drafted into the Cameron Highlanders. They were killed in the same attack on German positions on the Aubers Ridge (15 km south west of Lille), on 9 May 1915. They had been up since 0400hrs that day, but the attack had been delayed until 1600hrs, that familiar 'rush to wait' that characterises so much of army life. When the Cameron Highlanders were ordered up to the start line, they found that the communication trenches through which they were to move forward unobserved were already choked with men of another unit. As a consequence, only just over half the battalion were in position by zero hour when they were ordered to charge across open ground. As they emerged from behind the breastworks, they ran into a hail of machine-gun and rifle fire. Of the 350 Cameron Highlanders who crossed the start line, one man alone reached the German barbed wire.

Some of the sons of the parish had migrated in adulthood. Sergeant-Major John McKay from Bruchag farm, for example, had gone to Kenya. He died of sickness, the principal cause of death for those British posted to the King's African Rifles, but he is still remembered here.

Then there were the Canadian Brandanes. Dugald Boag grew up at Birgidale Butts (barely 1½ km west of here) but migrated to the prairies. He volunteered in December 1914, even though he was 36 years old, and rose to the rank of Sergeant in Princess Patricia's Canadian Light Infantry (PPCLI), a unit formed specifically for this conflict. He fell at Passchendaele, 30 October 1917. Along with the Somme, Passchendaele must be rated among the very worst battles of the war. The planned attack had been delayed because of almost incessant rain since August. The ground was not simply waterlogged but, by dint of shelling, reduced to a series of deep ponds, mud and slime, ground so dangerous that in places to leave the duckboards risked drowning in mud. A decision was made to attack before winter rendered further advance impossible. On the night of the 29th, the PPCLI moved forward to the start line. The night was clear, so Germans defending the higher ground saw the troop movements and prepared themselves. At 0550hrs on the 30th, the British barrage began and three minutes later Dugald and his fellows climbed out of their trenches. No sooner were they 'over the top' than the Germans put down a heavy barrage of their own as the Canadians advanced across the morass. It was, predictably, a slaughter. Dugald Boag probably died in the first few minutes. Within the first hour the regiment had lost 80 per cent of its officers and sergeants. Yet the survivors of this terrible mayhem did not flinch from their task, capturing the high ground towards which they had advanced. Out of the 500 or so riflemen who crossed the start line, by dusk there were only 180 left.

Daniel Black grew up in the delightfully innocent setting of Kerrycroy and became, like his father, a carpenter. He, too, moved to Canada and enlisted in 1915, aged 25. In August 1918 he won the Military Medal, rushing forward to capture a machine-gun post single-handed. Four weeks later he was dead. He was only 28.

Daniel Black

Frank Saunders was the son of the manse, born in 1881. He spent his childhood here, attending Rothesay Academy before going on to Glasgow University. He followed his father into the church, becoming a minister in Kirkcudbrightshire. When conscription was introduced in 1916 he could, presumably, have opted for the Chaplains' Department, a relatively safe choice. Instead, he enlisted in January 1916 and just over a year later was commissioned into 5th Battalion, Argyll and Sutherland Highlanders.

Frank Saunders

Morris Meredith Williams' Cartoon of Figures NE (4th) Panel, design for the Scottish National War Memorial (Scottish National Portrait Gallery).

Following the Bolshevik Revolution, Germany had been able to move all its troops from the Eastern to the Western Front, launching massive attacks through April and May 1918. The Allies were able to contain this frightening offensive, but not before Haig had issued orders to all troops that they must not retreat, come what may. The line held and the tide turned. In July the Allies began to push the Germans back from the River Marne to the Aisne. On the evening of 31 July, Frank and his fellow officers received orders to attack at first light the following morning. Their battalion was already reduced to less than half strength, barely 250 men led by six officers. In order to cover their allotted frontage, they had to put every man into a single line, perhaps evoking a regimental memory of 'The Thin Red Line' at Balaclava, 1854. After a preliminary bombardment of enemy positions, at 0449 hours the Argylls fixed bayonets and climbed out of their trenches to advance across open ground. The dense combination of early morning mist and a smoke screen was such that the officers led, revolver in one hand, compass in the other. Their objective was the village of Beugneux (15 km south of Soissons) and 'Hill

158' south of it. We can imagine the scene, the troops walking steadily but blindly forward towards the German positions through the mist and smoke, then very suddenly these luckless men, both Scots and Germans, face to face: an intense exchange of fire and charging the enemy down. The Argylls captured their objective but at heavy cost, including all six officers. It was Frank's 37th birthday. His place of burial remains unknown, which must have given added anguish to his widow. A grave at least affords a focus for grief.

What is there to say of them, each a victim of the failed policies of the chancelleries of Europe, beyond the obvious: that these policies inflicted a wilful and profound desecration on human life? Perhaps we must leave it to those who fought and who, like Wilfred Owen, could articulate the true dimensions of the tragedy, his words themselves like bugles, calling the fallen from sad shires. Owen was killed in the last week of the war but Private Harry Patch lived until 2009. He had fought at Passchendaele. He was Britain's last surviving veteran of the trenches. Aged 110, he gave his considered verdict: 'War is the calculated and condoned slaughter of human beings.' May our elected leaders take note.

The memorial was unveiled in 1921. John Saunders, the bereaved parish minister, was too ill to conduct the dedication service himself and it was performed by Rothesay's minister (and historian), J.K.Hewison. Those assembled sang the *'Old Hundredth'*. Pipers from the Bute Mountain Battery played *'Lord Lovat's Lament'*.

The beauty of the ceremony gave no hint of the acrimony surrounding the memorial's erection. The small memorial committee which had formed itself had resolved to list the war dead simply by name, without military rank or the regiment to which they belonged. John Saunders asked the committee to allow this decision to be reconsidered at a meeting of the subscribers. It would, he said, 'be a deplorable thing to have anything but the greatest possible unanimity in connection with a sacred memorial for the glorious dead.' Mr Esplin, the committee secretary objected to this suggestion on a point of 'standing orders' of the committee. Mr Saunders observed that no such standing orders existed. 'Whereupon,' according to *The Buteman*,

> Mr Esplin said that he would not allow himself to be insulted in that way, and rising from his seat at the table he made his way to the door. The Chairman then said that if Mr Esplin was going, he would go too, and twitted Mr Saunders with always wishing to have his own

way in everything… [and said] he would attend no public meeting of the subscribers.

The subscribers, however, evidently had their way, for rank and unit are both specified. We are left perplexed by the contrast between the heroic sacrifice of those driven into the slaughter, whose names are engraved on this memorial, and the day-to-day pettiness of our more usual behaviour.

Take the track running to the left of the memorial.
Enjoy the lapsed-coppice beech trees along this road. These were planted ornamentally, for beech is otherwise not of much practical use except for firewood, unless you plan to make kitchen chairs. Beech, an introduced species, is common enough in Bute, but is a rarity in the Western Isles (see p.332).

On your right you will pass a late nineteenth century reservoir. The fine brickwork of the reservoir settlement housing is a delight. It is no surprise that it was designed by Robert Rowand Anderson, when he was rebuilding Mount Stuart in the early 1880s, to ensure the water supply to the estate and to Kerrycroy. It probably replaced a reservoir made necessary by Robert Thom's dexterous channelling for his water mills of the previous source here (see p.302).

Cross roads. On your right the track leads down to New Farm. Dan Edgar recalls life here in the 1950s. An admirer of Burns, in 2009 he remembered the farm from his childhood:

It reminds me now of *The Cottar's Saturday Night*, almost as if I had been there. My grandmother, Flora (Bell) Middleton, was the driving force in the household. She would read the Bible by paraffin lamp or candlelight every evening as we sat around the table. I can only assume my love of language stems from those candlelit sessions, and the subliminal effect of the beautiful poetry and prose of the King James Version of the Scriptures.

There was no running water and no electricity at New Farm until about 1955. My grandmother cooked wonderful meals on the old range. The hot water system was a giant kettle, permanently hung on a swee over the fire, periodically topped up from an enamel pail. The water came from a spigot outside. The water came from a natural spring. The toilet was an old stone outhouse a hundred yards from the house. It was a square box, with a couple of bars on which to sit to do one's business. There was straw in the bottom of the box and you just threw more straw on top when you had finished. The box was mucked out once a week. Within sight was the reservoir that supplied Mount Stuart with running water, and serviced the swimming pool. I realised that something was not quite right.

My grandfather, Angus Munn Middleton, by then in his eighties, had been a drystane dyker but had been hurt in a rockfall. I remember at the age of ten being with him when the factor gave him a harsh dressing

Dan Edgar with his grandfather, Angus Munn Middleton.

down for possessing [and grazing], as I recall, one animal too many, my grandfather his cap in his hands, his head bowed. Even at that young age I knew it could not be right. No wonder my politics were shaped at an early age. When I was older and grew to love the poetry of Burns, I recognised what I had witnessed:

> Poor tenant-bodies, scant o'cash,
> How they maun thole a factor's snash   [*abuse*]
> He'll stamp an' threaten, curse an' swear
> He'll apprehend them, poind their gear   [*impound*]
> While they maun stand, wi' aspect humble,
> An' hear it a', an fear an' tremble!

>> 'Twa Dogs: A Tale', in *Poems, chiefly in the Scottish Dialect*, 1786.

The land around here used to be frequented by poachers. Samuel Rippie was caught poaching nearby in November 1889. He appeared in court in January when he entered a plea of not guilty. The gamekeeper said in evidence that he took two rabbits out of the prisoner's pockets. At one blow Rippie demolished both the gamekeeper's statement and his own defence by indignantly informing the sheriff that the witness was not telling the truth. He had, he said, only one rabbit in his possession.

On your left you will in due course pass three houses, the second being Dixon's Dam, an old dwelling, perhaps dating back to 1820. It acquired its name from one of Thom's small auxiliary reservoirs built to retain water destined for Loch Fad, and eventually to drive the cotton mills in Rothesay (p.302). We can reasonably suppose is that it refers to the engineer who carried out the work here on behalf of Thom. The dam and reservoir are long since gone. We do not know when Scoulag Moor first became farmland. It may not have been until the late eighteenth century, during the agricultural revolution. If you look across to the grassy turf part of the hillside beyond, you may notice the telltale signs of runrig, or 'ridge and furrow', ploughing. We know it was farmed for most of the nineteenth century, until perhaps sometime around 1880 when the 3rd Marquess decided to let the land revert to moorland for shooting game.

It was somewhere along here during smuggling days that there was supposedly a cache of contraband. It is said that if anyone came wandering down the road while the goods were being moved, a black coffin left on the road would 'rise up and begin to walk towards him.'

After 3.5km the road begins to descend to Loch Ascog. You will pass a plantation of conifer, edged with beech. Shortly after, as you descend, look out for a sign on a gate on your right, directing you to Mid-Ascog. Take it and cross a couple of fields, then pass through a neck of woodland (through which another of Thom's silted-up cuts passes, to feed Loch Ascog.) Cross the next two fields. Turn right, following the track. Turn left up the tarmac road. As you reach the top of the hill, you will see the track off to your right to Ascog Millburn, a separate walk, p.85.

As you descend into the valley, you will see Windyhall Farm on the opposite hillside overlooking Loch Ascog. In 1807 a Mr Stobbo, a surgeon by profession, was farming Windyhall. He is a nice example of those caught up in the spirit of agricultural ferment in Bute in this period. That same year he introduced John Wilkie's iron frame plough, described at the time as 'the best plough ever used in the county of Ayr, or probably in Britain.' It was an improved version of the Berwickshire farmer James Small's literally groundbreaking 'swing' plough of 1763. With a feathered share and curved mouldboard, these ploughs cut the furrow and turned over the sod with minimum friction. Wilkie improved it by lengthening the mouldboard, and giving it a greater twist, thus turning the sod more thoroughly.

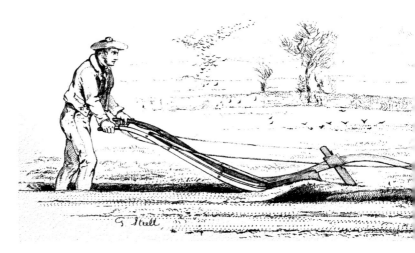

Stobbo's neighbours began to sidle up to him to borrow the Wilkie plough 'for a couple of days'. By 1810 his neighbours were clamouring for him to procure similar ones for them. In 1809 he introduced a drill-barrow for turnips, and within a couple of years he was lending it to sixteen neighbours. He must have been relieved when six other machines were brought to the island. Stobbo had clearly started something at Windyhall. He would have found it very satisfying to learn that in February 1866, well after his own demise, two prize-winning greystone turnips were grown at Windyhall, 'the respective measurements being 39 inches and 37 inches in circumference.'

Follow the road back to Rothesay. Once over the hill just keep following the road down hill.
You will pass through a beautiful beech plantation. The leaf cover of beech allows very little light onto the ground, popularly known as 'summer darkness', which is why few ground plants will grow in beech woodland.

A few paces beyond the Rothesay Golf Clubhouse, you can turn right to take a quieter road back to the Serpentine (map, p.20) and back into town.

John Wilkie's iron frame plough (compare with what it replaced, on p.259).

Harvesting at Windyhall in the 1920s. The two Harvey brothers on the right, with a couple of farm hands. Their brother, Jack, died of wounds in May 1918. In April 1917 he had won the Military Medal, something his surviving brothers could be proud of.

Kames Castle

PART 3

North Bute

North Bute only became a separate parish from Rothesay in 1844. At the time it had no coherent centre. Port Bannatyne was simply a collection of but-and-bens, housing fisher families. Elsewhere there were steadings, moorland and Kames Castle, home for over three hundred years, until the early 1800s, to the Bannatyne family.

This section is composed of two walks, and an exploration around Ettrick Bay, plus a few notes on settlements facing the eastern Kyles, including Rhubodach, where at the time of writing it is only possible to take a pretty stroll opposite Burnt Islands. At some point a more satisfying walk may be opened up to include the evocative site of Balnakailly.

174

WALK

9

Port Bannatyne and The Kames Estate

Distance 6km: 2½ hours
OS Map 2

BEFORE YOU WALK

This walk is from Port Bannatyne to Wester Kames, to Croc-an-Raer, thence back via Easter Kames, Banntyne Mains, down to Pointhouse (Ardbeg) and back to Port Bannatyne. The Kames estate, covering the valley and hillsides facing Kames Bay remained a distinct entity from the Middle Ages until 1863 when it was finally acquired by the Marquess of Bute. The walk is replete with anecdotes, which you may wish to skim before setting out, or read fully once sat down with a cup of tea.

Start at the stone quay in Port Bannatyne.

The stone quay was completed in 1801. It had been commissioned in 1797 on the instruction of Lord Bannatyne, the local landlord, 'for the general benefit of that part of the country as a place where vessels passing up and down the Clyde, Loch Fine or Kintyre might be with safety.' In 2009 there was still a picturesque hulk beside the stone quay, the last of three wooden fishing boats still in use in the 1960s.

In the early 1800s there was a small fishing community living here, self-sufficient in curing their own nets and sails. Before the advent of Indian cutch, oak or saugh (willow) bark was brewed up to produce the tannin mixture for curing the sails and nets. This brew was purchased from one of the two barking houses, one of which, with its adjoining fisher dwellings and storage, is still standing. These are the last buildings on the left, going up Quay Place (opposite the quay), and were built around 1804. The other barking house no longer exists but was close to the War Memorial, where the main road from Rothesay joins the Shore Road in Port Banntyne.

Port Bannatyne, however, is essentially like Kilchattan Bay, a late nineteenth century development, which displaced the handful of fisher

Port Bannatyne with fishing nets on the shore.

dwellings that had been here since the eighteenth century and possibly earlier.

Among the fisher folk here in 1805 was a small colony of millenarian Christians, followers of a hellfire and damnation preacher called Donald McArthur. Writing in the *Rothesay Journal* in 1852, a Mr McGavin remembered coming to the shore in 1813 where he accosted a member of this colony:

> I was desirous of seeing some of your friends here, because they are everywhere spoken against. 'Ah,' said the fisherman, 'if we were more like Jesus Christ, they would speak far more against us. It's our shame that they speak so little against us, and is a sign we are growing too much like the world.... [Donald McArthur's] work began at Dunoon where the first conversions took place. It was there that I was awakened, and there were half a dozen families there. We considered whether we should settle at Greenock or come to Bute, and agreed to come here, and many of us went to America, so that we are now few as well as poor.'

Donald McArthur seems to have started his mission around 1800. His preaching was, in the disapproving words of William Aiton, 'a delusive frenzy' by this 'native of Argyllshire, who was bred a shoemaker, and afterwards became a herring-fisher, and whose education spread no farther than reading English.' Yet, whatever McArthur lacked in education he certainly made up for in oratory. His silver-tongued rhetoric rendered him hugely popular on the shores of Loch Fyne, Cowal, Bute and the Cumbraes where people flocked to hear his warnings that they were all doomed. If reports of McArthur's preaching are remotely accurate, he makes Stella Gibbons' comic creation, Amos Starkadder, seem bland by comparison:

> When he [McArthur] spoke out his great swollen words of vanity about the roasting, burning and roaring of the damned in hell, some of the hearers who had never heard such modes of expression, began to move their heads from side to side like the motion of a pendulum, and to increase the motion to a surprising degree of velocity, till often they were drenched in sweat. They next started up, making unnatural screams, fell down, tumbled or rolled on the ground; foam issued from their mouths and blood from their noses. These shoutings were infectious, for whenever one began others followed and the sound increased to a surprising degree.

Perhaps it was Aiton's description of McArthur that inspired James Hogg's imagined preacher of Auchtermuchy:

> Nothing in the world delights a truly religious people so much as consigning them to eternal damnation.... All who heard him were amazed, and many of them went into fits, writhing and foaming in a state of the most horrid agitation.
>
> James Hogg, *Confessions of a Justified Sinner* (1824)

McArthur, however, was destined to face a severe personal crisis, and he must have wondered if he himself had not been damned. For it was on the very shore here on 20 October 1805 that, according to *The Edinburgh Annual Register*:

> while M'Arthur was celebrating divine service in the midst of his congregation, [the local Justice of the Peace, John Campbell of Southall] had violently seized upon his person, forced him on board a vessel bound for Greenock,.... marched him along the road as a common felon, and delivered him to Captain Tatham, the regulating officer for that quarter, as a person fit to serve in his Majesty's navy. That officer.... speedily conveyed him out of the jurisdiction of the Scottish courts. After being detained for five weeks on board different ships of war, and suffering, as he alleged, every species of indignity and hardship, Mr M'Arthur was discharged on the express order of the Lords of the Admiralty, and furnished with a certificate that he was never

again to be impressed into his Majesty's navy.

McArthur was released on the grounds that clerics were exempt from the press. It says little for McArthur's disciples that they seem to have meekly stood aside as their leader was abducted, unless direct divine intervention was part of their belief system.

Forgiveness does not seem to have been McArthur's strongest suit but who can blame him? He knew perfectly well that he had been deliberately targeted and he consequently decided to obtain maximum damages. Campbell justified the seizure by accusing McArthur of 'preaching immoral and seditious doctrines'. This argument struck the Edinburgh Court of Session as irrelevant, which found in favour of McArthur, who apparently walked away with £2,000 in damages (something in the order of £66,000 in today's money).

Possibly fearing another assault or perhaps his head having been turned by the possession of such riches, McArthur seems to have deserted his flock here in search of fresh pastures in New York State. But in the New World he slipped from view, outdone perhaps by the stiff competition to be found in that land of millenarian preachers.

As you walk towards the boatyard and the stone mole:

The mole is to provide shelter for a boat marina. During the Second World War, Kames Bay was the scene of fervid salvage activity. Damaged and torpedoed merchantmen were brought into the bay, and when the bay was full others were taken into Rothesay Bay. Malcolm McMillan was a junior salvage diver and remembers:

> Port Bannatyne was the salvage centre for the whole of the North West Atlantic approaches. All the damaged vessels came here. Vessels were bumped by the enemy off the west coast of Ireland. The casualties that did not make it were buried at Croc-an-Raer. I remember one ship, the *Coronda*, a four-mast merchantman carrying whale oil from the South Atlantic, was hit down aft, where the magazine was, below the living quarters. It was terrible.

Twenty six men had been killed when an aerial bomb hit the *Coronda*'s magazine. In those days, of course, neither Malcolm McMillan nor his colleagues received any counselling for the psychological ordeal of what confronted them below decks.

> I was a shipwright diver, and with others made sufficient repairs for the marine casualties to be taken to dock. We once went to the north

of Skye where there was a stricken vessel, an American 'Liberty' ship, 7,000 tons, prefabricated and assembled in ten days. We made a temporary repair with layers of alternate canvas and rubber down each of the cracks in the hull, sufficient to refloat her. We put thick plates on her to get her around the Mull of Kintyre. We would measure the buckling hull with a plumb-line strung between the two masts. Because of the danger that it might founder *en route* for the Clyde we had to stay on deck the whole time. We used compressed air to force the water out of the hull.'

Work was carried out also for Royal Navy submarines at a large steel floating dock in the bay.

Follow the road north-westwards along the shore, pause at (but do not take) the turning to Ettrick Bay.

With the growth of the herring fishing in the nineteenth century it was inevitable that the shore became festooned with nets, or 'deepins', drying or being mended. By the late 1850s there were 25 herring skiffs. By now, however, Port Bannatyne was rapidly becoming 'a choice summer-retreat of strangers for sea-bathing'. Consequently, while it had a permanent population of only about 330 inhabitants, a growing proportion of its house were villas, suitable for those who came for recreational purposes. The politeness of the holiday-making middle classes began to clash with the work-a-day needs of the fisher community. Duncan Hoyle, who became the proprietor of the Kames estate in 1850s decided to impose order. 'We have the shores of our beautiful bay desecrated by a line of naked poles… with black dingy nets which endanger the lives of passengers on the highway.' So he made the fisher folk move both their boats, their net drying frames and other paraphernalia well away from where they had customarily had them, so as not to impede the newly laid highway as it turned up towards Ettrick Bay. The fishermen, led by James Lamont who owned the Quay Place barking house, were furious but impotent. Hoyle had his way, but acquired great unpopularity among the permanent population.

Continue walking along the edge of the bay for another ½km to the first track on your left, by the cottage, marked 'Through Road for Walkers'.

This is Sawmill Cottage. As its name implies, it is the last vestige of a sawmill here in the nineteenth century, established in the 1850s for local boat building. The water wheel was mounted on its flank wall. The building had previously been used for a lint mill, which marks the beginning of Scotland's transition from a rudimentary economy producing raw materials to one that could hold its own in European manufactures.

In order to address this economic backwardness, compared with England's prosperity, a Board of Trustees for Fisheries and Manufactures was established in 1727, intended among other things to 'carry to perfection linen manufacture'. Scottish linen had a poor reputation for rotting easily (since lime was used for bleaching) and for being sold in underlength or under-width bolts. During the middle decades of the century massive efforts were made to develop the industry.

Linen was used for anything from canvas sails in the Atlantic (probably providing for the local fishing boats too) to the finest shirts or table linen for London society. Scottish linen had tended to the cheaper end of the market since lint, or flax, was a side crop within a subsistence agricultural system. To produce high quality lint required a dedicated and skilled workforce. In 1762 the Trustees for Fisheries and Manufactures decided to invest their funds in Bute, which could feed directly into Glasgow and Paisley's burgeoning weaving industry. The mill here, like the one on the Lade in Rothesay, did not spin the flax. Rather, the mill performed the 'scutching', the breaking of flax stems necessary before combing out the fibres (on the process for linen production see p.298). The actual spinning would still have been done by hand in the dwellings of northern Bute. A couple of Glasgow firms were successively given inducements to use and develop Bute's spinning capacity. They probably supplied local women with spinning wheels.

For a while the linen thread spun here was woven on the island into coarse fabrics like osnaburg. A Rothesay merchant, William Risk, kept a warehouse stocked with osnaburg, which he exported to the West Indies plantations to clothe slaves, the destination of most of the linen produced in the west of Scotland. This market took an increasing share of Scottish linen production: 24 per cent in 1766, rising to 78 per cent in 1810. As with salted herring, Bute's growing prosperity was built on the demands of the plantations and their slave population. But by the time slavery was actually abolished, in 1833, cotton had largely displaced linen. In 1776 Bute was producing 5,000 spindles annually (each spindle having approximately eight miles of continuous thread), yet that year the Glasgow spinning firms withdrew, almost certainly because they foresaw what was happening: a rise in the cost of raw lint and a halving in the cost of raw cotton during the years 1776-1780.

However, the mill here may have continued to operate, for it was still described as a lint mill when adapted for timber in the late 1850s by Duncan Hoyle. Hoyle had been born in a thatched cottage opposite the lint mill. His was a rags-to-riches success story. He had gone to Australia where he had made a fortune in the gold fields, and increased it by running a pub in St Enoch's Square, Glasgow, a tribute to the unquenchable thirst of that great city.

If you are wondering if anything preceded the lint mill, it was probably the Kames corn mill built in 1491.

After 150 metres, you will pass the scene of a tragedy that took place in March 1968. The Camerons were a family of Travellers, a couple in their late eighties and their 36 year-old son, Alexander. They were traditional Travellers, possibly descended from the Gaelic tinsmiths, who had been something of a special caste in Highland society for many centuries, indeed possibly since Iron Age times, as people who could work magic with metal. Yet, equally, the Camerons may have been descended from remnants of the Jacobite army. Jacobite clan names are common within the Traveller community. With Redcoats scouring the Highlands 'to pursue and hunt out these vermin amongst their lurking holes', to quote Butcher Cumberland's own despicable words, there may have been many clansmen who joined Travellers to acquire a new identity and thus escape destruction.

By the 1960s those Travellers still living in crude shelters were a dwindling minority. Most were in caravans, either horse-drawn or motorised. Yet the Camerons still used the traditional 'gelly', a shelter made of bent saplings or hazel wands. They had covered these wands with old bags and plastic sheeting, where once there had been tarpaulin. Perhaps these shelters were largely unchanged from those of early humans, who would have covered bent saplings with skins. The Camerons and others still using gellies kept warm with a wood or coal stove for cooking, probably home-made from an old tin or oil drum, with a 'reek' or stove pipe through the roof. Needless to say, these were a terrible fire hazard. All the Cameron's worldly possessions were kept in a 'hurly', a pram. After they had gone to sleep the shelter caught fire. Severely burnt on his limbs, face, chest, Alexander managed to crawl along the track, presumably back to Sawmill

Travellers in their traditional bow tent in Kintyre. The Camerons' bow tent must have been similar, covered in plastic rather than tarpaulin.
© A. Stewart.

Cottage, to get help. His mother, Isabella, died in hospital the next day. His father, 89-year old George Cameron, seems to have survived. By an irony of fate, George had been born only a few yards away. One wonders where he had roamed during his lifetime. Isabella came from Travellers at Tyndrum. Her funeral in Rothesay saw a mighty gathering of friends and relatives, word of the tragedy having flown rapidly across the Traveller network.

At that time there were probably about 450 Traveller families in Scotland, roughly 2,000 people in all. Today, far from dwindling, there are probably in the order of 750 Traveller households, possibly totalling 3,000 persons all told. The decision taken in Edinburgh half a century ago to ensure that every county created designated camp sites and decent shelter, rescued the Travellers from the danger of imminent oblivion after half a century of economic collapse. This collapse was manifest in three principal ways: mass production destroyed the market for metal working; the internal combustion engine displaced horsepower; and cheap plastic goods displaced woven baskets.

After another 150 metres, you will pass a track on your right running uphill, to Hilton Farm. Had you been here on 16 August 1875, you would happily have tripped up this track for, in the words of the *Glasgow Herald*:

> A pic-nic of something like American proportions took place at the site of the old slate quarries on the farm of Hilton on Tuesday last. About 100 assembled together, composed principally of young farmers and their sisters and sweethearts... Dancing went on merrily on the green, and an adjournment took place in the evening to the farm

of South Colmac, where Mr and Mrs Simpson gave every facility in providing tea and the use of their large barn....

What would you not have given to be present at this Arcadian scene? We have lost so much community cohesion since then.

WESTER KAMES CASTLE

Who would not wish to live in this utterly charming fortified house? It would be nice to claim that what you see is the original structure, which was probably built around 1650. However, by 1895 only the vaulted ground floor survived, the walls barely two metres high. Lord Bute, the then owner, commissioned Robert Weir Schultz (p.111) to rebuild the castle, inspired by what little remained. What you therefore see is the castle as imagined by one of the leading Arts & Crafts architects of his day, although Schultz's design was never fully completed. You will see a course of thin red bricks on the tower, distinguishing modern fantasy above from ancient architecture below. The rest of the frontage has a few more indicator red bricks. Were it not for these red markers (Schultz was scrupulous about declaring his 'invention'), the castle would have been harled, in keeping with standard practice in the seventeenth century.

Wester Kames after and before it was rebuilt.

Fortified houses of this kind were symptomatic of the lawless conditions endured by many parts of Scotland periodically until the end of the seventeenth century. Except for its border country, England had no regions of equivalent turbulence, for it had enjoyed the stability and comparative prosperity of a highly centralised state for longer than any other country in Europe.

Myth claims that Wester Kames was a Mackinlay property until the end of the thirteenth century. It was then apparently granted to the Spens family. The first Spens here was supposedly a scion of Clan Donald who served Robert the Bruce as his 'dispenser'. What we know for sure is that in 1445 the Royal Chamberlain ordered 130,000 slates from Wester Kames, from the quarry on the hillside above, to repair the king's castle at Dumbarton. When Wester Kames itself was rebuilt in 1905, the slates came from the same quarry, naturally.

Pass through Edinbeg farmyard and continue walking until you reach the church at Croc-an-Raer, and turn into the graveyard.

Tragically the church building is now a ruin. At the end of 1980 the congregation was advised that £50,000 was required to render the roof safe. They simply had not the money and most churchgoers in any case attended St Ninian's in Port Bannatyne. It was sold for one penny. An asset stripper removed the lead and slates, and disappeared. Architecturally it is now of little interest, but remains a much loved, albeit crumbling, landmark.

In addition it has lost the two features which had distinguished it, though both miraculously survive elsewhere. The church had an old-fashioned long table for Communion, in keeping with the seventeenth and eighteenth century form of Presbyterian celebration, a style fast disappearing even at the time the church was completed in 1836. These tables are now a great rarity (there is an example in the National Museum, Edinburgh). The table ran three-quarters of the length of the building, separated from the pews on either side. At the east end of the church the double doors opened into the vestibule under the tower, and were only used on Communion Sunday. In the words of A.S. Borrowman, one of the last ministers before the closure:

> During the singing of the Communion hymn, the people leave their pews, and singing proceed into the vestibule, the door is thrown open and the members [returning into the body of the church] take their

places on either side of the Table. It was necessary to have several sittings, those who had received communion leaving the church by the doors either side of the pulpit at the west end, so that the only persons finally left in the church would be the officiating minister and any elders assisting him. Mercifully, the rarity of this table was recognised and it is now in a museum in Perthshire.

The other feature was the stained glass window made by the Glaswegian firm, William Meikle & Sons, and installed in 1896 at the beginning of the firm's fame. It is in the nature of greed to be hasty and Croc-an-Raer's despoiler rushed off with his ill-gotten lead and slates, ignoring this, the most valuable item. Somehow it survived, no one throwing stones through the glass. Twenty years later an American couple hoped to purchase the ruin, to turn it into a holiday home. When that proved unfeasible, they decided to rescue the window they so much admired, putting it into the hands of a local stained glass expert and craftsman, Alec Galloway, who lovingly restored it. It now enjoys a new existence in Louisiana.

Panel from the Meikle window at Croc-an-Raer church: 'In the end of the Sabbath, as it began to dawn toward the first day of the week, came Mary Magdalene and the other Mary to see the sepulchre…'

Croc-an-Raer's chequered history says much about the disputatious quality of the Kirk. Officially, it was named North Bute Church but local people called it by its locality, Croc-an-Raer, or more properly *Cnoc-an-Rath*, 'hillock of the fort', a hill fort just west of Lower Ettrick Farm.

Rothesay parish church had customarily held a Gaelic service on the Sabbath morning and an English one in the afternoon. In 1834 the Rothesay elders decided to abandon the Gaelic service in favour of two

English ones. This caused outrage among 1,400 Gaels, most of whom lived in north Bute and many of whom were recent incomers from Argyllshire. The church here was built at the Marquess of Bute's expense partly to assuage this indignation. So Croc-an-Raer offered a Gaelic service in the morning under the comforting aegis of their old Gaelic-speaking pastor, Alexander MacBride, and perhaps more reluctantly one in the Sassanach tongue in the afternoon. The church could seat 700, but on its first Sunday 'the church was filled to overflowing, and many were obliged to return home for want of accommodation.' As if to drive the point home a Gaelic missionary was engaged to officiate in Rothesay for those there too infirm to get to Croc-an-Raer.

By 1843 the dust, it seemed, had settled on the linguistic storm and the Rothesay elders, filled with contrition, had decided to build a dedicated Gaelic-only chapel in Rothesay's Old Vennel [still there in 2009, but long since closed, in what is now Russell Street]. However, a far larger cataclysm was to burst upon the scene that year, namely the Disruption. Since 1712 the laird in each parish had enjoyed the right of choosing the minister, regardless of the wishes of the congregation. On the whole this had led to a more liberal slant, since few lairds wished to be harangued each Sunday by narrow-minded firebrands. Yet however beneficial that regime had been, it was also incontrovertibly undemocratic. In that year, 1843, the question of democratic choice of minister split the Kirk more spectacularly than anything before it, certainly since the Covenanter conflicts of the seventeenth century.

One third of the Church of Scotland's ministers resigned. Alexander MacBride was one of them, faithfully followed by his congregation. It was only a fortnight before a seasonal service of Holy Communion. MacBride asked if, exceptionally, they could use the building just once more for this service since no one else would be using it. Passions were high and charity temporarily in short supply, so he was refused. MacBride and his 470 communicants, the entire tenantry of the parish, defied the torrential rain to celebrate the Lord's Supper on the road and in the field opposite. Oh, sweet martyrdom! Following which, the dissenters met in the open when fine and in the top floor of the Port Inn when wet until they were able to build a 'Free' church of their own in Port Bannatyne. The Disruption in the life of the Church was not healed until 1929. In the meantime, by 1895 Gaelic had virtually disappeared and was no longer a requirement for the minister at Croc-an-Raer.

CROC-AN-RAER GRAVEYARD

Graveyards always contain their own discreet rewards. Look out for:

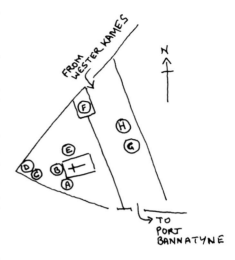

(A) **The Hogarths**, a fishing family at St Ninian's Point (see p.75). Death was the close neighbour of every family until the twentieth century. John Hogarth and his wife, Jane Nelson Waugh, living at St Ninian's Point, buried two daughters, Agnes in her infancy and Isabella at the age of 15. That was not so unusual. Yet one branch of the Hogarths was particularly well acquainted with sorrow. Mary Malcom, remembered on a nearby stone, married James Hogarth, a fisherman at Port Bannatyne in 1856 and bore him eleven children, of whom three were deaf and incapable of oral speech: her eldest, James, her sixth, Jane, and her tenth, Kate. She buried her seventh child, Gilbert, aged 20 months in 1870, her ninth, Mary, aged only 5 weeks in 1872. The sea took her son, Malcom, when he was thirty in 1900, yachting off Milford Haven. Five years later, in 1905, it also took her man, James, aged 73. His skiff sank following a collision with another boat off Arran. It seems he got entangled either in the sail or the running gear. His body was never recovered. Ten years later she lost her youngest, another Gilbert. He had gone to Canada in search of a better life. With the onset of war, he had enlisted in the Alberta Regiment. He was blown to bits in a desperate counter-attack to defend the Ypres Salient on 23 April 1915, one of 55,000 Allied soldiers whose mortal remains were never recovered, their names inscribed on the Menin Gate. Every evening without fail, the traffic halts and a bugle sounds the *Last Post*, a daily passing-bell for the blasphemy perpetrated upon them. Mary's grief was not yet enough. Another son, William, died in 1918, aged only 55.

(B) **The Revd John MacArthur** took over an empty church as Minister here in 1843 after Alexander McBride had led the entire congregation out. Think of his awesome task rebuilding a congregation and his unpopularity with the members of the new Free Church who now gathered in Port Bannatyne, perhaps still a little damp from the rigours of their first Communion as a Free Church. It cannot have been much fun for him but, as the gravestone states, he stuck it out for 25 years.

(C) and (D) **Simpsons** and **Hunters** respectively. Both were nineteenth century incomer farming families from Ayrshire. There are many in today's farming community that can claim descent from one or both families.

(E) **James McFie** of North Park, Inchmarnock, who died in 1901. He, it probably was, who rowed across to St Ninian's Point with his rabbits (p.76).

(F) **Duncan Hoyle**, briefly master of Kames. His is the tall stone cross surrounded by railings, close by where you entered the graveyard, once gleaming white marble, now turned almost black.

(G) **The merchant navy seamen** buried at the line of white limestone graves, 21 men from the *Coronda* (p.177), or at least as many body parts as could be found, are interred in seven graves. Their fate is too terrible to contemplate for long. Here are two things to marvel at: that the merchant seamen came from such varied international backgrounds and also the strong presence of men from the Gaidhealtachd, the Gaelic inscription reading: 'Eternal rest grant him, O Lord; and may light perpetual shine upon him.' Indeed, these stones seem to be the last permanent public evidence of Gaelic in Bute.

(H) **John Balloch** (1860-1947), to be found three graves to the right of the merchant seamen. His name is below that of his wife, Eliza Porteous, on the same stone. John Balloch was a famous piper. He joined the army, aged 18. Four years later, he piped the lead company of the Highland Brigade into action at Tel el-Kebir, 13 September 1882. He undertook his role with courage, only a few paces from the commanding officer who was shot down. The battle itself, however, was hardly an honourable episode. It was undertaken to overthrow a nationalist leader in Egypt inimical to British interests. It commenced the British Occupation of Egypt, which decisively ended with the Suez débâcle in 1956. Having blighted Egypt with 70 years of occupation, Britain went on to damage profoundly the prospects of the indigenous people of Palestine and Iraq. Balloch, of course, was simply a soldier, doing his duty. He was posted to India where he tutored Gurkha pipers and composed a number of tunes, some of them still well known. Having retired in 1899, he rejoined the King's Own Scottish Borderers in 1914 and served with them till 1918.

Across the main road is a mound, now planted with fir trees which give the place a strongly interior feeling. The stone wall surrounding it is late eighteenth century, but what lies inside is largely a matter for conjecture. Once thought of as a prehistoric site, it is probably medieval. Possibly thinking it to be a prehistoric fort or burial mound, it appealed to one nineteenth century owner of the Kames estate, James Hamilton (see below), as a place to be buried, hence the rather tumbled down tomb. He had must have fallen out with his wife, Harriet, since he stipulated he was to remain buried *alone*. If she had had her wits about her she could have emulated my own forebear and hit back by inscribing her husband's stone with the prescription: 'Prepare to meet thy God'.

Walk back towards Port Bannatyne along the main road, but note almost immediately the small grove at the road junction.
This is where Travellers would camp seasonally, even in the post-war years. A row of red-roofed houses had been built by the Council just west of Croc-an-Raer Church, apparently to accommodate Traveller families. Others camped along here to do casual work on the neighbouring farms, for example Acholter on the hillside behind. But, as they did not hesitate to say, since the latter decades of the nineteenth century it had become harder and harder all over the country to find somewhere to camp: 'You see, at one time you *could* go along the road, over a hedge and into a wood, and put up your tent – and nobody said anything to you.' By 1900, however, Travellers were increasingly unpopular. In August 1905 three were taken to court in Rothesay for camping on farmland without consent. *The Buteman* reported it under the tendentiously hostile caption: 'The Tinker Nuisance: Promiscuous Camping Out'. As one of the accused told the bailie, 'they [the Travellers] must go somewhere out of the road, as they could not stay about the streets. He protested volubly that he was only on waste ground among the whins…. The Bailie said it would be a good job if they never came back to the island…. They could not allow people like

them to come here and set up camp wherever they liked [and]….he gave them a strong warning not to come back. They were determined to stamp out this sort of thing in the island.'

However, while the bailie was duly gathered to his forefathers the Travellers' presence was not stamped out. They continued to spend time on Bute and this was one of their favourite camping places. Their casual work for local farmers included lifting turnips or tatties, described by a Traveller living on the mainland:

Ah've seen us doe the neep thinnin an we shawed [top and tailed] the turnips tae. Ye had a thing fer cuttin them – a tapner – bent like a henk fer grass. If ye taen two dreels [drills/furrows] up and two dreels doon, that was yer raw. Whit ye done was cut the nebs an shaw aff them. Ye stoopit doon as ye wir gaun along. Then sometimes ye got dung spreadin wae forks or a graip…. The best was the thinnin o the neeps for ye could work late at night on clear nights. The worst was potato gatherin. Ah niver liket hit.

Robert Leitch, *The Book of Sandy Stewart* (1988).

You may also imagine the scene in the evening, for traditional Travellers were addicted to music-making, so there would have been a piper or a fiddler and any number of voices, happy to sing songs ancient or modern. The rest of us had pretty much already lost our oral culture by the 1950s, yet here you probably could have witnessed the last guttering flames of an ancient culture on the edge of extinction. In place of it, we all now have television, in front of which we sit in soulless passivity, slowly being amused to death.

After ¾ km you will pass on your right the hillside farm of Cranslagmory (Gaelic for 'the border of [the lands of] the Virgin Mary'). On 8 March 1853 you would have seen forty ploughs there with their Clydesdale teams. It was the Bute Farmers' Society annual ploughing match, when 'A refreshment was ordered to each ploughman at his Lordship's expense.' The winner? Hugh Duncan of Scoulag (west of Mount Stuart), who also walked off with the Highland and Agricultural Society's medal and, perhaps on the strength of it, moved to Langalchorad (p.156).

Shortly after, Kames Castle will come into sight on your left.
Kames Castle has been described as 'the oldest inhabited house in Scotland'. The original building was a five-storey keep, built probably in

THE DIAMOND BEETLE CASE

1 Lord Hermand.	4 Lord Armadale.	7 Lord Hope.	10 Lord Craig.	13 Lord Woodhouselee.
2 Lord Baimuto.	5 Lord Cullen.	8 Lord Campbell.	11 Lord Glenlee.	14 Lord Robertson.
3 Lord Bannatyne.	6 Lord Polkemmet.	9 Lord Dunsinnan.	12 Lord Meadowbank, Senr	15 Lord Newton

Lord Bannatyne in the Court of Session, third on the left, leaning forward intently, chin resting in his hand, July 1808. He was known among his peers for his 'involved phraseology'.

the sixteenth century, but possibly earlier. Much of the upper part of the tower is modern. The castle's outbuildings were built in 1912, following extensive fire damage. Kames Castle was once the centre of an estate covering much of this valley and the hill country either side, as well as Kames Bay. The Bannatynes acquired the estate in the early fourteenth century, probably from the Stewarts. The last Bannatyne to own it, William MacLeod Bannatyne, Lord Bannatyne (1744-1833), inherited it from his uncle and adopted his mother's maiden name on inheriting the estate. He was appointed sheriff of Bute in 1776 and proved an energetic improver of the estate, even though he was largely absentee on account of an illustrious legal career in Edinburgh, in which he had followed his father, Roderick MacLeod. He had a remarkable memory. As an old man in 1832 he recalled from his early childhood, 'his father drawing on his boots to go to make interest in London in behalf of some of the men in trouble for the '45, particularly his own brother-in-law, the Clanranald of the day.' Like his father he, too, had radical tendencies and an instinct to do what he believed to be right, regardless of disapproval by the ruling establishment.

Lord Bannatyne closely followed improvements on the Bute estate and implemented similar measures at Kames. Indeed, he paid for the first road across to Ettrick Bay. He had a passion for the economic and cultural well-being of the Highlands and in 1784 was a founder member of the Highland and Agricultural Society of Scotland. Bute farmers featured among the winners of the Society's medals for agricultural achievement. He must have been duly pleased. Just imagine his proprietorial delight had he lived to see the ploughing match at Cranslagmory Farm over the road, ploughing so good as to win the Society medal.

Lord Bannatyne seems to have been a jolly, kindly and genial man, described by one contemporary as 'an honest merry old gentleman'. A child living at Ardmaleish remembered him thus:

> He wore knee breeches of red plush, with white stockings and silver buckles in his shoes. His vest was also of red plush dotted all over with black specks which made me think that it had been plastered over with black currant jam and dried.

His best likeness, by Henry Raeburn, sadly hangs 400 miles away at Polesden Lacy in Surrey.

Lord Bannatyne was a poor manager of his wealth. In debt, he leased Kames in 1806 to Captain Edward Sterling, who later wrote so bombastically for *The Times* that he is credited with gaining the paper the epithet 'The Thunderer'. In Bute Sterling left the impression that he had once been a captain of dragoon guards, very dashing, very grand. Perhaps we should ascribe this economy with the truth to his ebullient journalism, for his name eludes the published army lists of the period. In reality he seems to have been a local militia captain in Ireland, thus perhaps less Flashman of the cavalry and more Captain Mainwaring of the Home Guard. His son, John, born here, became a well-known writer and friend of Thomas Carlyle.

In 1810 Lord Bannatyne sold the estate to a fellow Edinburgh lawyer, James Hamilton, the man buried in the Croc-an-Raer mound. Duncan Hoyle purchased the estate after Hamilton's death, in 1854. He held it for barely nine years before selling it to the Bute Estate. Hoyle, however, was largely responsible for the creation of Port Bannatyne (see below).

In the 1960s the castle and outbuildings became a holiday home for children with cerebral palsy. A decade later, in the years 1972-84, it was a local authority home for 32 children from families in adversity. It would be good to think that the beauty of the place and the kindness of those charged with caring for them provided a process of healing. Today Kames Castle provides high quality self-catering holiday accommodation.

Continue walking down the road but 200 metres before the T-junction, turn up a track on your right, and bear right up 'the Garrison Road'.

This lane is now delightful, but it may not have been viewed as such two centuries ago. At the top stands Bannatyne Mains, once home farm for the estate but now no longer a farmstead. It was the billet for the Militia and possibly for the Port Bannatyne Company of Volunteers, both raised as a response to a nation-wide state of panic at the prospect of an invasion by Bonaparte. A company of Volunteers was formed in 1798, composed of about 70 men in all, 'to be exercised for three hours in every week'. Local men flocked to join, less out of patriotic ardour than to obtain exemption from the dangers of conscription by ballot into the hated County Militia. After they had been briefly disbanded during the phoney peace of Amiens, 1802, 598 men volunteered for the 366 vacancies with the Bute Volunteers. We know from Captain Neil Jamieson's letter of resignation in 1806 that while on the one hand the government neglected the volunteers it had asked for, on the other, the Bute Volunteers were a lackadaisical shambles: 'I find it impossible for me to get my Company to attend drill so regularly as I would wish…'. Lest you think that young Jamieson alone was unable to get a grip on his men, the Kingarth Volunteer Company captain resigned on the same grounds and at the same time. Perhaps this in part explains why, in 1808, the Volunteers were combined with the conscript Militia into 'The Buteshire Regiment of Local Militia' (for more on the Militia and Volunteers, see p.54). The latter were kitted out in scarlet with yellow facings (the livery of the then 98th Foot, later the Argylls), white breeches and lace cravat. So you may imagine the scene here in 1808: someone in a fancy captain's uniform would relentlessly march you unwillingly up to the top of the hill to your billet, and in the morning march you down again. Bannatyne Mains was locally known as 'the Barracks' for over a century, a name still remembered by older people in 1960.

At the top of the lane turn left along the road.

You have a chance to peer over the wall into what may have been the crude billets for the militiamen. So, even at night, while on training they must have had a dog's life.

The Kyles of Bute Hydro, as seen from the steamer pier.

Continue down the road, passing small villas on your left. When the road takes a hairpin turn left, stop by the old gate pillars on your right.

These stone entrance pillars of the Kyles of Bute Hydro are all that is left of this enormous 88-bedroom hotel. The original hydro was built in 1877 but it spectacularly burnt down the night before Christmas Eve, 1909. Fortunately the 44 guests were roused from their beds and no one was hurt, except for one imbued with more valour than discretion, who joined the fire fighting. Without any fuss a larger version was built within two years, this time with electricity supplied from the tram company depot down the hill. But it was the exotic new bath section that caught the imagination of the *Rothesay Express*:

> a splendid group of baths including Turkish, Russian, plunge, spray and swimming ponds, all supplied with hot and fresh and salt water.

Baths were one thing but, since these establishments were all teetotal, a hydro's reputation depended equally upon the provision of first-rate food and this could only be achieved by keeping livestock ready at hand, close to the premises. Barely a year after its splendid re-opening the pigs got loose, creating mayhem in local gardens and apoplexy among their owners.

In 1942 the hydro was requisitioned by the Royal Navy to become HQ for the 12th Submarine Flotilla, re-christened HMS *Varbel*. Port Bannatyne, the Kyles and Loch Striven became the epicentre of Britain's submarine capability, where virtually all the training took place. The 12th Flotilla concerned itself with midget submarines and human torpedoes. So low was the expectation of survival in these craft that recruitment was

Midget submarine.

limited to volunteers, single and under 24 years of age, men of exceptional courage. Midget submarines were so cramped that even sitting down on the floor of the vessel, there was barely head clearance, except at the periscope-dome, where a very small man could just stand straight. The Flotilla's moment of glory came in 1943 when six midget submarines penetrated German defences to put the *Tirpitz*, Germany's première battleship, out of commission for the rest of the war. In the words of the admiral responsible:

> they went out into the night in their tiny craft to face a thousand miles of rough seas before they reached their objective, which itself, to their knowledge, was protected by every conceivable device which could ensure their destruction before they could complete their attacks. And the *Tirpitz* herself was tucked away close under the cliffs at the head of a narrow fjord sixty miles from the sea.

Their success was only achieved with considerable loss of life.

After the war the Royal Navy left the Hydro. For a while the hotel revived its custom. In her autobiography Jess Sandeman, who managed the Hydro, recalled one guest, Sir William Burrell, asking her to phone his agent at London auctions: 'One day, particularly anxious to get a jet necklace he kept saying, "Tell him, bid another hundred." His bid was successful.' Burrell told Jess, '"I'll probably never see it myself…. I made my money in Scotland, and I'm leaving everything for the people of Scotland to see, especially the people of Glasgow."' Look out for it next time you are at the Burrell and, when you have a glass in your hand, remember this extraordinary benefactor.

Perhaps more could have been done to adapt the Kyles Hydro to the rapidly changing post-war world but it must be doubtful, for the public mood had changed. Sadly it closed in 1960, and nothing remains except the gateway.

Turn right along the unmetalled track just below the Hydro gates, and follow it. When you reach the main road, cross over and walk down the right hand path of two opposite. Walk down to the Shore Road and turn left.

Immediately on your left you will find the Pointhouse Burn, which goes under the road to the sea. It takes much of the run-off from the high ground above Ardbeg. It is also the boundary between Ardbeg and Port Bannatyne.

On the far side of this burn are the remains of the Pointhouse estate, comprising an enormous garden with a modest house (now derelict, standing opposite the offices of the bus depot on the main road). It was the property of a successful Rothesay-born merchant, John McDougall. (You may wish to skip the ensuing story and turn to p.198 but if so, save the tale for later. You will not regret it.)

McDougall had started his career around 1800 as a shipping agent. Moving to Glasgow, he acquired some small brigs of his own. He always insured both vessel and cargo at full value, in case of misadventure. It was just as well, for McDougall, it seemed, frequently had bad luck. Vessels foundered, but providentially the crews were always saved. McDougall showed his appreciation by feasting the underwriters, and thus acquiring a reputation for generosity. Despite his apparent losses his business prospered, so much so that he could afford to build a house here.

He had been joint owner of the *Friends of Glasgow*, which sank off the Dutch coast on its way to Hamburg in the early summer of 1816, laden amongst other things with cotton yarn, coffee, cocoa, refined sugar and salted herring. Four years later, in July 1820, the *Mary,* another ship he partly owned, left Glasgow bound for Trinidad. It was laden with calicoes, and he insured the vessel and contents for approximately £40,000 (roughly £1.5 million in our terms). It took an unorthodox route out of the Clyde via the Kyles of Bute, close by Pointhouse in fact, but later foundered off Ireland.

Very shortly thereafter, Mr Colin Gillespie, a calico printer in Glasgow, out perhaps for his lunch break, was accosted in the street by a woman peddling her wares, mainly calico pieces. He immediately recognised some pieces he had himself printed and sold to McDougall, calicoes that had supposedly gone down on the *Mary*. Gillespie went straight to the Customs House. When challenged, McDougall confessed to other offences including the fact that the *Friends* had not foundered by accident either: the crew had holed its hull. The Revenue men dug up his garden here at Pointhouse and found: 95 pieces of printed calico, each 28 yards long, 11 boxes of 'crown glass', 37 Saragossa shawls, gingham lengths, muslin and other materials besides, all off the *Mary*. The 'wilful Casting Away, Sinking or otherwise Destroying of Ships or Vessels with the felonious intent of defrauding or prejudicing the owners thereof, or the owners of goods shipped in them' was a capital offence.

Now on trial for his life, McDougall seems to have suffered some kind of mental collapse. He was tried in the Court of Admiralty in Edinburgh, first in regard to the sinking of the *Friends*. Despite his confessions in custody, his Counsel advised him to plead not guilty. Furthermore, his Counsel announced the prisoner to be in a state of mental derangement. A long discussion ensued during which learned doctors were called in evidence. McDougall had indeed been consigned during his incarceration to a lunatic asylum, where he had been put into a 'whirling chair', intended either to allay his disorder or to see whether he was 'only feigning insanity', an apparatus that sounds as if it might render the sanest of us insane. In court, McDougall wisely held his face in his hands throughout the proceedings but it did him no good. The lawyers had been arguing about the state of his mind all day until everyone, it seems, had quite run out of breath. In the words of the *Glasgow Herald*,

> The Judge-Admiral, after summing up the evidence very shortly, repelled objections founded on the plea of derangement. The Court then, at the request of the Jury (it being 2 o'clock in the morning), adjourned till ten o'clock.

Juries and court officers in those days were evidently made of iron compared with now.

Things were at their worst for McDougall when the court reconvened. He had been deemed sane, so how could he possibly avoid the gallows? The evidence was overwhelming. The jury, however, quite unexpectedly came riding to his rescue, as the official minutes of the trial explained:

> a doubt did pervade the Jury as to a point which was not noticed as

doubtful by the Counsel on either side, or by the Court, namely, whether it was the design of the prisoner to prejudice the Underwriters on the Vessel, or merely to prejudice the Underwriters on the Goods, which latter class of persons are not mentioned in the Statute.

Doubtless to the extreme vexation of the Judge-Admiral, McDougall could only be found 'guilty at common law' but not of a capital offence. Fearing another fiasco in the case of the *Mary* (which was postponed *sine die*), the judge imposed the maximum penalty possible, transportation for life.

One senses behind the jury's perverse nitpicking, a real desire that McDougall should not hang. It was less than a year since three radicals had been condemned to extreme public punishment: to be hanged, drawn and quartered. In the first case, in Glasgow, the executioner hanged and beheaded his victim but baulked at further quartering, sensing the mounting horror of the spectators. In Stirling, a week later, another executioner had no such compunction. His victims, a couple of men apparently intent on affray but not actually guilty of committing it, suffered the full sentence. How could educated men, like those who sat on McDougall's jury, not have been shaken to the marrow by such judicial barbarity?

McDougall was duly sent south to the Thames Estuary where he spent about six weeks in a prison hulk, most probably the converted 74-gun ship of the line, HMS *Bellerophon*. Even in manacles this was a privilege, for the *Bellerophon*, 'Billy Ruffian' to her crew, had participated in three of Britain's most famous sea battles, the Glorious First of June (1794), the Nile (1798) and Trafalgar (1805). The *Bellerophon*'s glory days had ended abruptly in 1815 when she was assigned to the role of

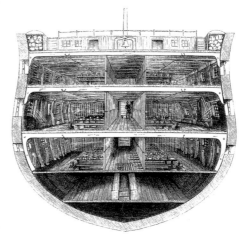

Section of a 74-gun ship of the line, converted to a prison hulk.

prison hulk at Sheerness, two lines of iron cages to be fitted on each deck, with a central aisle for supervision. The first prisoners were taken aboard the customised gaol early in 1817. Daily routine involved hard labour ashore during daylight hours.

In July 1821, six weeks after his trial, McDougall was transferred, along with 227 other convicts, to his transport, the *Lord Hungerford*, an East India merchantman bound for the Antipodes. On Boxing Day the vessel docked at Hobart, Van Diemen's Land, renamed Tasmania in 1856 to erase its dark reputation as a convict destination.

We have lived with John McDougall long enough that we should see him safely off his transport. He must wait a couple of days before disembarking, while reception arrangements are made and new convict clothes issued. He is filled with gloomy apprehensions. Yet, within three years a new regulation will give him hope. Condemned for life, he will be allowed to win local freedom after eight years' good conduct. Of course, he cannot know this yet, as he shuffles down the gangplank to his new life, dressed in convict clothes and fetters, but we know it and so can bid him farewell hopefully, wishing him good luck. He has delighted us long enough.

Start walking back along the shore to the centre of Port Bannatyne, till you reach St Ninian's Church, but keep an eye open for some of the fine villas along the shore front.
Now closed, this church is more than simply a monument to bygone piety. It was built largely as a result of local endeavour and opened for public worship in 1886. It cost £4,923 (in today's money approximately £275,000), and the congregation found itself with a debt of £2,500 (£140,000). Those who could donate money did so. Others thought of practical ways to help. Malcolm McMillan's grandfather, James Alexander McMillan, for example, was a boat builder with a small yard. He could not afford cash. So he gave his skill to build a yacht gig of the finest materials: yellow pine, teak wood and American rock elm. It took six oars. It was raffled among the wealthy steam yacht owners for St Ninian's, 'a winter's work to give the church some money.' What you see, therefore, in this shut-up church is in part the sad demise of a coherent and active community life.

Continue till you reach the remains of the old steamer pier.

By 1850 it was clear that Port Bannatyne's future lay with holidaymakers. In 1836 the Port had barely 400 inhabitants. Fifty years later the figure was 1,400, an increase of 350 per cent. A critical event in the Port's expansion took place in March 1857 when the Kames estate proprietor Duncan Hoyle built a wooden pier, the usual 'T' shape, for pleasure steamers and their expanding complement of holidaymakers. The pier was declared open with the unforgettable toast: 'May it answer the ends of its erection.' Indeed, it did, for by 1913 it was receiving around 2,000 steamer visits during the summer season. The arrival of visitors who did not simply wish to see Port Bannatyne from a steamer but also liked the idea of stepping ashore for a few moments, a few days or even a few weeks, helped encourage the development of the housing along the sea front. So did the laying of mains gas pipes from Rothesay through to Port Bannatyne in 1862, anticipating its development as a satellite settlement. The pipes were laid by the 'Kamesburgh' Gas Company, for Hoyle tried to erase the name Port Bannatyne which he thought unworthy of a village beginning to boast modern villas. His efforts did not outlast his own departure in 1862, probably because his favoured name unleashed confusion with Kames on the West Kyles. ('Kames' is a corruption of the Gaelic *camas*, a bay, rendering Kames Bay as absurd a tautology as River Avon.)

Hoyle may have failed with 'Kamesburgh' but he was successful in his efforts to transform the village. That same year a visitor wrote:

When I left this place a few years since, it was delighting in filth and dirt, and the old cognomen of Port Bannatyne and the inhabitants up in arms against the spirited proprietor of Kames Estate…. Now, on my return I find it is delighting in the name of Kamesburgh, the place nearly doubled in size, new and handsome houses and villas erected and being erected on every side, besides being possessed of an excellent steamboat wharf.

The steamer pier proved a great success, until the outbreak of war in 1939 brought its use to an end. By this time, Port Bannatyne had 30 shops, an almost incredible thought now.

Continue to the War Memorial.
At the back of the memorial is the plaque reminding us of what Port Bannatyne became in the Second World War. The whole of Britain's midget submarine and human torpedo training took place here, and the names of the exceptionally courageous young men of the midget submarines of 12th Submarine Flotilla who died are on the plaque behind the memorial. (On the left side of the memorial you will also find Malcolm Muldoon's name, see p.205.) Port Bannatyne remained the epicentre of British submarine training until the abrupt departure of the submarines to Faslane in 1957 (see p.19 for its impact), after which there was only a very small residual presence, HM Submarine *Attack Teacher*, composed of less than 20 naval personnel, until the early 1970s.

A FINAL WORD

The east end of Port Bannatyne was locally known by the nickname 'Grog Port' in the nineteenth century. It came by its name honestly, for even in the mid-nineteenth century there was still a shebeen which produced good whisky nearby supplying a secret market, as well as eight licensed whisky shops. In addition, however, there was an enormous amount of smuggled liquor. One resident, reminiscing in 1922, recalled:

> I could name a man – I knew him well – who often spoke of the narrow escapes he ran with the gaugers and the watchers [Customs officers], as they were called, when coming back from Kilmichael Ferry with what is called "the skin". It was full of spirits, of course. The skin and its contents were taken across from Kilfinan.

Bute must have been awash with illicit whisky brought from Loch Fyne by fishermen. There were any number of shebeens along the Loch Fyne coast willing to supply the skiffs. Lochgilphead alone, with a population of only 600 or so souls, had 23 inns which were reckoned to sell 5,600 gallons of whisky yearly. The herring fishers would go to many known places along the shore where they could purchase the stuff. There was, according to Angus Martin, chronicler of the Loch Fyne fishery, a Mrs Black, who 'would walk across the hills to the bay [Camus na Banrigh-earna, between Tarbert and Skipness] in her long billowing skirts, with skins of illicit whisky concealed beneath them.' The fishermen would put their skiffs in to shore and Mrs Black would peddle her skins over the bow.

Ettrick Bay

Ettrick Bay is a delight if you want an afternoon on the sands. It is easy to get to by bus and has a café which serves a mean cake. Local sites are listed, of which the following are worth walking to: St Colmac's Cross and the nearby stone circle; Kildavanan Point and also Jinty Bell's cave, which demands stout boots. They are all marked on the OS maps.

INTRODUCTION
People have used Ettrick Bay for recreation for the best part of two centuries and before then, during the Napoleonic Wars, it was a drill ground at low water for the local militia. In the mid-1830s Ettrick Bay sands were a well-known venue for horse racing. One August day in 1837 four thousand spectators attended the races, some travelling from Glasgow by steamer. It is nice to learn that, in the words of the *Ayr Observer*, 'several

People and donkeys at Ettrick Bay, c.1920.

An Edwardian family takes to the water at Ettrick Bay.

who had witnessed the gaieties of Epsom and Ascot were equally well pleased.'

Now that more people were coming out from Rothesay, it made sense to make provision for them. An enterprising inhabitant of Port Bannatyne established a bathing tent and refreshments in 1892, by which time such facilities were considered long overdue. Then small vaudeville troupes came to entertain the holidaymakers.

It was inevitable that the more affluent saw the bay as a wonderful development opportunity, in the same way that Kilchattan Bay had been developed in the late years of the nineteenth century. By 1909 several persons had applied to build villas along the shore. The local Member of Parliament lent his support to their applications, posing as a democrat against the landlord class. Fortunately the landlord, the 3rd Marquess, deprecated the idea as destructive rather than developmental. We owe him a great debt of gratitude. He was happy for people to come here to splash around in the sea, ride a donkey or eat ice-cream. But he did not want another strip of villas.

In 1909 'The Jesters' were providing entertainment and, so *The Buteman* said, 'no vulgarity will be permitted.' It was all very respectable, with sandcastle competitions for the children. In August 1919 an aeroplane carnival with two Avro biplanes piloted by men from the newly

Ettrick Bay, the model train, 1930s.

formed Royal Air Force was arranged on the sands, and 7,000 spectators turned out to see it. The following year flights were arranged, at a guinea a go. We are blasé today about seeing the landscape from the air, but imagine how irresistible and astonishing it must have been in 1920. Such trips became a fixture in succeeding years. Gardens and even a model railway were laid out, today all gone.

There are still a few people alive who remember playing here in the 1930s. Robert McLellan, born in 1921, grew up in Rothesay and recalled, 'When we were young we walked across the moors to Ettrick Bay and played football on the sand.' Billy Sprowl, born in 1934, remembered: 'In the 1940s and 50s there would be dances on Tuesday and Thursday nights at the Ettrick Bay Pavilion, accompanied by an accordion, but it would be rough dancing, the floor had been so often scrubbed that the knots in the wood stood proud of the grain.'

After the Second World War the Navy used the bay as an exercise area for laying dummy mines by submarine. A 75-foot fishing vessel would patrol the bay. A submarine would try to sneak in and lay the mines without disturbing the surface water, and without its periscope being spotted. It would have to lift this just above the surface every three minutes in order to take bearings. The practice was discontinued in the 1980s.

NEIGHBOURING SITES OF INTEREST, IN AN ARC FROM SOUTH TO NORTH

Jinty Bell's Cave. This cave, not much more than a cleft in the rock, is one kilometre south of the south end of Ettrick Bay. Walking along the shore for almost 1km, one must pass through a drystane dyke. The cave is 300m beyond the dyke, about 50 paces before Castle Cree, the Iron Age fort on a rocky outcrop almost isolated from the cliffs. If it has been raining you will find the ground heavy going getting there.

The story of Jinty Bell is a good deal more interesting than the cave itself. She was, in a sense, a direct spiritual descendent of the Irish Travellers who arrived in Bute in the late seventeenth century to live in igloo-shaped dwellings made of crude willow basketwork and covered in turfs near the seashore, where they could find mussels to eat. There were still one or two of these Travellers odd-jobbing in the 1950s. Yet Jinty was no Traveller by birth, for she was born more prosaically in Rothesay in 1846, her father being a local building labourer and her mother an incomer from Carradale. By the age of 13, Jinty was a factory girl in one of the cotton mills. In February 1884 when she was already aged 37, she gave birth to a son, Malcolm, somewhere in the High Street. The absence of a house number strongly suggests that he was born out of doors. Furthermore it was Jinty herself who reported the birth, marking the register with an illiterate's cross. Was she alone when she gave birth? I am tempted to think so. She was, of course, unmarried but the father's name was John Muldoon, a casual labourer.

By 1901 Malcolm was a teenager and stonemason's assistant in Rothesay but by then Jinty had been living in her cave for about ten years, the census that year recording her age optimistically as 46, her employment as 'farm worker' and her abode accorded some dignity as 'Upper Ardroscadale Cave'. Malcolm seems to have looked out for her, for if you visit her miserable dwelling, you will find the remains of a concrete lintel over the mouth of the cave. It seems he constructed an extension for her. Jinty used to hawk cockles on Rothesay Pier, something she had been doing before she fled to her cave. One of her visitors in 1902 remarked:

> Inside are two apartments divided by a curtain.... The bedroom is simply furnished – a bed on the bosom of Mother Earth and an alarm clock being its sole equipment.... The kitchen is quite

Jinty Bell standing in front of her cave, which her son had enlarged with a lean-to.

a cosy corner in its way, a stranded herring box taking the place of the more approved, but less substantial orange box, and being at once cupboard, dresser, table and lounge. The range is simple and effective - two large stones a foot apart for sides, with a bar or two of iron laid across…. the water supply a splendid spring in the brae above, is "keppit" in an old circular boiler.

In 1914, when Jinty was in her late 60s, another visitor described the scene:

A few empty herring boxes, a broken oar, and some oddments of clothing lay scattered about. Within, there was a bed in an alcove. The rock opposite was blackened with wood reek. The only "home comfort" noticeable was a small alarm clock, which ticked bravely in the midst of its ancient surroundings.

Malcolm was conscripted when he was already in his thirties, into the Argyll and Sutherland Highlanders. He was killed in action on the Western Front on 7 April 1917. Did the post boy bring Jinty the fateful telegram here in the cave? And what turmoil of feelings did the news provoke in her? We shall never know.

We are left with the central question: why did she eschew life in the community of Rothesay to live in this miserable crack in the rock? Did she fall out badly with her man and have nowhere else to go? Did she suffer some kind of mental breakdown? However jocular she seemed to those who visited her, one suspects that at a deep level she suffered profound sadness and alienation. That alienation is also indicated by her brief death details. At least she had left her wretched cave and died indoors, in a house in Mill Street in 1923, aged 77. Yet it seems she died alone. It was a police constable who reported her death.

Largivrechtan (Gaelic, for 'rocky declivity') **Farm** stands on the hillside overlooking the south end of the Bay. It was here one June day in 1927 that Robert Ronalson sat down in a field and tried to cut his own throat. Mercifully he made a hash of it, but was up before the Sheriff Court for behaving in a disorderly manner, 'alarming the lieges' and committing a breach of the peace. He arrived at court with a large bandage around his neck. 'He took things rather coolly, however, enjoying a smoke of his pipe while being brought by taxi to the Police Office.' Ronalson was newly married, his wife worked here at Largivrechtan, he at Glecknabae to the north. They had been married on 27 May but things went awry from the word go. He went across to Largivrechtan to sort things out, only to be told by her that it was over, as she had taken up with the ploughman. It was this that drove Ronalson to his desperate act. He must have been startled to learn from the unromantic Sheriff Hicks, 'there was no woman worth committing suicide for.'

Stone circle, St Colmac. This stone circle is about 13 metres in diameter. It is probably Early Bronze Age. It once consisted of nine stones. Four stones are still complete, another four are broken and the ninth is missing. The trees give the stones added aura, although, of course, they are less than a century old, whereas the stones must have been here for some 4,000 years or more. We are left in the dark as to the significance of this circle (but see p.234), yet persuaded that it must have been great, on account of the labour involved in its creation.

St Colmac's Cross. A deeply incised cross stands in the fields of East St Colmac farm. **(Walk up the drive of East St Colmac Farm, turn very sharp left on entering the farm yard and cross the perimeter fence by a style tucked into the corner, and then walk around the outer edge of the farm buildings).** It is probably a re-worked pre-Christian standing stone which has been exorcised of its previous meaning. It stands beside the site of Kilmachalmaig church, the final traces of which were removed by the local farmer at the end of the eighteenth century, probably to recycle the stones. The name 'Chalmaig', or Colmac, is an affectionate form of the common Irish name Colman.

Ettrick Smiddy. The smiddy cannot be visited but its story is of real interest. In the middle years of the nineteenth century, the blacksmith here was Daniel MacKirdy but he moved to Rothesay to a site in front of the castle. When the 3rd Marquess decided in 1876 to restore the castle he needed to clear the buildings that had grown up around it. So he had the smiddy and other buildings demolished (see p.249). With his compensation money MacKirdy set up shop in the High Street, but he died four years later. His successor, Andrew Baird, who lived to the ripe age of 91, distinguished himself less as a smith than as a designer and builder of an aeroplane, which he flew from the beach, here at Ettrick Bay. It was said to have flown 'short distances', which sounds ominous.

By the late nineteenth century Ettrick Smiddy was occupied by John Smith and his wife, Margaret. His grandson, John Thomson, also lived here since it was close to school, while his own farming parents were living a couple of miles away:

> I was born here. I attended Kildavanan school which is approximately 1.5 miles from here at the age of four, walking there and back every day [see below].... Every Friday my grandmother

Andrew Baird in his aeroplane in 1910.

would scrub the stone floors. The walls were simply whitewashed. Once the floor was washed my grandmother would take a wettened small round cake of something like pipe-clay, and make neat swirling patterns around the very edge of the floor, to 'finish' it off. The clay would dry off. She would vary the patterns from week to week. By the time the week was over, there was precious little of the pattern left. I suppose being a wee boy playing around, I had scuffed most of it. The cake of pipe clay was about the size of a 'peever', about half an inch thick and three inches in diameter. To play peever? It was more of a girl's game. They would mark about eight or nine squares in chalk on the road or pavement. You had to hop on one leg from one square to another, but you also had to nudge the peever into the next square as you hopped, the hopping and nudging all done with one move. If you failed, the next girl took a turn. Once the floor was finished my grandmother would lay a half-sack in front of the hearth. When it got dirty from the coal and ash, she would put a clean one down. That was our hearthrug.

I remember having tea here one day. My mother's mother had died when my mother was only four. My grandfather took up with another woman [Margaret, from Kilfinan]. She had no teeth and no falsies either. She managed to get by all right, but she was quite a sight when she was eating. That's what I remember. She could speak the Gaelic language fluently. She had left school at the age of nine, unable to read or write. My grandfather used to read the newspaper to her in the evening.

Every day we ate a plate of porridge and a boiled egg for breakfast, at midday we had soup, generally from chickens, which were killed the previous day and meat or the remains of the chicken with our potatoes, and supper was a repeat of the breakfast menu.

There has been a blacksmith's shop here since around 1800. My great grandfather Peter Smith [1828-1891] worked here in the smiddy. His family was from Campbeltown, originally in the fishing. His son, John, or Jake, took over. John's son-in-law, my father, Bryce Thomson, was born in 1892. He stayed at Ballianlay, three miles away. He came over here aged 15, in 1907, to serve his apprenticeship. He took a notion to the youngest daughter, Kathleen, and married her in 1917. In due course when I was born

[1921] Jake Smith became my grandfather.

My father received board and lodgings at the smiddy and was responsible for lighting the smiddy fire every day Mon to Sat. The hours of work were 8am-5pm Monday to Friday, and 8am-12am on Sat, with one week's holiday per annum (if they were lucky) There were, however, times when they had to work at night till 9.

As for my work in the shop, I picked it up by watching. Farmers could bring their horses for attention as these required shoes. But farmers coming along in winter would sometimes throw gravel onto the slate roof as early as 5am to bring us down to put studs on the shoes, to prevent the horses slipping on the ice. The square end of the stud was hammered into the shoes. During the winter these studs either wore down or fell out, or the shoe would have to come off as the hoof started to grow over the shoe.

There were two fires in the smiddy at one time. The coal used for the furnace was specially treated and washed. It was important to get a clean fire. The coal was delivered to Rothesay by puffer from the Ayrshire coast. The puffers came in to beach at high water, offload at low water when a horse and cart could collect the coal, and depart once they floated off with the rising tide. We would always keep a couple of tons of coal out the back of the shop.

There was a line up of workers, but when I was around there were only two workers and my grandfather. The workers were fed here during the day: breakfast, dinner, and working till dinnertime on a Saturday. They stayed in Port Bannatyne.

The farmers called twice a year on 15 May and 11 November to settle their accounts with my grandfather, when they would receive a dram in return. Despite that, if the account was £18 17s. 5d, they would make the cheque out for £18; they always rounded it down. They didn't know, of course, that my grandfather had already added a pound in anticipation. He would make up the accounts a day or two before. He would go upstairs, shut himself in the bedroom and open his large red ledger, filled with beautiful copperplate writing. It was a lovely thing. I don't know what happened to the ledgers. Woe betide you if you tried to go into the bedroom while he was making up the accounts. He would shout angrily if you opened the door. It was almost always the byremen or ploughmen who came to settle the account. When they came, my grandfather would give them time, for a dram and a blether. The farmers very seldom came to settle their accounts. They were too grand…. My grandfather got elderly and when he died, my father took over. The last commercial work ended in 1949, with mechanisation, the horses dying off, and all the plough ware and harrow ware died a death too. I worked…. in Glasgow and finished [with the smiddy] altogether in 1961-62. There was the odd pony that needed to be shod…. Electricity did not come here till the 1940s. Water came from the hill to the pump you can see outside, and we only went on the mains about ten years ago.

Drumachloy Bridge. The remains of what is probably an early nineteenth century bridge stand a few paces inland from the present one. It is said that the farmers of Drumachloy and Kildavannan, not to mention those on the road to Kilmichael, asked for the bridge but were refused. They hit upon a compelling reason why the bridge was vital: it would be quite impossible to attend Sabbath prayer if they were unable to cross the burn. The minister, at any rate, saw their point and ensured that the bridge was built.

Drumachloy Farm. This has been in the hands of the Lyon family since around 1800 (see p.275).

Kildavanan Farm. Kildavanan Farm is also farmed by a member of the Lyon family. John Thomson remembers one of the local characters of his childhood:

At Kildavanan [in the 1930s] there was an Irishman, Pat Gillespie. He was a drainage man, digging ditches. He worked very hard. He lived in the barn, up a ladder. In the end it killed him. He fell off the ladder in his eighties, drunk. He used to spend his money on a Friday night and drank too much. He'd pick up a policeman and lay him down.

Kildavanan School. The school is the oldest building in the row, on the left. Grace Weir was the teacher here for about eight years from 1898. She hailed from Ayrshire, her husband, David, from Kintyre. They had taken the lease on a farm on the Isle of Muck, only for him suddenly to die aged 42, in 1895. Grace, only 35, was now stranded with a dependent mother and four small children. She could not handle the farm herself but teaching was something she could do, and the

Kildavanan School, 1905. Grace Weir with her schoolchildren. Colin and Julia McCallum's daughter, Rebecca, stands third from the left in the front row. John Thomson's mother, Katie Smith from Ettrick Smiddy is in the front row on the right.

vacancy at Kildavanan came complete with a dwelling. From her photograph she looks a kindly soul but her work had its frustrations. She had to cope with the high absentee rate during lambing, sheep shearing, haymaking and harvest time. She got off to a shaky start, in mid-June that year: 'Had some difficulty in concentrating the attention of the children during the first three days owing to the volunteer Artillery Drill (see below) being in progress at the Battery', deployed at Kildavanan Point. Moreover, several children, or their parents, were lackadaisical about attendance, as her logbook shows: 'Am annoyed by the irregular attendance of the Ferry children... they were only here on Monday and Wednesday and they are fast falling behind in their classes.' And she had to cope with the different attitude of boys from girls: 'the girls read well: the boys are mumbling in their utterance, and monotonous in their style of reading.' So what, one wonders, is new? In December 1901 she received the ultimate excuse for non-attendance: 'The children from Kilmichael cannot come because of a bull which is kept grazing on the roadside.' It is difficult not to suspect a farmer's complicity. In April 1905 she crossed swords with the gamekeeper, regarding the natural world: 'McKellar, the gamekeeper, Chalet, has withdrawn two of his children because the teacher lectured his two boys and another for tearing down a little bird's nest and breaking the eggs.' Not surprisingly, the young McKellars do not feature in the school photograph that year. Grace, like her successor Maggie Blaikie, enjoyed the strong support of a local committee, none so assiduous in visiting the school and encouraging the work than Colin McCallum, farming at Kilmichael (see p.218).

John Thomson, whose mother, Katie Smith, had attended the same school, recalls from the 1920s:

> The school was a house with a rather small schoolroom attached and mainly supplied education for farmers' and their workers' children. There was only one teacher, Miss Blaikie, who took all the children through to the qualifying age of eleven, when they then moved to the secondary school in Rothesay. The number of children varied considerably and I remember as few as 6. We were supplied with double-sided slates (no jotters) and a slate pencil. Sitting through and listening to lessons given to all pupils appropriate to their age, resulted for instance in having to suffer the story of *Kidnapped* for 6 or 7 years. On the other hand, there were great advantages in being at a small country school. We could add, subtract and read much sooner than at formal school. I remember when we developed into the ink side of things, that the teacher had a double-sided blackboard. We were doing an essay. I got fed up and started flicking ink off my pen onto the paper. I was punished by being required to stand behind the blackboard for an hour, and then kept in at my desk late, after the other children had gone home. Another time, I remember I decided to end the last letter of each sentence with a little squiggle before the full stop. I was in trouble for that. There was no playground. So after I had eaten my piece, bread and bramble jelly, which had dried into the bread and was like toast, I used to try to climb the cliff behind the school. No one tried to stop you.'

My parents moved to a new house, Woodside Cottage round at Ballianlay [beside the turning down to Straad], and I joined them at the age of nine or so where I attended Ballianlay school, a similar small country school like Kildavannan and again with one teacher. I attended secondary school in Rothesay, the Royal Advanced Division Centre, from the age of ten to fourteen, walking three miles there and back every day. I had gone a year early because I passed the qualifying exam at the age of ten. I do not know how or why this happened. But I was put in with ten–year olds. One day the teacher saw me daydreaming and challenged me with questions about what she had been reading out to the class. Little did she know that I had heard it all several times before, because at country school one heard everything as the older children were being taught. I was familiar with everything. So when, to her surprise, I answered everything perfectly, she moved me up a year. It did not do me much good because I had to repeat the year when I was fourteen, since there was nothing after that age.

Kildavanan Point. Just beyond Kildavanan Point the 1st Bute Volunteer Artillery practised their gunnery with a couple of 65-pounder rifled muzzle-loaders, which were sited here in 1898. There is nothing quiet about guns of that size (see p.48). No wonder Grace Weir could not command the attention of her young pupils.

One Saturday afternoon in August 1953, the 851-ton Royal Mail steamer, *Saint Columba*, ran aground here. It had left Tarbert and was approaching Ardlamont Point (on the mainland opposite) when it ran into dense mist that had come down so quickly that it was unable to see the Ardlamont light. It proceeded slowly but blindly, and gently grounded 100 metres offshore here. Some 300 passengers had to be ferried ashore, without their luggage, though 'among them were young children, clutching small toys which they refused to abandon.' It took several hours to get everyone off. The timing, however, was fortuitous, for a reception committee of holidaymakers in Ettrick Bay raced round to give them a hand or rather a piggy-back ashore, since the lifeboats ran aground 10 metres offshore. Passengers and luggage were eventually reunited on the mainland, when the rising tide took the vessel off. It is said that the captain required passengers to surrender their tickets on leaving the vessel, a ludicrous piece of bureaucracy one might think. Yet he must have realised that it was only by a tally of tickets that he could be absolutely certain that every passenger had indeed been accounted for.

WALK

10

Scarrel Point to Kilmichael, via Torr Mor and Torran Tùrach

Distance 15km: 4½-5 hours arduous
OS Map 1

BEFORE YOU WALK

You have a choice. The recommended walk is arduous since there is no path over the high ground to Kilmichael. You need to keep an eye on the map as well as on the instructions. Only attempt this walk when fine weather is assured. Its rewards, apart from the exercise, are the exceptionally fine views, both across the West Kyle and down to Glen More, Bute's glacial valley. You are also likely to see roe deer and hares. It is heavy ground between Torran Tùrach and Ardnagave, above Kilmichael. This is significantly worse after much rainfall. If you choose this route take a mobile phone and tell someone where you are going.

Alternatively, you can take the cream off the cake by driving to Glecknabae (or all the way to Kilmichael, if the road there has been opened), and simply walk along to Kilmichael, taking in the three prehistoric burial sites of Cairn Baan, Kilmichael and Glenvoidean, along with the remnants of St Michael's church, and the Kilmichael ferry house. If you go for this option, the map will show you where to go, and you can turn to the appropriate page of the walk.

Start at Scarrel Point (there is a wooden seat on the left, looking out to sea, the first you come to after Ettrick Bay). There is room to park a car just off the tarmac. On the opposite side of the road there is a track inland with a sign saying 'Hill walk to West Island Way'.
Scarrel (in Gaelic, *Sgeir-gheal*) means 'seashore white rocks', ones covered by spring tides.

Go through the gate on the opposite side of the road and up the track as indicated on the sign post. Once through the next gate, cleave to the fence

on your left. Note the occasional blue markings. Follow these until told to disregard them. When you go through the next gate, turn right uphill, up the side of the field (or around the whin) until you are halfway up the field, then make for the gate in the fence at the top of the field straight ahead. Pass through this gate and go slightly left of straight ahead. You should find a wicket gate near the top of the hill. It will have blue markings. Go through it and, again, keep to the fence on your left.

This is Eenan Hill. It is difficult to know what the name might mean. In the nineteenth century a local historian thought is might be a corruption of Adamnan's Hill. If you do not find that convincing, here are two other possibilities: *eanaich* is Gaelic for matgrass, while an *eanag* is a plover. Both may be found up here.

Keep walking with the fence on your left.

As you ascend take the trouble to pause and enjoy the view of the lower part of Glen More (Gaelic for 'great glen'), beautifully scoured out by a glacier.

Cross the top of the next hilltop, Torr Mor (Gaelic for 'large hill'). **You will know you have reached it when you see ahead the power cables running over the hill from Achavoulaig** (Gaelic for 'field of the animal enclosure') **on your right to Glecknabae** (Gaelic for 'the birch hollow') **out of sight down the hillside on your left. Keep following the fence, passing under power cables till you reach the corner of the field. From now on there are no blue markers.**

Achavoulaig is now part of Drumachloy Farm, where the Lyons have been farming since at least the early nineteenth century, perhaps earlier. There were Lyons at Achavoulaig also in the mid-nineteenth century. John Lyon, the farmer here, bred fine livestock and even finer daughters, eight of the latter, at least six of them over six feet tall, but not a single son.

Continue in the same direction but cross the fence so that you are on the left of it and now keep to the high ground but stay a little on the east side as you pass the top of the next hilltop, Glecknabae Hill. You will realise why when you descend. First you will have avoided falling off Grey Craig, always a plus, and second you will find it easier to cross the burn a little upstream. Once over the burn make for the gate, ascend to find the trigpoint at the summit of Torran Tùrach (Gaelic for a 'turreted knoll').

From Torran Tùrach you will see below you, about 1km north-west, a thin ribbon of trees in a gully running westwards. This marks Aultmore (G. 'great stream') **Burn. You need to get to the north side of this burn, so descend, crossing the first tributary and make your way across the moss in the lee of the rocky outcrop, known as Creag a'Madaidh** ('dog crag')**, on the west side of the large plantation ahead of you and swing to your left (westwards) to cross the second tributary of the burn. On the north side of Aultmore** ('great stream') **Burn make your way westwards on the uphill side of the bracken and you will come suddenly upon Ardnagave (A), lurking in a small glen.**

There are the ruins of three buildings, each with its own yard, a well-preserved corn-drying kiln and enclosure dykes. It is difficult to know whether these enclosures were for enfolding or excluding livestock. Ardnagave (Gaelic for either 'dangerous height' or possibly 'cold height') seems to have been a functioning settlement until around 1830 when it was abandoned, presumably as a consequence of the massive changes in agriculture. It was a 'butt' of Kilmichael: the tenant paid rent in kind and also gave annual labour service to Kilmichael. The buildings have drystone walls. The roofs would probably have been of cruck construction (see p.253). The ends had stone gables, but along the two sidewalls curved timbers would have risen from ground level. These load bearers would have been tied at roof level by purlins, along the ridge and lower down, duly covered by wattle and turf, perhaps thatched over with rushes. The long axes of the buildings run downhill, good for drainage particularly when it is likely that humans had half of the habitation, with cattle kept in the lower part of the building. A partition of either stone or woven hazel wattles, daubed with a mix of mud and dung would have separated humans from livestock. The upper building contains an alcove, probably for an 'outshot' bed, on the west (sea side) wall.

Descend, making for the track on the far side of the glen, to the left of the sheepfold (B) on the hillside. Once across the burn, follow the track uphill for about ½km. As it begins to descend towards the sea, you will pass through a couple of old gateposts.

On your left but out of sight in the far gully, are the remains of Glenvoidean (Gaelic for 'Glen of Vows'), a settlement possibly dating back to the Middle Ages. It does not merit a detour. (It was a butt belonging to Lenihuline, a steading one kilometre to the south. The two

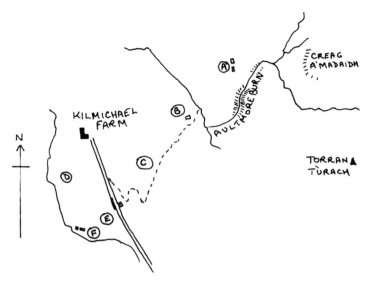

buildings stand within a circular enclosure. The lower house may be medieval. Some large upright stones have been used, possibly taken from the chambered cairn a little downhill.)

Follow the overgrown and sunken track. After 100 m it passes a power line post. Looking downhill 100 metres you should see a large cluster of whin, or gorse, just on the right of the sunken track. This whin bush (unless it is cut away) hides Glenvoidean chambered cairn (C).

Glenvoidean is a late Neolithic chambered cairn, a tomb first noticed in 1962 and excavated intermittently over the next decade. It is difficult for the layman to make much of it, beyond the astonishing arrangement of stones. Why was it sited here on a fairly steep slope rather than on the brow of the hill? What did it really represent: the memorial of a kindred group identity or only of an individual or series of individuals? What was the role of fire, since there seem to have been repeated burnings here? The dig revealed burnt material dating back to approximately 2900 BC. The site was used and enlarged by Neolithic people over a period of six centuries and again about one thousand years later as a grave by Bronze Age people. Pots found here can be seen in the Bute Museum.

Follow the overgrown track downhill until it takes you to the main track running from Ettrick Bay up to Kilmichael Farm.

Kilmichael Farm steading is a short way off to your right. Colin McCallum farmed here for 35 years, until 1922. He had come across from Kilfinnan. Beck Reid, now retired after a career in farming (at Shalunt north of Port Bannatyne), recalls:

Colin and Julia McCallum, celebrating their golden jubilee at Upper Ardroscadale in 1948.

> My grandfather, Colin McCallum, died aged 92 in 1952. He had a butcher's shop in Kames, and farmed Kilmichael until he moved in 1922. He ran it with his brother Peter. They are both buried in Croc-an-Raer. He kept both cattle and sheep but it was mainly the sheep that he slaughtered and rowed across to his shop. He made the journey every day for 19 years, and did not miss a day, for on the Sabbath he rowed across to attend the kirk. There were two generations of McCallums at Kilmichael.

It is a reminder that before the internal combustion engine, Kilmichael's communications with Kames and Tighnabruaich on the mainland side of the West Kyle were easier than with Rothesay.

Beck's mother, Georgina, remembered life at Kilmichael:

> I was born at Kilmichael. I had to walk to primary school at Kildavanan, three miles each way. After I left school (aged 14), I arose at 4.30 in the morning to milk the cows. I started work on the farm straight away. I milked cows, fed hens and when it came to harvest you bunched corn and tied it into sheaves. I also thinned turnips on my hands and knees, and gathered in potatoes....
>
> At Kilmichael you got a year's supply of coal at a time. You just put it in the yard. It came in on a sailing boat not as big as a puffer. May be about 30 tons. The shepherd would get about 5 tons for his cottage.

TO BE EXPLORED

St Michael's Chapel (D). As with St Ninian's, it is the site of this chapel which grips. One can understand immediately why people, almost all of whom came from across the water in Kames, wished to be buried here (the last burial was in 1927). One, at any rate, had been born in Bute: Duncan Currie, who died in 1900, aged 87. His father was a farm labourer at Rhubodach.

The altar slab of the chapel survives, and the wall recess may be an ambry, to contain the chalice and paten. The stonework suggests that the chapel had a beehive roof, thatched originally but possibly later of slate. Its supposed dedication is to St Maccaile, a follower of St Patrick, and the circular cashel around the chapel both suggest that the site was used for a church in the seventh or eighth century. Yet I cannot quite dismiss the suspicion that it may have been dedicated to the Archangel, St Michael. 'Micheal nam Buadh', Michael the Accomplished, was hugely popular in the Celtic church particularly on the western coasts and isles of Scotland, where he was considered patron saint of the boats and boatmen: seven locations in Argyllshire are dedicated to him, and at least one on Arran. More widely, he is patron saint of the sea, as indicated by sites such as St Michael's Mount and Le Mont-St-Michel. Maccaile or Michael? We are left speculating. There is no evidence of when the chapel fell into disuse but it was before the Reformation.

Michael's Grave (E). This chambered cairn stands very obviously in a field close to where the track running southwards becomes wooded on either side.

Kilmichael Ferry (F). There were two ferry sites for crossing the West Kyle, 'Old Ferry Craig', ½km north of the steading, which must have run direct across the West Kyle to Kames, and another more recently used, south of the steading, marked 'Ferry Port' which ran to Blair's Ferry just south of Kames. Here one may also find the old ferry house. It is currently hidden by thick tree growth, which may be cleared to expose it to view.

Ferriers were routinely required to provide food and shelter for travellers. The house here was known as 'The Bottle and Glass'. The ferry inlet may be found less than 100 metres north of the ferry house. At low water one can see the remains of the small quay, constructed in 1769 for the princely sum of £15 (£1,000 approximately in today's money), to service the Kilmichael-Blair's Ferry route 'where boats are kept in readiness at all times on both sides for the accommodation of passengers', as John Blain, the Rothesay Town Clerk noted. One can immediately see how skilful the ferrier had to be to get a boat in and out in anything but the calmest weather. Indeed, the principal landlord on the other side, John Lamont of Ardlamont, complained in 1819 that Blair's Ferry and Kilmichael:

> are both very unsafe to the anchoring of Vessels indeed I may add in Winter or when it blows impracticable and at the Bute Ferry it is very difficult to embark cattle.

By 1891 the ferrier was a woman, a Miss Cameron, who provided the boat and maintained the quay. Presumably she could handle the ferry too, although by 1900 she was on the point of retirement and employed a young lad to manage the boat. The ferrying of cattle had ceased by then. The end came as late as the 1930s, its survival for so long a commentary on the absence of motorised traffic in north Bute. In the early 1900s the ferrier's children trudged to Kildavannan for their schooling (see p.210).

Follow the main track back towards Ettrick Bay.

As you pass the lands of Lenihuline, the raised beach can be clearly seen on your left. There are three settlements up on the raised beach along this stretch, abandoned in the nineteenth century. The name in Gaelic was probably *leana-chuilinn*, meaning 'holly meadow'. Hollies still grow on the raised beach. Another theory is that it referred to the rental worth of the land.

After 1½ km, look out for the sign up to Cairn Baan on the left of the track. This sign, which can easily be missed, is just before there is woodland on the sea as well as landward side. The cairn is 500 metres up through the wood and is well worth the detour.

Cairn Baan (Gaelic for 'bright cairn') is visually the most rewarding of the Neolithic chambered cairns in Bute, for it is 60 metres long and dates to around 3000 BC. At its top end it is crossed by a very much more recent drystane dyke, built to define the extent of cultivated land, beyond which lay rough grazing.

Resume walking southwards.

This is a good stretch on which to contemplate the variety of trees and other floral growth alongside the track. A short commentary on different tree species may be found on p.331.

After about 1 kilometre you reach tarmac, passing Glecknabae (G. 'birch hollow') **on your left, a renovated old steading.**

Just beyond Glecknabae, about 150 metres directly through the first gate on your left is a Neolithic burial cairn. About 1,000 years after its construction, Bronze Age people put a stone coffin in it. Most remarkably, however, underneath the Neolithic material was found a Mesolithic midden, containing shells and bone-ash. However underwhelmed you may feel at the sight of this cairn, you are looking at a place that was intermittently used by humans for approximately 3,500 years, until c.1500 BC, which is very roughly the same time span which separates us from the Bronze Age people who last used it.

If you look up to the right of the cairn about 300 metres away on a shelf on the hillside is the ruin of Lenihall (in Gaelic: *leana choille*, 'field of wood'). If you are still bursting with energy, it is worth walking up. There was a steading here in 1440 but the present structure, which stands on an artificial platform dates from 1857 (as shown on the lintel in the central courtyard). Lenihall seems to have been abandoned just before the Second World War. In the 1920s there was, apparently, a woman living here who made a weekly journey into Rothesay. She would walk to Ettrick Bay from where she could take the tram. On the return journey she would be laden with the week's essential shopping. She had a thoughtful donkey, one given to kindness. It knew when she was likely to return to Ettrick Bay and would trot down to meet her and carry her bags.

After another 1.5 km look out on your right for a stone fish-trap on the shore, just about visible even at high water.

Fish traps of this kind were common in the coastal waters, and were probably used from Stone Age times. The layout is obvious. Wickerwork hurdles would be placed across the mouth of the trap as the tide turned.

Walk back to Scarrel Point (or to Ettrick Bay to pick up the bus).

The Eastern Kyles to Rhubodach

There is currently a very short marked walk from Rhubodach (meaning 'Bute Point') along the northern shore. Above, hidden in dense woodland, stands Balnakailly, a deserted settlement. It is possible that a marked trail will one day take walkers from Rhubodach to Balnakailly.

Ardmaleish. The Fyfes of Fairlie were boat building here in the nineteenth century. In its heyday, the yard here built the finest ocean-going racing yachts money could buy, the largest ever, the 66-ton *Rossa*. One of those who worked in Ardmaleish boatyard in the mid-1930s was Campbell Leitch, who died in 2007:

> When I left [school], I went to the boat building at Ardmaleish, working for MacFarlane Bute Slip Dock Company. There were forty of us, men and boys. We built yachts, 12 metres in length and masts 100 feet high. We built the 12 metre *Janetta*, which required a crew of four, plus a young fella. All the boats we built went down to Cowes. I did a 5-year apprenticeship and then got my full wages.... We made cruisers out of Burmese teak, properly fixed with copper. We worked in a team, say ten or so, and we took all winter to build something like the *Janetta*. We were the boat builders, but we had 'boat joiners', who built all the boat inner furnishings and fittings. We also built in mahogany, with elm timbers bent with steam for the ribs of the hull. The keel would be made of lead and hardwood.
>
> We had to make our own electricity for the lights to work by, with a hand-cranked generator. I remember one fella blowing a raspberry at another who immediately replied 'ye can fairt but you'll get nae lights.'
>
> Fishing boats? We used to repair them, for example the boats of

Hughes and Rae from Kilchattan Bay. But there was Dickie's of Tarbert, and also Smith of Tighnabruaich, very good boat builders.
A 26-ton luxury yacht was built here in 1959, *Melora III*, for a Kilmacolm businessman, Ian Laird. Designed by A. Mylne & Co., it was made of oak, with spruce masts and teak decking. Eight years later a 50-ton ketch, *Glenafton*, was built, but the heyday of luxury wooden yacht building was rapidly drawing to a close for Ardmaleish. Today Ardmaleish concentrates on repairs to vessels like CalMac ferries.

A decoy town was built during the Second World War between Shalunt, on the Kyles road and the Maids of Bute on the far north west side of the island, intended to create an impression of Greenock at night. It does not seem as if the Luftwaffe was taken in, since it only once dropped ordnance near Kilmichael.

The road up to Rhubodach. The road from Port Bannatyne to Rhubodah is very recent, although the crossing to Colintraive is old. Drovers may have had a track, but more probably simply walked their livestock along the land adjoining the shore. A proper road was only completed in 1939. No one was quite sure that there would be enough traffic to the mainland to justify the outlay. The road stopped short of the original plan to run all the way around the north end to Kilmichael.

The idea of laying a road around the north end has always fallen on stony ground. John Blain, for example, writing in about 1800, expressed the view that it simply was not worth it, a view which has held ever since:

From the shore below the farm of Baile na Coille [Balnakailly] to that at Kilmichael is a space of about two miles. People occasionally go across the north end of the island by that route through moss and muir. Strangers, however, ought not to make the attempt without having a guide to conduct them. A road might be made at great expense, but there is no occasion to throw away money on it.

There was also a distinct lack of interest in establishing facilities for travellers at Rhubodach. In 1769 the authorities (which probably means John Blain) reported,

that it did not seem to them that any further accommodation was necessary at Rue as the ferry boats are not at present kept on the Bute side and there are very good gravelly points upon one side or other of which the boats can touch with great safety at any time.

The Rhubodach-Colintraive ferry, over which the Campbells of South-hall (south of Colintraive) seem to have had control, grew in importance after the building of the road from Loch Fyne through Glendaruel to Colintraive, around 1805, to speed transit of the Loch Fyne herring catch to its market in Glasgow. With the decline in droving around the end of the century it seems to have fallen into abeyance.

Proposals for a regular ferry across the Kyles cropped up from time to time. The idea was turned down in 1939, but with the growth of motorised traffic after the Second World War one was inaugurated in 1950, thanks to the Marquess of Bute. The present CalMac ferry, however, dates only from 1970, following a long debate over the feasibility of a bridge, at that time estimated to cost £1.3 million, probably about £15 million today. Yet, was the ferry sited in the best place? See p.60.

Balnakailly (G. 'settlement in the woods') indicates by its name that the oak woodland surrounding it is ancient, several centuries old. There is a real aura to this site. The buildings consist of the remains of a dwelling and at right angles a byre, with a courtyard in the angle, and what seems to be a second dwelling set slightly apart from the main dwelling, and possibly other smaller more ruinous dwellings. The main building has sockets for rafters, and niches in the wall for the cruck frame. In the field on the north side of the dwelling are a couple of mature trees, an ash and a plane. The field boundary is banked. The settlement seems to have been abandoned sometime between 1840 and 1860, presumably because it was no longer possible to make a living out of the land. One of the resident families in the 1770s was McGilchatan, 'son of the servant of Catan' suggestive of a long presence in Bute, perhaps even descent from a monk at Catan's monastery.

Balnakailly lay on the route across to Glenmore, to Ettrick Bay and to Kilmichael. Coming via Glenmore and the high ground above Rothesay may well have been the preferred drove route. The coastal lands may have been too waterlogged.

PART 4

Background

Geology

The first to record the geology of Bute was John MacCulloch in *A Description of the Western Islands of Scotland*, published in 1819, when geology was in its infancy. MacCulloch stumbled into the subject by accident. He was a surgeon to the Royal Artillery at Woolwich. At war with Napoleon, he was required to monitor the quality of gunpowder. When the powder-millstones of Belgian limestone wore out in 1809, he was instructed to find a suitable British substitute. In his search, he travelled through Wales and Scotland, only locating the ideal silica-free material in Skye and Sutherland in 1813. Ironically, the limestone was so difficult to extract that no millstones were ever delivered, so it is just as well that others had held Boney at bay. It was on the basis of his acquired and vast geological knowledge that he published his great work. MacCulloch's book would have given you the basics but if you want a surer grasp of Bute's geology, go for the Bute Museum's publication by Julian Hill & David Buist, '*Reading the Landscape of Bute*' (2006), which includes dedicated geological walks.

THE FORMATION OF BRITAIN

For so small a land area, Britain boasts an unusually varied landscape. It is the consequence of a remarkably complex geology, parts of which are beautifully exemplified here in Bute. The principal reason for this variety is that the constituent parts of Britain were close to the edges of tectonic plates, subject to volcanic activity, earthquake and compression. Ever since the formation of the Earth, around 4.6 billion years ago, tectonic plates have floated independently of each other from their original cluster around the South Pole. Six hundred million years ago Scotland was part of 'Laurentia', while England and Wales were part of the 'Avalonia' plate

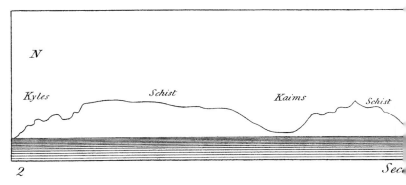

The geology of Bute: MacCulloch's geological cross section of Bute, 1819.

some 6,000 km away. By sheer coincidence, their eventual geological conjunction was along a line from Berwick to the Solway Firth, destined to form a political border 410 million years later.

During the movement of these plates, rocks were formed by different means: igneous rocks, the oldest, were formed from molten lava such as basalt (cooling at the surface) or granite (which cools in crystalline form within the crust), to be exposed by erosion. Sedimentary rocks like sandstone were formed by erosion and compression. Metamorphic rocks were altered by heat or pressure, for example slate or shale. It was a Scot, James Hutton, who first outlined such seminal ideas in his three-volume *Theory of the Earth*, in 1795. Hutton explored Arran, but not Bute. He concluded that 'The present is the key to the past', that we continue to witness the same processes: creation, erosion, deposition, change (or metamorphosis) and more erosion, even if they take place over extremely long periods of time.

BUTE

Geologically, Bute is defined principally by the Highland Boundary Fault running from Rothesay through Loch Fad to Scalpsie Bay. This fault was caused by the pressures as the Scottish and English land masses began to collide, causing the intervening ocean bed to be dragged under the plates.

(a) North of the fault lie the 'Dalradian' rocks, part of a wider Highland system. Dalradian rock is metamorphic, principally schist, parallel bands of quartz and mica of green-grey metamorphic rock produced

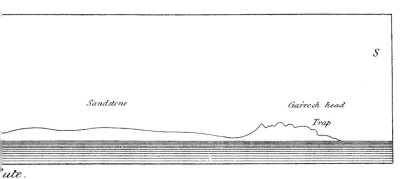

ute.

at high temperatures. But there are also phyllites, the oldest Dalradian rocks in Bute, produced at lower temperatures and of a more shiny green quality. The surface of northern Bute also contains plenty of younger sedimentary rocks, known as greywackes, laid down by fast-flowing ocean currents. These are composed of crudely graded grain particles, each of which can contain a range of grains from fine clay to coarse sandstone. There are good examples on the north edge of Scalpsie Bay.

(b) The fault between north and south Bute was moving for extremely long periods, spanning possibly 80 million years, the angle of movement varying. The remaining traces of these events are sufficiently complex that geologists are still trying to puzzle them out.

(c) The greater part of Bute south of the Boundary Fault is Old Red Sandstone, once part of a greater landmass known as the Old Red Sandstone Continent. In Bute this rock formed roughly 365 million years ago and is up to 2 km deep. There are several types of rock within the Old Red Sandstone area, principally limestone formed as a result of moisture evaporation; breccio-conglomerate, a composite rock of angular fragments of older rock cemented together; and brown sandstone, indicating iron oxide in its bonding material.

(d) Lava outcrops, sometimes called 'trap', as in MacCulloch's cross-section, occur in two principal districts of Bute. The first is composed of two areas running south-westwards, from Ascog to Loch Ascog, and again from the south side of Loch Fad to the area south of Loch Quien. The second is in the far south of the island, roughly eastwards from Lubas across to Hawk's Neb. These lava outflows occurred some 340 million years ago and are the consequence of the considerable volcanic activity in the western Midland Valley. This was the same period in which the rich tropical flora laid down the Coal Measures of the nearby mainland. The south of the island is characterised by volcanic vents, for example Suidhe Chatain; lava flows forming, for instance Glencallum Bay; and columnar lava visible at Dunagoil. Other lava outflows occurred more recently, only some 60 million years ago, when volcanic activity occurred across Western Scotland southwards to Antrim (the Giant's Causeway). There are two principal characteristics of this volcanic activity in Bute: (i) lava 'sills', essentially horizontal intrusions of magma, most dramatically exemplified as layers of the cap to St Blane's Hill, the result of volcanic activity centred in Arran; and (ii) lava 'dykes', which cut across the rock structures of both north and south Bute, mainly in a north-south direction and which owe their distant origin to volcanic activity centred in Mull.

(e) The last Ice Age, lasting until about 18,000 years ago, has left its mark on Bute and possibly erased traces of earlier ice ages. Although this particular ice cap did not cover Bute, the island was severely affected by erosion as glaciers moved southwards. Indeed, the overall shape of the lochs surrounding Bute are indicative of the general flow of these glaciers. Glen More is the best example of a glacial valley on dry land in Bute, but the two valleys of Loch Fad – Loch Quien and Kames Bay – Ettrick Bay also show the effects of glacial action. These glaciers left behind 'erratics' (rocks dragged into geologically different areas), striations, boulder clay, and a landscape of rounded hills.

Climate Change and the Landscape

The Last Glaciation lasted approximately from 115,000 to 16,000 BC, during which time there were spells of warmer weather between long periods of extreme cold.

When the ice sheet melted, between 18,000 and 12,000 years ago, sea levels rose by up to 120m to reach the present level around 6,700 years ago. However, this was in part offset by the uneven lift of north-western Britain, as it became relieved of the immense weight of ice, leading to sea regression as evidenced in the raised beaches in many parts of Bute, now up to 30 metres above current sea level. In fact, around 7000 BC, the sea level was probably about 4 metres higher than today. The lifting process is still happening, with the west coast of Scotland rising at 2mm yearly while East Anglia, for example, is falling at the same rate. However, another process, the melting of polar ice, ensures a global rise in sea level. Variable climate has led to radically altered sea levels at different junctures since the ice cap started melting.

Around 9500 BC, the climate rapidly became warmer and drier, with a succession of tree species transforming the tundra landscape into deciduous woodland: first juniper, hazel and birch on open ground, the latter liking drier acidic soils; aspen and sallow occupying wetter ground; alder taking the wettest ground of all; and later oak becoming dominant on richer soils and providing canopy. By 3500 BC Bute was dominated by oak and hazel, both of which remain plentiful.

The upland at the northern end of Bute, like most of the Highlands, was impoverished and turned acid by climate deterioration, not only in prehistoric times but later. By 1000 AD most of Scotland's tree cover had been significantly modified and in many places had totally gone, to be replaced by moorland. The natural process, alongside human intervention, continued during the 'Little Ice Age' of the sixteenth to eighteenth centuries AD, when it became colder and wetter than in the preceding millennium.

This impoverishment results from high rainfall, which washes the basic minerals out of the surface layers. A cold climate slows the disintegration of plant debris and since the acids produced are not neutralised, a layer of highly acid raw humus forms on the surface. Among broadleaves, only birch can flourish on this type of soil. All conifers tolerate this acid soil more willingly. Where the surface remains waterlogged, deep peat develops, sometimes as blanket peat bog. The plants that can sustain life under such conditions are limited, principally to sphagnum moss, certain sedges, heaths and one or two other species. Heather colonises drier peat areas. Peat, the traditional fuel of wood-impoverished areas, is of no use agriculturally unless drained and heavily manured. It is only on particular slopes, for example ravines, where sufficient mineral and other nutrients have built up, that other broadleaves like rowan and oak can still grow, for example on the northern slopes of the island.

Prehistory

One of the most tantalising features of prehistory is the paucity of artefacts to illuminate the lives of the people. We have the detritus of foodstuffs, stonework of various kinds, a few implements and in the later phases funerary and fortified constructions. It is often difficult to make much of these. The acid soils of Scotland have been particularly destructive of organic remains, for example timber.

Although the phases of human prehistory are conventionally dated Mesolithic (Middle Stone Age) and Neolithic (New Stone Age), Bronze Age and Iron Age, there are of course no neat dividing lines. The technologies, practices and probably culture of one age overlapped with the advent of new ones over a long time span.

Modern man emerged roughly 100,000 years ago. The first critical evidence of us being significantly different from other hominids dates back some 70,000 years, probably the time of the final phase of language evolution, and to our first recorded expressions of an artistic and religious impulse on cave walls more recently, little more than 10,000 years ago.

THE MESOLITHIC PERIOD

We cannot know for sure when humans settled in Bute, but the first sign of human habitation in Scotland is in Clydesdale: a piece of charcoal from a wild service tree (*Sorbus torminalis*). It dates back to the early ninth century BC, but the date of first habitation will probably be pushed back further as fresh evidence comes to light. Only 40 years ago archaeologists reckoned that humans did not settle Scotland much before 3000 BC. Today the wild service tree will no longer grow willingly much further north than London, so we know that Bute's climate was substantially warmer and drier than today.

There is virtually no trace of the Mesolithic people in Scotland except the detritus of their foodstuffs, flints, which must have been imported, fashioned quartz and microliths, bone hooks and harpoons. Most Mesolithic artefacts were made of perishable materials, wood and animal skins, which have disappeared, or which if they survived have been ploughed out. Mesolithic study awaits the discovery of a waterlogged site, where much more may be found to help bring these people out of the shadows.

So far, in Bute there are two known late Mesolithic sites: a shell midden at Glecknabae, just north of Ettrick Bay, and another site at Little Kilchattan, on the north-west shore of Kilchattan Bay. The people here seem to have lived off nuts, fruits, molluscs, fish, wildfowl, small game, seals and possibly other large mammals, now extinct. They used stone, bone and antler implements. They were probably nomadic, moving on once food resources were temporarily exhausted. There may have only been one kindred group in Bute, which may have split to establish a second settlement when it grew, but that, of course, is only a guess.

There is nothing for visitors to see, save objects such as imported flints or microliths in the Bute Museum, so you may well wonder why you should have any interest in these people. Consider their timescale: these hunter-gatherers, possibly our forebears, existed as a culture for over 4,000 years before the transition into the Neolithic period. That is a time span nearly as long as that between the Neolithic people and ourselves. The frustration lies in knowing so little about them.

THE NEOLITHIC PERIOD

The early Neolithic people probably arrived because of an improvement in the weather conditions, rendering sea travel feasible. They must have travelled in curraghs (wicker boats covered in hides) settling in Ireland and along the western seaboard of Britain. The first signs of their arrival in Scotland occurred around 4000 BC, with the appearance of domesticated livestock, and a little later with the cultivation of plants (six-row barley and emmer wheat). These people may have remained primarily hunter-gatherers, for there was almost certainly a long overlap between the Mesolithic and Neolithic culture, as there also was between the Neolithic and the Bronze Age when flint knapping skills, for example, were still in use. Woodland clearance, which Mesolithic people had probably begun, greatly increased during the Neolithic period as people became more sedentary and invested more effort in their place of abode. Livestock rearing and agriculture demanded widespread tree clearance, which must also have accelerated peat and acid soil, or podsol, formation.

Indeed, it was in the Neolithic period that permanent communities began to form. The transition from nomadic to sedentary communities possibly represents the most significant moment in the political development of human society. Judging by hunter-gatherer societies which have been studied, Mesolithic people operated in small and highly egalitarian transient groups with mechanisms – joking, teasing or temporary ostracism, for example – to prevent individuals gaining dominance. In contrast, Neolithic people formed social hierarchies for an ordered sedentary life, and to achieve this they reverted to the behaviour of primates. Ambitious alpha males must have applied fear and violence in order to control others. Alpha males are still hard at it, some domestically, others in the work place or politically. The conscious use of fear and violence in politics has a long pedigree. With the end of Mesolithic social organisation, it seems, we were cast out of Eden.

The Neolithic people who settled in Britain are our direct and principal ancestors. Their DNA accounts for roughly three quarters of British genetic make-up. According to the genetic evidence, they had emerged from an Ice Age refuge in what is now the Basque region straddling the Pyrenees. Their DNA may have been pretty much identical with the Mesolithic people, who may indeed be our oldest forebears. We do not know yet. Each of the subsequent invasions, Gaels, Anglo-Saxons, Norsemen and Danes left a genetic 'signal', but not one of them accounted for more than one tenth of overall British genetic make-up. This finding is sufficiently recent that, even in the context of a book about Bute, it deserves mention.

Celtic languages probably arrived from south-west Europe with early Neolithic settlers between 4000 and 3000 BC. These languages may have fragmented into two main groups before their arrival here, or fragmented after settlement. Strathclyde was a Brittonic-speaking region until it was slowly overcome by the expansion of Gaelic settlers at a later stage. From this one can speculate that the early Neolithic people of Bute spoke some version of Brittonic, as did the Picts and the people of Cumbria, Wales and Cornwall. Welsh is the sole survivor of this branch of Celtic. Gaelic became established in Ireland and later in western Scotland and Man.

By 3300 BC, these Neolithic people had developed a local monumental culture, now known as 'Clyde cairns', tombs distinguished by the great stone slabs used to line each side of a tomb and to roof it. The entrance opened directly into the burial chamber. In 1946 the leading exponent of Scottish archaeology of his day, V. G. Childe, realised that their closest parallels were found in the Pyrenees (we now know why). Having studied tombs in Bute, Arran and Kintyre, he noted that 'Each tomb corresponds to a natural agricultural unit, generally still or till recently farmed by a community and in each case comprising a stream, a strip of good arable below, and a tract of pasture above the tomb.' As one walks the landscape in Bute this is a useful image to bear in mind. Within the tomb grave-goods included round-based vessels with a ridged rim or with lugs. Some of these vessels, for example beakers which first made their appearance in this period, were more highly decorated, as found at Glenvoidean (near Kilmichael) in Bute. Perhaps such tombs were not for one person alone, but symbolic monuments for the entire kindred group.

THE BRONZE AGE

Around 2000 BC, at the beginning of the Bronze Age, the weather was warmer and drier than today, and pollen analysis indicates a significant increase in arable farming and tree clearance for cultivation. Houses were circular, with large upright timbers forming an inner circle, on which the roof rested, sloping down to the outer wall, and up to 6 metres in diameter. They do not seem to have been fortified, but lay within their field system. Since Bronze Age sites tended to be on the better drained areas of more fertile land, the vast majority of examples must have been ploughed out since. What we are left with principally is the funerary evidence: tombs, or cists, slab-lined rectangular pits with cover stones, well exemplified in Bute.

A distinctive feature peculiar to the western seaboard of Europe is the henge or stone circle. The earliest belong to the Neolithic period, but the majority are Bronze Age. In Bute there are the remains of two henges, one in Blackpark Plantation just inland from the head of Kilchattan Bay, and the other near St Colmac, similarly sited inland of Ettrick Bay. These are particularly fertile sites and one might speculate that the circles may have had some kind of ritual fertility purpose. It seems that, in common with societies all over the world, stones were seen as some kind of spiritual embodiment of the kindred or of its individuals. Think of our war memorials and graveyards. Like our very distant ancestors, we are still standing in front of stones. They offer permanence in contrast with our transient lives.

From about 900 BC the weather deterioration, forcing the abandonment of hill farms, where much of the land turned to peat, or podsol. With scarcer resources, competition must have been fierce for fertile lowland areas. It seems that cattle reiving became a feature of inter-communal conflict. From about the same date the bronze industry began to expand rapidly. Many artefacts of violence of this period have been found: spear and axe heads, coinciding with the first appearance of defensive forts and

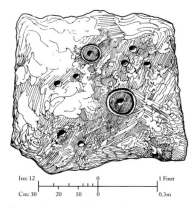

Cup and cup-and-ring marks.

enclosed settlements in the seventh and sixth centuries BC.

In Bute the best-preserved remains of the Bronze Age are the cists or cairn tombs, but there are also a few examples of the cup or cup-and-ring marks on stones, more widely scattered across Argyllshire, marks which continue to mystify archaeologists. Bronze Age folk were in some respects sophisticated compared with their forebears. In 1887 an early Bronze Age grave was found close to Kerrycroy Burn (near the entrance to Mount Stuart). A remarkable 107-piece jet necklace lay under the skeleton. Forget the necklace. The real sensation was a 2cm perforation in the left temple of the skull, that of a young woman. She may have suffered terrible headaches or epilepsy. Whatever the reason, she had been trepanned, an operation which she had survived. Alas, we do not know whether she was also cured. It is the first known case of surgery, let alone brain surgery, in Britain. The medical profession in Scotland has a long pedigree.

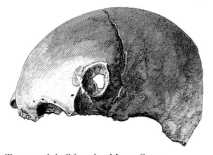

Trepanned skull found at Mount Stuart.

THE IRON AGE

Iron was introduced to Scotland around 700 BC and led to a slow decline in the use of bronze. Since iron could be obtained locally, it also led to a decline in maritime trade networks. The spread of defensive enclosures indicates an increase in conflict. Duns, or forts, were constructed with stone, sometimes laced with timber, as strong points. While these offered strong defences they were usually too small to hold more than a few people and no livestock, but they were redoubts to which people could flee. Dunagoil, at the south end of the island, provides an important exception, for thanks to the rock formation, it combines a strong hill fort with a defensible bailey into which animals could be and probably were driven. Several hill forts may be found in Bute, most of them sited to ensure good visibility, and presumably communication, to others.

Crannogs were built in lakes, using stones and wood, sometimes with vertical piles to provide circular wooden housing above the water level. Crannogs may have offered an effective defence for a small group, but their chief purpose was probably for storing grain beyond the reach of rats. There are traces of crannogs in Loch Quien and the Dhu Loch. The former is sited close to good agricultural land.

Plan of Loch Quien crannog, as drawn in 1889.

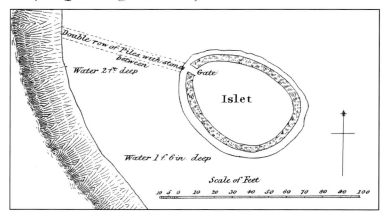

History

THE EARLY CHRISTIAN PERIOD, AD 400-800

The sea dominated the history of western Scotland until very recent times, indeed until the invention of the steam and internal combustion engines. It joined rather than isolated the communities of the region. It was land, not sea, which was difficult to cross.

In the early Christian period society formed around secular and religious foundations with wide sea-based networks. A Brittonic-speaking kingdom emerged in the Clyde region, probably consisting of client kindred groups and centred on Dumbarton, the strategically placed *dun* of the Britons. Local rulers may have seen Christian missionaries as offering useful contact with superior economic, cultural and political powers in mainland Europe. At a more profound level, these missionaries purveyed universal ideas rooted in human behaviour, replacing localist divinities. Ninian, or a group of monks for whom his name has become emblematic, established a monastery at Whithorn in Galloway in the mid-fifth century. This seems to have been a Brittonic extension of the abbey established at Tours in Western Gaul in c.375 by St Martin, the first great exponent of western monasticism. Galloway at that time was part of a Cumbrian state probably centred on Carlisle, but Whithorn itself was well placed on the great sea routes.

The wider region had been in the throes of a violent contest between the Brittonic world of Cumbria and Strathclyde, Irish Gael raiders from the west (the Brittonic St Patrick had been a victim of one of their raids), and to the northeast, Brittonic Pictish military encroachment. The spread of Christianity across linguistic and dialect frontiers at this time had a miraculously pacific impact, which allowed for a burst of creative scholarship and art. Ninian extended his influence well beyond Whithorn, to the Clyde and also across the Campsie Fells into the land of the Picts. Whether Ninian ever reached Bute must be doubtful, but the sixth century chapel on its west coast dedicated to him indicates the extent and durability of his influence.

By the late sixth century Bute was still Brittonic speaking, but became increasingly under the influence of Gaelic culture, as inroads by northern Irish settlers since the fifth century began to have an impact. A Christian missionary, Catan, came to Bute from Ulster in the late sixth century intending to found a monastery. He sent his nephew, Blane, back to Bangor for training and on Blane's return handed the monastery and bishopric into his care. In due course, probably around AD 600, Blane seems to have established his own monastery, the one that remains, unless his name was simply associated with Catan's foundation. Blane also established a monastery in a *dun* in Pictland, Dunblane, and another near Dumfries, Kilblain, indicating the ease with which people seemed able to cross the linguistic boundary between the Gaelic and Brittonic language groups.

It was around this time that Columba established his monastery in Iona. As one of the O'Neills of Tara, Columba personified the twin political and religious colonisation of western Scotland by the Irish Gaels. In Bute several place names testify to the intense Gaelic-Christian activity of the ensuing period: Inchmarnock (St Marnoc), St Colmac (St Chalmaig) and Kilmichael (Maccaile, allegedly a servant of St Patrick), not to mention Kilchattan and St Blane's. And, of course, the people of Bute have been known for over 500 years as Brandanes, after St Brendan who is supposed to have come to Bute.

It is thought that Kildavanan, apparently named after the great abbot of Iona and biographer of Columba, Adamnan ('Wee Adam'), was a staging post on the route between Iona and the river Clyde. Travellers carried their light-weight curraghs overland, from Crinan to Loch Fyne, and then again from Ettrick shore to Kames Bay.

VIKING RAIDS AND SETTLEMENT, 800-1100

The Gaelic rulers used large curraghs, wooden framed craft with skin covers, powered by sail and oar. By the seventh century they had seven-bench craft powered by fourteen oars, and decreed that every twenty houses across Bute and Cowal had to provide the manpower for two of these vessels.

Yet they could not compete with the powerful vessels of the Norsemen, clinker-built longships designed to well-nigh hydrodynamic perfection, and manned by at least thirty-two and often nearer fifty men. In 794 Vikings made their first devastating raid on the Hebrides. The following year they pillaged Iona and Skye. In 798 they raided Man. For the next century monastic and other settlements, including Bute, were subject to periodic raids and devastation.

About a century after their first raids, the Norsemen embraced Christianity and sought to be buried in the very places, like Iona and Bute, which they had previously so ruthlessly sacked. Just as significantly, they began to colonise the western seaboard of northern Britain. Taking Gaelic wives they melded culturally into the Gaelic world. It is difficult to picture the society that prevailed in Bute, but it is likely to have been based on clientship. The lower order, the 'base' clients, were probably in forced servitude, obliged to render food, military service and hospitality in return for land and protection. An upper class of clients were of noble or warrior status, companions of the chief. Politically, the Hebrides and Argyll became contested territories between a succession of Hebridean sea-kings: Norse rulers and local 'Gallgael' warlords, the Gaelic-speaking descendants of Norsemen.

During the eleventh century, the kingdom of Scots slowly sought to consolidate and extend its control beyond the Midland Valley and the Lothians. The kingdom of Strathclyde, so close to Bute, had been absorbed into the Scottish kingdom by about 1050. But the hold was tenuous. The Clyde islands and most of the western seaboard of Scotland remained in the hands of the Norse-Hebridean sea-kings, while to the southwest Gaelic-speaking Galloway also remained fiercely independent.

THE SEA-KINGS, THE KINGDOM OF SCOTS AND THE STEWARTS

In the twelfth century the Scottish kings introduced a new warrior class of Anglo-Norman knights into their lands. Unlike the independently-minded tribal groups of the highlands and islands, these knights held their land directly from the king and undertook to serve him on the battlefield when he needed them. These bonds of hierarchical loyalty were replicated by those beneath them. The feudal system had already demonstrated its potential for a stable, secure and centralised state in England.

A Shropshire magnate, Walter FitzAlan, entered Scottish royal service in about 1136 and was appointed High Steward – hence Stewart – to the king. He was also endowed with extensive lands in Renfrewshire and Ayrshire, where he settled knightly members of his retinue. His fiefdom was intended to be a bulwark against attacks by the sea-kings or the lords of Galloway on the Ayrshire coast or up the Clyde. Another Norman knight was granted lands on the north bank of the Clyde, to confront the

Seals of Walter the Steward, and his son Alan, both armed and on a charger, icons of noble status.

Gaels to the north and west. These appointments were intended to stabilise the Clyde estuary frontiers of the kingdom.

In 1164 Walter's mettle was put to the test when the legendary sea-king, Somerled, Lord of the Isles, sailed up the Clyde and attacked Renfrew with a large mixed force of men from Argyll, Kintyre, the Hebrides and Ireland. Walter's smaller force defeated the invaders and slew Somerled. Yet it was probably only towards the end of the century that Bute itself was wrested from Somerled's grandson, Ruaridh.

From this time Bute became a substantive part of the Kingdom of Scots. Walter's son, Alan, was acknowledged as lord of Bute, an island on the front line of defence of the Clyde and a potential springboard for advancing royal authority into Cowal and beyond. Given the fine anchorage in the bay it is not surprising that a castle was built at Rothesay to garrison it. It is one of Scotland's first stone castles, originally probably a massive round keep. As a Crusader, Alan may well have learnt the best defensive architecture from Saracen castles in Palestine.

It is indicative of Bute's strategic position that Håkon IV of Norway sent another of Somerled's grandsons, the Norse-Hebridean leader Uspak, with a force of 80 warships to attack Rothesay castle in 1230:

> And they sailed south round the Mull of Kintyre, and so to Bute. The Scots sat there in the castle; and a certain steward was one of the Scots. [The Norwegians] attacked the castle, but the Scots defended it, and they pour [*sic*] out boiling pitch the Norwegians hewed the wall with axes, because it was soft [perhaps the mortar had not set.]…. Many Norwegians fell before they won the castle.
>
> *The Saga of Håkon Håkonsson* (c.1265)

Uspak, however, was compelled to withdraw owing to the approach of a rescue fleet. He himself had been mortally wounded in the siege and died shortly after in Kintyre.

In 1263 the Norwegians attacked Rothesay Castle for a second time, this time led by Håkon himself. The siege was part of the Norwegian response to assaults on Man, Ireland and the Isles, so it was an attempt to punish as well as to take back control of the Clyde approaches. Rothesay fell to Håkon, but he had to fight Stewart forces, including Brandane spearmen, on the hills above Largs. While the actual battle was inconclusive, the strategic outcome was decisive. Håkon died on his way home and three years later his son, Magnus, decided formally to cede control of Man and the southern isles to Scotland. But for brief raids in support of the English 30 years later, Bute had finally – after 450 years of contest – seen the last of the sea-lords.

THE STEWARTS AND THE WARS OF INDEPENDENCE

No sooner, however, had the kings of Scots dealt with the threat from the sea than a more serious challenge developed to the south. England had long coveted control of Scotland. When war broke out with England's King Edward I over the Scottish succession in 1296, the Stewarts supported the national cause: the right of Scots to choose their own king without English interference. When English pressure was too great the Stewarts submitted, but sidled back to the national camp when pressure relaxed. They gave sanctuary, for example, to Wallace's ally, the Bishop of Dunkeld who

> To saiff his lyff, thre zer [three years] he duelt in But
>
> Leifyde as he mycht, and kepyt ay gud part,
>
> Undir saifte [protection] off Jamys then Lord Stewart.
>
> Blind Harry, *Wallace*, book viii.ll.936-938, c.1488.

The first documented reference to 'Brandanes' is in an account (dated c.1420) of the battle of Falkirk, 1298, near the beginning of the wars of independence:

> Thare Jhon Stuart upon fute [foot],
>
> With hym the Brandys thare off Bute
>
> Andrew of Wyntoun, *The Orygynal Cronykil of Scotland*

In 1301 a mixed English-Islay fleet occupied Rothesay and its valuable bay. Bruce only recaptured it in 1306. In 1309 James Stewart, lord of Bute formally acknowledged Robert Bruce as lawful king of the Scots. Five years later he led Brandanes into battle at Bannockburn,

> of Argile and of Kentyre,
> and of the Iles, quharoff was syre
> Angus of Ile, and Bute and all tha
>
> John Barbour, *Brus* (1375)

James Stewart's son, Walter, sealed the alliance with the house of Bruce by marriage to King Robert's daughter, Marjory. It was during Walter's close association with the Bruce that Rothesay became important politically, the most striking material indication being the remarkable Bute Mazer, probably made in 1316 at the instigation of the Keeper of Rothesay Castle. After Walter's death in 1326, Robert, his son by Marjory, became Steward of Scotland.

In the meantime political fortunes had reversed. An English army triumphed over the Scots at Halidon Hill in 1333 and Edward Baliol was installed on the Scottish throne as an English puppet. Baliol dispossessed the fief holder of Bute, Robert, but was unable to take Dumbarton, where both he, now heir apparent, and King David II had taken refuge. By now, however, the idea of Scottish independence was firmly rooted, not least because the Scottish clergy were determined not to be subservient to the Primate of All England. There was more religious merit, thundered the Bishop of Moray, in fighting the English than the Saracen.

It is the measure of a remarkable and pervasive national spirit in the feudal age that the unarmed populace rose against Baliol's garrison at Rothesay Castle. When the latter sallied forth against them on the slopes of Barone Hill,

> ....the Brandanes in their habitual agility took up stones in their hands and threw them at the sheriff's men like a shower of hail and they brought about very considerable slaughter, killed the sheriff, seized the rest who were running away, and furnished themselves with booty and weapons from them.
>
> Walter Bower, *Scotichronicon* (c.1440)

Shame about the bloodshed, but there is something peculiarly satisfying about the triumph of civil indignation against unrepresentative government.

Of course, there was retribution to come. The English were incensed and in 1335 landed troops in Bute, ravaging it. In part this may have been because Robert was heir presumptive to the Scottish Crown, though he

The Bute Mazer. This drinking vessel is one of Scotland's great treasures, now in the National Museum. The central boss was fitted into an existing bowl shortly after Bannockburn, between 1314 and 1317. The silver rim is of a later date, c.1522, bearing the name of the then owner, Ninian Bannatyne of Kames. The silvergilt boss, with Scotland's earliest heraldic enamelwork in the centre of the bowl is of great significance, replacing the original base. The lion couchant represents the Crowned Head of Scotland. Between its paws lie the arms of the High Steward, Walter, husband of Marjory, Bruce's daughter. He is the honoured senior magnate, later briefly Regent of Scotland. The other escutcheons signify the loyalty of Firth of Clyde nobles. To the right, anticlockwise, are the arms of John Menteith, Lord of Arran (a cadet branch of the Stewarts, hence the similarity of shield); Susanna Crawford, Lady of Loudoun, hereditary Sheriff of Ayr; John FitzGilbert the Keeper of Rothesay Castle. Since he furnished the High Steward's table in the castle, it must have been John FitzGilbert who had the boss set into the mazer, and it must have been for an occasion when all these magnates were gathered around the table, probably with their king. They would all have drunk from the mazer, symbolising mutual loyalty. The next shield is that of John's father, Walter FitzGilbert, lord of Hamilton and a powerful magnate in Renfrew and Lanark. The sixth escutcheon represents the one magnate with no direct connection with the Clyde estuary, Sir James Douglas, the close companion of the Bruce in his struggle against the English.

only became king, as Robert II, in 1371 when he was aged 54. Both before and after his coronation he spent much of his time at Rothesay. It is from Robert II's natural son (mother unknown) that the earls and marquesses of Bute trace their descent.

Robert III, his lawful son, succeeded to the throne. In 1398 he appointed his firstborn son as Duke of Rothesay, a tradition of the Scottish monarchy in practice to this day. Robert granted Rothesay the valuable and privileged status of a royal burgh, yet from this time onwards Bute ceased to be important in the political history of Scotland.

There is, however, a sad coda to add. Robert III, certainly not one of Scotland's more impressive kings, had already had to come to terms with the murder of his wastrel firstborn son in 1402. Four years later his second son, James, still only a boy, was captured at sea while en route for France. It seems the English were acting on a tip-off. They were to hold him for 18 years:

> When King Robert heard of his son's capture while sitting at supper in his castle of Rothesay, he was moved inwardly in his heart on hearing the messenger; his spirit failed directly, the strength of his body dwindled, his face grew pale, and in his grief he ate no more food until he breathed out his spirit to his creator.
>
> Walter Bower, *Scotichronicon*

ROTHESAY AS A MILITARY BASE, 1400-1700

In the fifteenth century Bute was briefly sucked back into the struggle between the independent sea-borne tribal chiefs and the land-based kingdom of Scots, for the island was a symbol of royal authority on the boundaries between the sea and land-based political worlds. Of the sea-borne tribes, Clan Donald was the pre-eminent. From the 1430s the MacDonalds refused to pay dues to the Crown for their estates in Kintyre. In 1454 Donald MacDonald came with 5,000 men on a fleet of 100 galleys, ravaging the Clyde approaches, including Bute.

From about this time, however, the Crown began to enjoy an alliance with Clan Campbell, which sought to challenge the dominance of Clan Donald across the western isles from Kintyre to Skye. In 1464 the Campbells, led by the Earl of Argyll, joined James III's expedition to bring the MacDonald Lordship of the Isles back under royal control.

Like his predecessors, James IV had to use Rothesay as a base for imposing royal authority throughout the west. In 1493 he finally suppressed the MacDonald Lordship of the Isles. He was back in Rothesay the following year, having also just subjugated the MacDonalds of Kintyre, and again in 1499. Before his untimely death on Flodden Field in 1513, James had issued instructions for the strengthening of Rothesay Castle, as a bastion against the recalcitrant tribes of western Scotland. His son, James V, visited Rothesay in 1540 on completion of an expedition to assert his authority over the clans of the western highlands and isles. It is probably the last time a Scottish king stayed in the castle. The defeat at Flodden proved a critical setback for royal authority across the Gaelic-speaking western coastlands. Clan Donald immediately reasserted its independent ways.

Bute remained vulnerable, partly because of its position on the Clyde approaches but also because symbolically it represented the Crown. It remained a target for the English too, when they felt the need to give the Scots a good whipping. In 1544 Henry VIII decided to browbeat the Scots into his planned marriage union of the two crowns: his seven-year old son Edward to the infant Queen Mary. When the Scots became uncooperative, his forces gave support to local allies to ravage Bute, a crude reminder of the consequences of a failure to please England. Henry gave instructions that Rothesay should be assessed as a permanent base from which to control the western approaches to the Scottish Kingdom, a scheme which seems to have come to nothing.

A century later, Bute was again engulfed by conflicts not of its own making. An Irish rebellion in Ulster in 1641 triggered a massive influx of fugitives – over five hundred – who threw themselves '…upon the charitie of there freinds and other weill affected christians within the tua paroches of the said Ile of Boote.' This invasion must have affected at least a quarter of the households on the island. Brandanes shared their food with the refugees for four months before government relief came, and the rebellion subsided.

A second conflict, one between Crown and People, threatened the people of Bute much more directly. While in England this conflict took the form of a quarrel with Parliament, in Scotland the quarrel was with the Kirk. Given its geographical situation, Bute found itself straddling mental fault lines which had arisen only relatively recently: between Gaelic and Scots speakers, between King and Covenant, and between Catholic and Presbyterian. Each fault line differed in its geographical boundaries:

some Scots-speakers in the Lowlands supported the Crown, while in the Highlands some Gaels, most notably the Campbells, came out firmly for the Covenant against the Crown.

Bute seems to have been reluctant to be involved in the struggle and certainly reluctant to supply the manpower which the Presbyterian army required. When Alasdair MacColla, MacDonald chief and royalist leader in the west, marched victoriously through Cowal in 1645-46, Bute's leaders unsuccessfully tried to avoid the terror of a visitation. They were aware of the devastation wrought in Argyll, where, in the words of one of MacColla's officers, 'were left neither house nor hold unburned, nor corn nor cattle that belonged to the whole name of Campbell.' But MacColla's men had old scores to settle. They remembered that Brandanes had assisted in the suppression of the MacDonalds of Kintyre in 1615. Having entered Bute, MacColla's men, part of 'the Highland Horde', were quartered on its inhabitants, burning and plundering where they wished. As always, there were some in the community who collaborated with MacColla's men. When order was restored the Kirk brought Bute's royalist collaborators to book, a very much milder retribution than that visited by the Campbells on those who had raised their hand against them in Cowal and Kintyre.

Then, five years later, Rothesay was again garrisoned by foreign conquerors, this time English Parliamentarian troops who stayed from 1650 until 1659. They demolished enough to ensure that the castle would not be defensible in future, but they left the gatehouse as a habitable dwelling. Even this fell victim to the ravages of military conflict, this time the recklessness of the 9th Earl of Argyll. The earls of Argyll had successively supported Knox and the Reformed Church. When, in 1685, James VII implicitly threatened a return to Catholicism, Argyll rebelled and seized Bute. It was a bungled and short-lived event. In the words of Bishop Burnet, he 'landed in the isle of Bute; where he spent twelve days more, till he had eat [sic] up that island.' In the words of an eyewitness his forces, 'in going through the Isle of Bute, committed many abuses, by plundering people's houses, killing and hoching kine sheep and lambs....' They also burnt the castle gatehouse (see p.30).

LIFE IN ROTHESAY BEFORE 1700

Robert III had elevated Rothesay to the status of royal burgh in 1401, by which time it must have been an old settlement. He followed an established practice that where there was a royal castle, it was also desirable to build trade, justice and administration. By its new status, Rothesay might defend its trade interests but it was also subject to Crown fundraising. It enjoyed export trade privileges and had sole market rights for its hinterland, including Arran and the Cumbraes and, until the establishment of Campbeltown as a royal burgh in 1700, possibly the produce of Kintyre. The attraction of becoming a burgher was that you could sell your land if you wished, a privilege certainly denied those living in the countryside. Rent-free inducements may well have been offered to English, Norman or Flemish traders to settle. It is perhaps no accident that when Martin Martin visited Bute, around 1695, he reported that 'the oldest man now living in this isle is one Fleming, a weaver in Rothesay.' He was in his nineties. Non-Scots incomers to Bute have a long history. Martin could not resist including an intimate personal detail about Fleming, 'his neighbours told me he could never ease nature at sea.' One can only sympathise.

Exports would have been principally wool, flax, hides, animal skins and herring to local if not foreign markets. The principal market destinations abroad were England and Flanders. Being on the west coast was a disadvantage, so while consignments would have been weighed at the burgh tron and sealed, they were probably consigned to another burgh, for example Linlithgow, for onward export.

Be under no illusions when thinking of this royal burgh. It was little more than a handful of dwellings up the High Street beyond the castle, with barely one tenth of the island population. Ordinary dwellings might have had stone footings but would have been flimsy single storey structures not much better than those in the countryside. Behind each house would have been a plot of land to cultivate and keep livestock ending at a back lane, parallel with the High Street.

The burgh would have been dependent on the countryside for its most basic resource, population. Urban families in Scotland tended not to survive for more than three or four generations. A trickle of incomers would have kept this pitifully small burgh viable. And, of course, it would have been dependent on the countryside for export commodities, principally livestock, destined either for the mainland or abroad. Brandanes probably only visited the mainland exceptionally, for that, too, was 'abroad'.

The market place was beside the castle, probably close to where the present mercat cross stands. The commodities traded locally would have included grease and tallow for candles and rush-lights, soaps and lubricants; antler, bone and horn used for small implements, hooves for oil to lubricate leather; dog dung for tanning; feathers for arrows; baskets made of willow and hazel wands. One may conjecture the presence within the burgh of a blacksmith, cooper, weaver, tailor and brewster, the latter often a woman. Noxious activities, like curing and tanning skins, were essential for the export market. They would probably have been kept firmly outwith the High Street area, well away from the burghers' nostrils. A cuckstool probably stood close by the mercat cross, in which miscreants could be pelted with ordure, mud and suchlike from passers-by. The burgh mill was below the castle, on the Lade in what is now John Street. People of the burgh, including holders of burgh lands beyond the dwellings themselves, were required to use it, so it was a significant source of burgh revenue.

The royal burgh can hardly have got off to a flying start since Scotland, like most of Europe, had entered a long period of deteriorating weather from about 1320. A series of plagues, most notably the Black Death in 1348-9, and failed harvests led to acute population loss by both disease and starvation. Like France, Scotland had a particular problem: England's imperial appetite. Repeated wars well into the sixteenth century cost the population heavily, not least through English depredations on land and sea. This left a lasting legacy of distrust of England, certainly till the Union and some might argue to this present day. It also meant that Scotland endured centuries of economic adversity. Inevitably Scots looked back to a golden era, before Alexander III's accidental but catastrophic death in 1286 that paved the way for persistent English interference and, coincidentally, climate deterioration.

Life was regimented in a way we would find profoundly unacceptable now. For some years in the 1630s the burgh was even roused in summer at 5am and 'stood down' at 8pm, by a piper marching through the streets. A small concession was made in the winter months: an hour longer in bed. The piper was abandoned in favour of a drummer, who was one third cheaper. Were the pipes too noisy, too expensive, or was it that they

Rothesay Castle in the nineteenth century, with the smiddy and other buildings clustered around it.

were associated with unruly roistering and so incurred po-faced disapproval? We are unlikely ever to know.

Rothesay remained seriously poor until the eighteenth century. In 1652, during Cromwell's Protectorate, Rothesay was excused sending a representative to the Dalkeith conference convened to consider a union of the three crowns, simply on account of its poverty. In 1690 a survey of Scotland's 68 burghs rated Rothesay 68th in terms of wealth. Few then would have believed that a century later it would enjoy a burgeoning economy.

ROTHESAY AFTER 1700

By the mid-eighteenth century the town extended from the Lade (now covered by Dean Hood Place) in the west, to the foot of what became Bishop Street in the east. The north sides of Montague Street and West Princes Street were open seashore. This shore ground was overgrown with whin, or gorse, and was a dumping ground 'upon part of which the seamen dub a filthy and noxious mire', probably a pungent combination of human ordure and fish offal. Cattle were still driven out of town daily to the common grazing. There were poultry in the streets, scratching away at the midden heap outside each house. Until the mid-nineteenth century almost all the houses on the High Street were no more than two-storey structures, many with passages to allow cattle to be accommodated in between. Rothesay was hardly a pretty sight.

According to John Blain, arriving as town clerk in 1761, the town looked 'half in ruins'. As he was not offered a salary but only received fees, he had a vital interest in reviving Rothesay's trade, which he ably did. He started to smarten the place up. He banished middens from the streets, and had the puddles and ruts in the streets filled in with gravel from the shore. He introduced building standards regarding construction and the headroom indoors. New dwellings had slate, beginning to displace 'clay-built' tenements with strange thatched roofs and smokey wooden chimneys that would not draw properly. On the shore, now Victoria Street, a few small tenements, resembling fishermen's huts, for a while survived. The narrow confines of the burgh's buildings were expanded, for example in 1761 to develop the land around the Gallowgate on the west side of town and that beyond the Watergate to the east. The north sides of Montague Street and West Princes Street remained on the shore. Blain's regulations affected new building, but it would take at least a couple of generations to transform the town to what we now see. As late as 1774 there were still only 1,000 or so people in Rothesay out of an island population of 5-7,000. While by the 1830s Rothesay could still be described as 'a bustling little town with low mainly thatched cottages clustered around the castle', its population was rapidly growing and already exceeded three thousand.

Life on the Land

RURAL LIFE, 1200-1700

Scotland's medieval farms were entirely ploughed out by the end of the eighteenth century, so we have little to go on. Outwith the burgh of Rothesay itself, there would probably have been only tiny fermtoun-type settlements across the landscape, some possibly not even with stone footings, and neither hedgerows nor drystane dykes, nor indeed sown grass. Without land drains, low-lying areas would have been waterlogged and unusable. Trees would have been very sparse, though some were protected, intended as timber for building. Most trees, particularly ash, hazel and willow, would have been grown as coppice for fuel, for farm implements, fencing to be cropped every ten or so years, and willow on a shorter cropping cycle for weaving baskets.

The field system was divided into 'infield' and outfield' for each small fermtoun. Infield constituted the best land, annually under crop usually on a 3-year cycle of oats, oats and bere. Oats were favoured because of their tolerance of inclement weather and acidic soil. Bere (four-row or six-row barley) also did well on sandy soils, particularly on raised beaches and where seaweed was abundant. Its advantage over barley was that it could be sown later, when the earth was warmer and drier, and cropped earlier, vital considerations in Bute's climate. The infield stubble, in theory, would be grazed after harvest to put a modicum of manure on the land. Even so, the yield was not expected to be more than threefold, which as an old maxim indicates, left no surplus: 'ane to saw [sow], and ane to gnaw, and ane to pay the laird witha'.' Anything in excess was a sure sign of God's bounty. From about 1450, beans and peas may also have been grown. From 1678 those living on Rothesay burgh land risked a fine if they did not devote one quarter of their arable to legumes, an indication of the reluctance to grow them. Perhaps people did not understand that legumes benefit a subsequent cereal crop, since they release nitrates into the soil. Periodically rye, flax and hemp were also grown.

The rest of the land, the outfield, was less productive, and was assigned to oats in sections until these ceased to yield. Then that part of the outfield would be grazed and so rested and manured. The outfield would have been several times larger than the infield.

The infield and outfield would have been in 'runrig', long strips of land.

These strips were probably allocated among tenants on a periodic rotational basis, as practised in Arran. One can still see the traces of runrig on the slopes of Kelspoke (see p.130, where ploughing is described). The perimeter of the outfield would have been marked with a crude stone and turf dyke. Outwith the dyke lay uncultivable land, moor and bog, used for grazing and for collecting rushes and turfs for roofing, bracken for litter, and peat and whin for fire and for kindling.

Grain would have been threshed and dried in a corn kiln. From prehistoric times until the early nineteenth century, corn kilns were a common feature of farm life across Scotland, needed for drying grain before grinding. In Bute remains may be found at several locations.

A kiln is composed of a long flu and a circular kiln chamber (about 1.5 metres in diameter), the ground plan rather like a keyhole made of stone and daub. Some may have been roofed with thatch. Others seem to have been open to the skies. To dry the corn, a fire would be lit either at the bottom of the kiln chamber, or in the flu. When it was glowing but no longer with flame, the corn would be spread where the heat would slowly dry it out, on a linen sheet or some such surface. If the harvest had been brought in wet, a frequent condition given the climate, the corn would have to be dried in sheaf, before stacking and threshing. Corn kilns fell into disuse because the potato displaced oats as the staple. In any case, those who still produced grain found it more efficient, given the rise in cereal prices in the late eighteenth century, to send their corn to be dried at the mill, where there would have been a common kiln.

Previously the corn would have been milled in a rotary quern, which displaced the 'saddle' (push-pull) quern around 100 BC (both can be admired in the Bute Museum). Grinding by rotary quern persisted into the nineteenth century in remote parts of Scotland. A quern once owned was never sold or hired, only given or lent. The upper stone rested on a spindle on the nether stone, so finely adjusted that the two stones never met but husked the grain near the centre, grinding the meal out to the edge.

With the advent of watermill technology, people lost their individual milling rights. Landlords compelled their tenants to use their watermill. At least four mills, at Rothesay, Kames, Scalpsie and Kilchattan, were in operation by the late fifteenth century. Millers had a reputation for rapacity. This coercion was bitterly resented. Landlords sent their servants around their estate smashing the nether quern stones, usually only the upper part surviving.

Keeping grain dry in the barn was the first imperative for survival, dryness in one's dwelling a good deal less important. A barn would invariably be more watertight than a dwelling.

Most dwellings were flimsy. In the late fourteenth century, Jean Froissart noted that Scots were

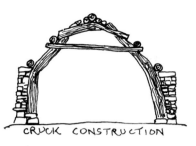

CRUCK CONSTRUCTION

none too worried about having their homes destroyed by the English for it would take only three days to repair them, in his words, 'only five or six poles and boughs to cover them'. Even if he exaggerated, their dwellings were, frankly, hovels. They were shaped like ridge-tents, the ridge provided by a stout pole or slim tree trunk and secured to a series of A-shaped pairs of leaning boughs. Horizontal hazel wattle would be tied to each leaning side, then a layer of vertical wattle. The wattle may have been daubed with a mix of dung, mud and animal hair to seal it. Turfs and finally thatching would probably make the structure reasonably weather proof. Slates were far too heavy. More sophisticated dwellings would have used cruck construction (using the inverted angle between branch and tree trunk to create the same ridge-tent shape) with stone footings to prevent the timber ends from rotting.

By 1650 dwellings were not much better than they had been three centuries earlier. In the words of a Cromwellian soldier, they were simply 'low thatcht cottages full of smoke and noisome smells. In many places their families and catell be under one roof.' Livestock, kept at the lower end of the dwelling, helped to provide modest heating. There would have been a central hearth for heat and cooking, the smoke from the dung or peat filtering out through the roof. Peat cut from moorland was still in use for fuel in 1800, although by then Rothesay was getting supplies of coal from the mainland.

Inside these dwellings, pottery cooking vessels had widely given way to metal ones by 1400, platters would have been of wood, and bowls made of staves, like a half-barrel. There would have been bracken, heather or rush litter for animals at one end of the dwelling, and for people at the other.

Stones from the fields were too rounded to provide stable building blocks, except for walls that did not have to support the outward thrust of a roof. Without wheeled vehicles and carriageable tracks, quarried and dressed stone could not be brought to site. Carts were commonplace in most English villages by 1300 but rare in Scottish ones until 1750 or even later. If you wonder why Scotland was technically so far behind, the climate ensured that there was seldom a grain surplus beyond survival and payment of rent. Sleds and packhorses were quite sufficient to take any unanticipated surplus to market.

Women performed the domestic chores: spinning, preparing food, rearing hens and mucking out the animal end of the dwelling. Most importantly, they also were responsible for all the milking, for which they hoped for a mellifluous voice. Every milkmaid knew that crooning sweet melodies pleased their cattle, inducing them to give freely of their milk. Thus had cattle been milked since time immemorial, with invocations to the watchful, caring saints:

Come, beloved Colum of the sheep fold,

Come, mighty Bride of the kye herds,

Come, mild Mary from the mists,

Make bountiful to me the cow of my love.

And what cow in milk could possibly resist such sweet blandishments?

Women were also called upon for lambing, shearing and bringing in the harvest. Manure would be used to fertilise the land, except where there was such a dearth of fuel that it had to be made into bricks and dried for this purpose. Indeed, the local term for cow dung, bachruns (derived from Gaelic *buachar*), came to mean fuel 'used by poor people instead of peats'. Children were required to act as scarecrows, to protect newly sown seed, and to herd the livestock to prevent them entering the arable during the day, and to fold them at night.

People ate oatmeal every day. It was just as well, for Bute was already described by 1549 as having 'very fertile ground, namlie for aitts'. Forget Samuel Johnson's mockery of this Scots diet two centuries later, for we know from Froissart that Scots had long since found oatmeal to be the best of foods. Oatmeal set them apart:

These scottysshe [fighting] men are right hardy…. within a daye and a nyght they wyll dryve theyre hole host xxiiii myle…. behynde the saddyl they wyll have a lytle sackefull of oatmeal … [and] make a lytle cake… and that they eate to comfort withall theyr stomaks. Wherefore it is no great marvel though they make greater journeys than other people do.

Jean Froissart, *Chronicles* (c.1370, trans.1525).

Ordinary people also ate some meat, cheese, butter and milk, but one should be suspicious about the words of an Italian visitor in the early fifteenth century who reported that 'They eat flesh and fish to repletion, and braid only as a dainty.' From around 1600 it seems that meat became scarcer, oatmeal became overwhelmingly dominant and animal products were used usually only to enrich broths. The deteriorating climate and population growth may have had something to do with this, but it may equally have resulted from the increasing export of live cattle to England, following the union of the two Crowns in 1603. Whereas in previous centuries the Scots ingested the original contents of the hides they exported, from now on they supplied much of the Roast Beef of Old England (on droving, see p.277), settling for a vegetarian diet supplemented by herring, fewer dairy products and by the late eighteenth century, eggs. Whatever its shortcomings, compared with today's junk foods, it was probably not a bad diet, even if it lacked greens. There simply was never enough of it.

By 1300 the north end of the island, probably roughly from the Kames-Ettrick road northwards, had been designated royal forest. Forests were essentially places for game, not necessarily with trees although tree and shrub cover for game was clearly desirable. Presumably deer, hares and anything else edible were hunted. Rules and punishments may have been in force to ensure no unauthorised person exploited the hunting, but we cannot be sure. The Stewarts, as Normans, would instinctively have wanted to apply draconian laws forbidding all other users and it is unlikely that the more egalitarian Gaelic custom, allowing anyone to pursue quarry across forest, was allowed. In any case, by the end of the fifteenth century the forest was probably tenanted as rough pasture, and this may have been going on for a long time. Nevertheless, as late as the mid-sixteenth century this area was still described in leases as 'Forest'.

There was a hierarchy of tenants in Bute, as elsewhere. At the top of the social scale, Robert III's half-brother, John Stewart, was appointed Sheriff of Bute and was granted Barone, Grenan and Ardmaleish. The present Bute family is descended from him. The Bannatynes had lands all over the island, in Bruchag, Lubas in the south end, but also Dunalunt, Shalunt, Drumacloy, Scarrel, Glecknabae in the northern part of the island, and were established in Kames by 1500. The Glass family held an estate in Ascog (there was still a Glass living there in the 1820s) and another held Ardnahoe, probably in return for military service. Then there were lesser tenants, among them the McConnechys, who held Dunagoil and Ambrisbeg in the fifteenth century, relinquishing the latter in 1867 after tenure, so they claimed, of more than 600 years. They anglicised their family name to Duncan, still a common name in Bute. The family McCaw/McKay held Garrochty in the far south of the island from the sixteenth century until 1853 when the last McKay died. The McKirdys, a distinctive Bute name even today, possessed lands for centuries in several parts of the island, including Stravannan, Bruchag, and Kerrymenoch, lands not taken over by Lord Bute until the late eighteenth century.

Lower down the social scale there would have been landless folk. In 1100 these would have been effectively slaves but even in 1521 there were people who 'have no permanent holdings but hired only, or in lease for four or five years, at the pleasure of the lord of the soil.' One can see how they were unlikely to make any investment in soil that was theirs for only a few seasons.

Fortunately, in the sixteenth century a fundamental change in land tenure, known as feu-ferme, gave many people the chance not only to spend their working lives in one steading, but also to pass it on to their children, and therefore to improve it. The tenants of Bute purchased feus from their landlord in 1506, the Stewarts being in urgent need of money. It was the single most important factor in the improvement in agriculture in Bute before the advances in the second half of the eighteenth century. As a result, compared with England, Scotland became remarkable for continuity of tenure. At a time when the population was declining, not increasing, younger sons were not necessarily ejected on reaching their majority, but often given parcels of their father's landholding. Furthermore, they married the daughters of local landholders, creating a complex but powerful network of kin relationships. Five hundred years later, remarkably, that pattern to an extent still persists in Bute within the farming community. Farmers' wives themselves are farmers in their own right, usually coming from local farming families.

The sixteenth century also saw a beginning to the liming of soil, and the enclosing and consolidating of landholdings. In 1720 the island's landlords instructed their tenants that they must no longer harrow the land with wooden pins 'whereby the ground is not sufficiently pulverised, but must make use only of iron pins in their harrows'.

It would be nice to say that by the seventeenth century life was much easier. Certainly the population began to increase again after the appalling losses of the Late Middle Ages but that put pressure on resources, for instance denuding the landscape of trees. Tree loss had become an issue from the fifteenth century, with the Parliament repeatedly enacting legislation to prevent wanton tree felling and encourage replanting, but clearly in vain. By 1700 Bute was a largely treeless landscape. Whatever the modest improvements, compared with England agriculture remained primitive and unproductive.

We have a nice description from the Lothians of the kind of work burden carried by women on the land by the 1650s (and probably much earlier):

> [They] are to Shear dayly in Harvest, while their Masters Corn be cut down. They are also to be assisting with their Husbands in winning their Masters hay and Peats, setting of his Lime-kills, Gathering, Filling, Carting, and spreading their Masters Much, and all other sorts of Fuilzie [manure] fit for Gooding and Improving the Land. They are in like manner, to carry th[e stack]s from the Barn-yards to the Byres, Muck, Cleange, and Dight [clean out] the Byres and Stables, and to help winnow and dight the Cornes.

Truly, a woman's work is never done.

As for the general level of health, the plant collector, James Robertson, visiting in 1768, noted how poor it was, the result of deep ignorance and lack of basic hygiene: 'Children are subject to Worms and ffevers and the common people to the Scurvy and itch.'

The period from 1300 until the mid-eighteenth century was profoundly miserable for ordinary country people. Years of famine or plague were frequent right up to the eighteenth century. Indeed, from 1695 until 1702 harvests were catastrophically awful on account of successive cold wet summers. As a result, up to 10 per cent of Scotland's population, it was claimed, was reduced to begging, so many thousands, perhaps tens of thousands, must have died of hunger. Average life expectancy was well below 35 years. We must assume that this applied as much to Bute as to other parts of the country. We are right to marvel that humankind, certainly in the inclement conditions of Scotland, survived at all. Before the agricultural and scientific improvements of the mid-eighteenth century, life in Bute was not for the fainthearted.

BUTE'S AGRICULTURAL REVOLUTION

In the early 1700s the backward state of Scottish agriculture shocked the few English people who ventured over the border. They had never seen such ignorance. A century later, Lowland Scotland led the world in agriculture, with English landlords sending to Scotland for experts to ensure best practice on their estates. Bute took a full part in that redemptive revolution. This transformation was an unintended by-product of the Union of 1707. Summoned to the Westminster parliament, Scotland's representatives were astounded by the orderly fertility of the English landscape: an Arcadian vision compared with the desolation at home. As a result lairds began to invite English farming experts to advise them on how to modernise their own farmlands. There had been piecemeal improvements before, but we know that economic life in places like Bute was rudimentary: 'The inhabitants are all countrymen and cowheards who feede cattell and spin and make some woollen clothe which [is] carried to be dyed and dressed at Glasgow', as a Cromwellian tax officer reported from Bute in the 1650s.

Those landowners, like the 3rd Earl of Bute, who established themselves in London soon discovered the imperative of making their estates yield enough for the outrageous cost of London life. They had to transform agriculture from subsistence to a market-driven system. This required many measures, viz: scrapping the infield-open field system to enclose and consolidate landholdings; improving arable and pasture soil by the burning and liming of the landscape (Bute being particularly well placed with limestone locally available (see p.159)); sowing imported rye grass to improve pasturage; increasing productive land by draining mosses and reclaiming moorland; planting woodlands to provide the timber and underwood for building, farm implements and fuel as well as planting tree windbreaks for crops; improving the livestock through the introduction of new English breeds, and providing root crops to carry livestock through the winter; modernising implements, for example replacing the heavy wooden Scotch plough by a lighter iron one, which could be drawn by a single pair of draught horses and driven by one man; finally, introducing carts and other wheeled vehicles (though it was not till after 1760 that Bute had its first proper road, or indeed its first wheeled vehicle).

These measures got off to a slow start principally because improvement

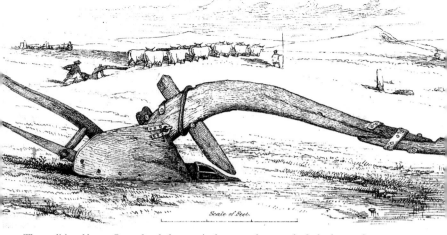

The traditional heavy Scots plough that required up to twelve oxen (in the background) to cut a furrow.

required extremely deep pockets. A handful of lairds and agricultural banks across the Lowlands who underestimated the financial challenge spectacularly bankrupted themselves. As usual, those with money, intelligence and determination reaped rich rewards, while the poor, the ignorant and the passive were elbowed aside. This must have happened in the fermtouns of Bute as elsewhere. It was only after the 1750s that Bute's agriculture very slowly began to improve.

The best description of the wretched conditions in Bute is found in William Aiton's *General View of the Agriculture of the County of Bute*, published in 1816:

> Many of the Earl of Bute's tenants, at and for some time after the middle of the last century, had no leases, but were mere tenants at will; his Lordship had a steelbow, or right to one half of the crop. There were no carts in the island. Too many cattle were kept, and they were neither productive of milk nor had the food to fatten them. Six horses were generally yoked into a clumsy plough of the Scotch kind …. The crops were seldom more than three, often little more than two seeds, the ground overrun with weeds, the ridges crooked [some superstitious ploughmen deliberately made them crooked to thwart the devil's liking for straight furrows], and large baulks between them; fallows, green crops, and sown grasses were unknown in the county…. The farms were small and generally occupied by more than one, often by three, four or five tenants, all joined in possession [i.e. fermtouns], and the barbarous arrangements of croft [infield] and outfield, the

former getting all the manure, and the latter kept in a state of absolute reprobation, prevailed over the island.

Lord Bute had already acquired an interest in botany (see p.105). From botany to agriculture is not so large a jump. Four years in the political wilderness from 1741 fuelled his interest in turning Bute into an island arcadia. He must have been affected also as an eyewitness to the wretched consequences of the famine following the failed harvest of 1740, mercifully Scotland's last. He returned to London in 1744 but continued to take a keen interest in the transformation of the island. He abolished the 'steelbow', the traditional arrangement whereby a landlord supplied tenants with seed or livestock but took 50 per cent of the yield. It was a system that generated mutual mistrust: the landlord's factor would suspect tenants of hiding part of the crop to avoid paying dues, while the tenant would resent the extortion of half his crop. Lord Bute offered tenants a straightforward fixed rent and a lease of 19 years to ensure a more predictable income for himself and to encourage investment in the land by his tenants. He also abolished compulsory labour service. He introduced experts in arable or livestock husbandry to take up vacant tenancies, a shepherd from Sanquhar at Kilmichael and an English arable improver to reclaim 700 acres at a farm in Kingarth and to instruct the tenant. He realised that demonstration models were a necessary persuasion for, in Aiton's words, 'such was then the ignorance and prejudices of the native inhabitants, that the generality of them demurred exceedingly to accept of leases for nineteen years.'

Lord Bute persevered. Oversized herds of poor quality cattle decreased, rather than increased, income. So he built a sloop to carry surplus cattle to the mainland markets, transporting his tenants' cattle free of charge. He introduced a scheme of bonuses for the best-bred cattle, for butter, cheese, the best dunghill, for wasteland brought under cultivation, and also for spinning flax, a hint at the growing importance of the linen industry (see p.298). By 1775 some English shorthorns, which produced better beef and more milk than local longhorn cattle, were being imported. To improve poor quality local draught horses, Lord Bute imported a Suffolk stallion for siring foals, again available free of charge to his tenants. He also brought in two English wrights, one to make improved ploughs, the other to build carts for an island still without proper roads. It was a timely measure, for the newly appointed town clerk of Rothesay, John Blain, embarked upon a dynamic programme of road building from 1761, from Rothesay to Kingarth, to Greenan Mill, and even to the ferry at Kilmichael. Blain was still building roads at the end of his career, in 1814, by which time he could report 'almost every farmer in the island has carts now,' an indicator that yields had started to move well beyond subsistence level.

By 1772 we know that the first results of the improvements were already evident, for that remarkable Welsh traveller, Thomas Pennant, noted how Bute was already leading the field:

> In the article of enclosure, it has the start of the more southern counties of this part of the kingdom: the hedges are tall, thick and vigorous: the white thorns [hawthorn] and wicken trees [rowan, see p. 334] now in full flower; and about 2,000 acres have thus been improved. The manures are coral and sea shells, seaweeds and lime….

Pennant also tells us what was being grown:

> The produce of the island is barely [*sic*] oats and potatoes [which had probably arrived in Bute in the 1740s]. The barley yields nine from one: the oats four [in fact a poor return]. Turnips and artificial grasses have been lately introduced with good success: so that the inhabitants may have fat mutton throughout the year. A great number of cattle are also reared here.

Furthermore, he was impressed by the farmers:

> notice must be taken of their skill in ploughing even in their rudest days, for the ridges were straight, and the ground laid out in a manner that did them much credit.

However, Pennant spent only a few days in Bute, insufficient, one suspects, to find out what was still wrong in much of the island.

Five years later, in 1777, Lord Bute appointed a new factor, Peter May, who must have seen the shortcomings at a glance. May came from the east side of the country where his work for the Board of the Annexed Estates, handling 13 large estates forfeited by Jacobite magnates, brought him into close contact with the most experienced improvers of his day. He undertook a detailed survey of each farm owned by the 3rd Earl, producing maps that indicate the significantly greater proportion of farmland devoted to arable, compared with today. Where there were cattle, he noted, 'the cows are small and the brood of indifferent quality', seldom weighing more than 20 stones.

Beyond the 1,700 acres of Lord Bute's estate, much of the farmland was still profoundly backward, with infield barely producing fourfold on the seed, and the outfield – 'the returns would astonish you', noted May, barely two and a half fold, 'so poor a crop is not worth culture.' Even within Lord Bute's estate, things had not gone well: 'the south side of the island is mostly cornfield and has cost Lord Bute an enormous expense inclosing and dividing the land with ditch and hedge. But I must observe with regret that they have not been attended to and are now in wretched order.' Without an industrious factor, Lord Bute's improvements were bound to fall into neglect. As May also observed, 'Upon the whole we are not wanting in the means of improvement, but we are greatly in arrear to industry.' He soon put that right, with a level of skilful diligence quite unprecedented in Bute.

It might be thought that the agricultural development of Bute could now ensue without difficulty. But this intense process of development demanded huge labour, enclosing with drystane dykes (see p.276), hedging and ditching, enriching the soil with lime, coral (crushed coral and sea shells, principally from Inchmarnock), seaweed and manure, as well as the routine tasks of each farm. This demand for labour coincided with a sharp rise in competing demands: for the herring industry (p.283), for the navy (p.292) and for privateering, so that as May observed in 1781, 'The farmers are much distressed for labourers…. The island is destitute of servants.'

As any visitor to the island soon discovers, most of the landscape is now part of the Bute Estate. It was not so when May arrived. In view of his proven skill and success, May was instructed 'to pick up any bits of land without waiting to give advice.' We reap the benefit of this policy. In Britain where so much of the coastline has been euphemistically 'developed', we have in Bute a well-maintained and beautiful landscape, unblemished by a rash of coastal bungalows and access roads.

The Butes established a reputation as good landlords. The 3rd Earl had made significant efforts to improve the lot of the farming population. His son, the 1st Marquess, made his views regarding the security of his tenants abundantly clear when a vacancy arose for the farm of Balnakailly, at the north end of the island in 1798. Writing to his factor, he said:

> 'having made it the unerring rule of my life to disturb no person holding land under me, be it where it would, who was willing to agree to my terms and who conducted himself well, I desire also you will consider what I now say as an instruction from which you are never to deviate.'

It seems as if Lord Bute was well aware of the general tendency of factors to deal with tenants over-zealously, even to the point of cruelty, on behalf of their masters.

NINETEENTH CENTURY AGRICULTURE

By 1800 the innate conservatism of impoverished farmers was a thing of the past. The island was covered in networks of hedgerows and drystane dykes. Bute's farmers had become convinced of the value of systematic and sophisticated crop rotation and manuring, mindful that 'Muck is the Mother of the Meal Chest'. In fact liming and manuring with seaweed had demonstrated that the old outfields could be virtually as productive as the old infield. A review of agriculture in the Western Isles in 1811 identified Bute (and Islay) as exceptionally advanced in virtually every aspect of productive land use, compared with other islands.

Tenant farmers were now eager to realise their potential. In 1806 they established a Bute Farmers' Society (renamed the Bute Agricultural Society in 1901), resolving to meet to discuss their specific agricultural and breeding interests, and to carry out experiments relevant to Bute's conditions. Moreover, Bute enjoyed its first ploughing match, the 1st Marquess providing improved ploughs as prizes. There had already been much improvement. In 1760 six horses were still used to draw the plough. Improved breeding of horses and the design of lighter ploughs meant that by 1800 only two horses were now necessary. Then came other implements like turnip-drills, and new-fangled threshing machines.

William Aiton, writing in 1816, still spoke of cattle as 'a confused jumble of various breeds, some of Irish extraction, some from Argyllshire, some of the Galloway race which are hornless'. But he also noted that one third were now of the Ayrshire dairy breed, introduced from 1803 and destined to dominate the dairy scene in Bute for over a century. Their introduction was the work of incomers who knew a thing or two, men who had taken tenancies along the road across to Ettrick, at Edinmore, West and Mid St Colmac. By the middle of the century Bute's Ayrshires were so good that a selection were sent to the Paris Exhibition of 1856, to show French farmers what was what.

The growing demand for beef in England meant that cattle prices had risen fourfold during the eighteenth century. Improved breeding doubled the size and weight of cattle. In the meantime, cottagers started to keep pigs and poultry – it seems for the first time – for home consumption.

For the rest of the century, the records indicate the assiduous efforts of the farming community to perfect their skills. The *Bute Record of Rural Affairs*, published in 1860, provides ample evidence of the annual competitions for ploughing, crops and livestock rearing. On the whole there seems to have been keen competition between farmers. Strict rules were introduced in ploughing matches in 1840, which put a quick stop to an outbreak that year of 'disagreeable bickerings'. But the spirit of competition clearly reflected an obsession with perfection. No less a person than Robert Thom (p.303) observed in 1843 that Bute's ploughmen are 'capable of competing with the best in the Country, much of this is owing to the ploughman's ambition to gain a medal of the Highland and Agricultural Society of Scotland.'

There was also a strong spirit of mutual assistance. In 1828, the Society established a weekly market in Rothesay and purchased two weighing machines, one for Port Bannatyne and the other at Kingarth Smiddy (now part of the Kingarth Hotel) to serve farmers otherwise without this useful facility. When a new tenant arrived at the neglected farm of Drumreoch in Kingarth, many farmers rallied round and gave him a darg, a day's ploughing. No fewer than seventy ploughs turned up:

the day being exceeding fine, and the horses in first rate condition, the ploughmen set to work with much spirit, and turned over a great breadth of land, part of which appeared never to have been cultivated before, and some of it for nearly half a century.

Such was the new found level of prosperity that the minister, John Buchanan, writing about his parish of Kingarth in 1845, exclaimed,

It will astonish a farmer, who is accustomed to make the price of an acre of Turnip pay for a year's supply of coals for his family, to learn, that fifty years ago, "the farmers being employed the most of the summer in cast and leading of peats [for fuel], could not provide manure for their farms."

Speaking of turnips, by the early 1850s the McAlisters of Mid-Ascog, one of Bute's most famous farming families, were winning turnip and potato competitions annually, thanks to their skilful use of 'Goulding's Manures' one of the new proprietary products on the market.

Inevitably certain members of the Society were convinced that they had found agriculture's Holy Grail. One proclaimed in 1841 that 'Thorough draining is the foundation of all good husbandry.' The following year

Overton Mains, Kilmacolm, Renfrewshire, c.1850, illustrates completion of the revolution as it must also have been in Bute: neat slate-roofed buildings, an orderly farm yard, a purchased metal gate, mature windbreak trees. A full stackyard on the left declares harvest home. Beyond lie orderly enclosed fields. On the right, exotic conifers have been planted. The farmer stands well dressed and proudly at his farm gate. A century earlier the scene would have been of hovels and unproductive open fields, and the family in ill-fitting crude clothes.

another knew for sure that 'The sheet anchor of all husbandry must depend upon a large store of dung.' Yet another insisted that a very precise method of liming was the real talisman. If a farmer found bone manure to be successful, he would be expected to share his experience at a Society meeting. Indeed, the Society was a glorious soup of enriching ideas, a mirror to the untold riches gently composting in every member's midden.

The mania for perfection in all things extended even to 'the form and neatness of the Stacks and Stack-yard.' In 1844 the prize went to Mrs Hall of Ardnahoe (p.153). Nor was the neatness and cleanliness of the steading and cottage ignored. In 1836 the Society decided that the mistress of the household, not the master, should be entered as competitor, for it was the woman, as in the case of Mrs Hall, not the man who had done the real work. In this, too, the Society was well ahead of its time.

Other features of farm life remained deeply traditional. For example, until the second half of the nineteenth century bringing in the harvest was probably done in exactly the same way as it had been in the seventeenth century. Teams of usually seven labourers, a 'bandwin', would take two ridges of ploughed land at a time, cutting the grain with sickles: three women to each 5-metre wide ridge. The seventh, the 'bandster', cut the tied grain into sheaves and set it up in stooks. Working well together, such a team could cover over two acres daily.

The six-monthly hire of farm labour, 'feeing', was institutionalised but it is unclear when it began. The system must be deeply rooted in Gaelic culture, the Celtic year being divided into two halves, winter commencing with Samhain (All Saint's Day) and summer commencing with Bealltain (May Day). Feeing lasted in Bute until the advent of the minimum wage and mechanisation in post-1945 Britain. A happy employee would contract another six months with his farmer. Others would assemble on Feeing Day, set for November and May, in Guildford Square in Rothesay to contract out their labour to farmers in need of help.

On Bute reputations for skill, diligence, laziness or clumsiness would be well known, except with regard to those innocent-looking fresh-faced 14-year olds, just out of school, who had yet to prove themselves, and the substantial number of labourers who, attracted by Bute's farming reputation, came from the mainland in hope of work. Once the bargain was struck, labourers 'flit' on the last Saturday of May and November to their new abode. Rothesay folk kept their fingers crossed for a fine feeing day, otherwise there would be inebriation and disorder around town. At one of these feeings *The Buteman* reported, 'There was a large turnout of stalwart men and buxom women whose powerful frames and blooming cheeks spoke volumes in favour of a country to a town life.' One must wonder whether these paragons of fitness and health would have agreed. Here is John Thomson's recollection:

> On these two [feeing] days the country workers and byremen who wanted fresh employment would gather in Guildford Square, just on the corner where the Esplanade Hotel is now. They might have left their previous employ for any number of reasons. They might have been refused a small increase in their pay, they may have disliked the food, or the farmer or the farmer's wife. Anyway, it was on the feeing days that they sought a new employer, who would press a coin into their hand, a shilling or half-a-crown as earnest of the contract. It was on these days, too, that farmers made up their accounts, to pay their workers. They always rounded the final figure down. They were a mean lot. The farmers treated their workers very hard. John Dickie,

John Dickie with his sour milk cart.

for example, at Cranslagvourity farm, ran the milk car. His milking floors would be spotless. He had a bothy above the stables, where he kept his workers. I can think of another case where there was a stable for four or five horses, and a loose box in which two men slept.

Thus labourers were worked hard, paid little and required to live in extremely primitive circumstances on the farms, often the unheated loft of a barn with no privacy whatsoever. Conditions for most farm workers remained harsh, rudimentary, cold and uncomfortable until the 1940s.

SOCIAL CHANGE IN BUTE 1760-1900

Between 1760 and 1830 rural society underwent a massive change, after which everyone was worked a good deal harder. Better yields and also inoculation against smallpox led to a rapid rise in population. Migration as a result of agricultural change and population growth was higher in Scotland than in England and many parts of Europe. By 1800 Scotland was more urbanised than England, indeed it was one of the most urbanised societies in all Europe.

Urbanisation massively increased market demand and the logic of this, so the agronomists and political economists argued, was to carry the agricultural revolution and the clearances to their conclusion. The most thorough clearances took place in the Lowlands and south Argyllshire, Bute lying plumb in the middle of this region. Unlike the Highlanders thirty years later, those cleared off the land mostly found an expanding job market, locally in Rothesay, on the south bank of the Clyde, in Ulster or as far away as Canada.

At the time that people were pushed off the land it was fortunate that Rothesay was growing rapidly. While the rural population of the parish declined, the burgh population more than doubled in a generation, from 1,158 in 1766 to 2,607 by 1790. The burgh's ability to absorb surplus workers was a consequence of the establishment of the customs house, which attracted regional and Irish shipping; the growing herring fishery; and from around 1780, the establishment of cotton spinning. Rothesay also attracted folk from the poorer districts to the north and west. In the century 1750-1850, the island's population grew three fold.

Nevertheless, not everyone prospered. Both Rothesay (covering all north Bute) and Kingarth parishes had lists of paupers, to whom alms and material assistance were regularly given. In 1801, the 1st Marquess, a man inclined to generosity and kindness, instructed his factor:

> Too much attention cannot be shown to the poor, to which I shall cheerfully contribute. A scheme for supplying them with porridge at an astonishing cheap rate has been imagined with success in the North of Scotland, and I conceive, Mr May, may be equally practised in Rothesay.

The Reformation's emphasis on education, evidenced in the kirk session records, slowly paid off. Male illiteracy in the Lowlands, around 75 per cent in 1650, fell to around 35 per cent by 1750. In the Highlands schools were created to teach Gaelic-speaking boys English, and since Bute was still overwhelmingly Gaelic, English was taught here in the parish schools. Whatever its motive, it is difficult now to approve of this assault on the indigenous culture.

While by our own standards women were still decisively disadvantaged, the Reformation brought a degree of equality. Marriage depended thereafter on mutual consent. Parents could not enforce marriage or, indeed, prevent an unsuitable one. Divorce was easier than in England. Before the end of the seventeenth century a woman had acquired the right to write her own testament without her husband's approval and to control the fate of her immoveable property. She also acquired strong views on her more moveable property: in 1661 the High Court of Justiciary must have been taken aback by a case on the mainland in which a woman called down the Devil upon her husband for selling her cow.

Before the agricultural revolution in Scotland, laird, tenant and farm labourer lived in closer intimacy. Their children attended the same school. The laird-tenant relationship never had the deference that was characteristic of the English rural scene:

Princes and Lords are but the breath of kings,
"An honest man's the noblest work of God."

But by the time Burns wrote these words the inter-class intimacy of the sixteenth and seventeenth centuries was in decline, the result of the transition from subsistence to a market economy during the second half of the eighteenth century. A slow separation of classes based on wealth was under way. The larger landholders ended up as landlords or tenant farmers.

A new hierarchy emerged below the tenant farmer. Since agriculture now depended so much on skilful horse work, a good ploughman took first place, able to find work at his own choosing if his employer proved unsatisfactory. Not far behind him were shepherds and cattle men with first-class experience, but at the bottom of the pile were orra-men, odd-jobbers who had to be told what to do. Many small-holders were pushed off the land, some ending up as labourers, others migrating to the growing towns.

In the sixteenth century rural Brandanes had probably made their own footwear, possibly tanning their own leather, but by the mid-eighteenth century this was no longer so. Virtually all men wore bought clothes: badly fitting short coats, breeches and blue bonnets, which they only took off while saying grace, while women wore brightly coloured plaids to cover the head and shoulders. Wearing shoes while walking was widely considered an extravagance. They were only put on for 'best'.

The agricultural revolution also led to a transformation in housing. We have a glimpse of Bute's tumbledown fermtoun buildings from William Aiton: 'the houses of their tenants were very mean, the fire on the floor, and the condition of the inmates far from being comfortable'. Roofs were still covered in thatch, held down by straw ropes. Thankfully such dwellings disappeared in favour of well-built farmsteads of quarried and dressed stone, mortared, and complete with proper fireplace and chimney, even if the floor might still be packed earth. Mills and smiddies were built to cater for the improved yield and the need to keep horses shod and metal implements in good repair.

Every household had its spinning wheel, a woman's task regardless of

Dwellings in Bute before the impact of the agricultural revolution were probably like Pennant's depiction of an Islay stone dwelling, the thatch held down with straw ropes.

rank (the wheel had displaced the distaff during the period 1730-1770), so weavers were well supplied with yarn. In 1700 most people ate off wooden trenchers, usually communal ones. Only the richer folk used pewter. Clothes were kept in the kist, the chest for the family's clothing. By the end of the century, almost no home was without table linen, pewter and pottery dishes, and a chest of drawers for clothes. People still used oil lamps, simple crusies, the wick supplied with fish or animal oil, which made a terrible stench. Some stuck to rush-lights: a single rush lasted about half an hour. Potatoes had come to Bute in the 1740s and by the early 1800s had become the staple diet, in Aiton's words,

> eaten alone, or with salt, milk, fish, and flesh; beaten into a paste; formed into puddings, and baken into bread. They are now very much used in feeding of horses and cattle.

At last vegetables, mainly kale but also root crops, accompanied meals, and fruit was bottled or turned into jam. All food was cooked in an iron pot that hung on the swee, the metal arm over the fire, a piece of kit still widely in use in the countryside in Bute as late as the 1950s. Many people drank illicit or smuggled goods: whisky, brandy or tea. Drinking tea was widely thought of as a vice for most of the eighteenth century, but it slowly gained approval as it began to displace alcohol.

CLYDESDALE AND TRACTOR: AGRICULTURE IN THE TWENTIETH CENTURY AND BEYOND

By the 1920s Bute enjoyed a high reputation for the excellence of its agriculture. Individual ploughmen and cattle breeders were known for their skills well beyond the island, distinguishing themselves in competitions across the western Lowlands.

But in each decade there had been some change or innovation. During the 1914-18 War, horse-drawn binders were brought onto the island because of the loss of manpower. Womenfolk of the farms were still talking in the 1950s of the backbreaking work bunching the sheaves behind the reaper from the days before 1914, or after 1914 when the binder was unable to cope with crops flattened by adverse weather.

Only 60 years ago almost everything on the farms was still done with horse power, as it had been for centuries. As recently as 1953, in the words of a retired farmer, Elizabeth Johnston, 'my husband took over to Inchmarnock a plough, chain harrows, cultivator and rake…. Any man with a horse and those implements could think of taking on a farm.'

One breed dominated the scene: the Clydesdale. This powerful beast had been bred in the mid-eighteenth century using Flemish stallions in Lanarkshire, in the district after which they were named. All today's surviving Clydesdales claim descent from a mare purchased in 1808 at Carstairs. By 1900 there were at least 140,000 Clydesdales in Scotland. They were *the* farm horse. They carried out all the heavy work, particularly the ploughing. The breed was introduced to Bute in the 1840s by James Simpson, an incomer farmer from West Kilbride. As elsewhere, it rapidly became Bute's draught horse *par*

Sowing by hand, a posed postcard image from Galloway, c.1890.

Completion of the stacks at Auchintirrie, near Ballianlay.

excellence. Farmers bred and broke in their own horses. A stallion visited the island every May. In 1938 the going rate was £2 per service, but an additional £3 was payable if the mare became pregnant. The stallion was still visiting in 1946, when there were 490 or so working horses in Bute, and six full time farriers.

In 1950 dung from the midden was still forked onto a horse-drawn cart for spreading in the fields, also done by fork. Many farmers still used a sowing sheet. In the words of Mrs Johnston, 'the farmer stepped across the furrows with a measured stride, rhythmically flinging out the seed with alternate hands, completing the cultivation, harrowing and rolling after the oats were in the ground.' In late June the hay was gathered in large conical rucks for a month, roped against rough weather, and later stacked at the farm. In August 'the sheaves were loaded and carted to the stack yard to be built into neat round stacks with conical thatched tops, which were such a feature of Bute's stackyards.'

In the 1920s and 1930s girls in their teens were still being trained to milk by hand. *The Buteman* routinely carried advertisements for experienced milkers. But this was about to change. In 1951 Scotland's very first milking parlour was installed at Kerrytonlia. This rendered the byre obsolete. The cows were now moved, a batch at a time, through the milking unit. Buttermaking went the same way. Until the 1950s, butter churning had been largely done by horse power. The horse was harnessed to one end of a beam attached at its far end to a horizontal wheel and would continuously walk around the wheel, which was connected by gears to a churn. The last one disappeared from Bute in 1957.

Ploughing with Clydesdales.

By the 1950s Bute's farming had entered a ferment of change quite as profound as the agricultural revolution two hundred years earlier. Mains electricity came to rural Bute in 1947-8, providing instant power. Few refused it. Yet the principal agent of change was the tractor. The first had come to the Bute Estate as early as 1919, and four more arrived in 1938. But then the war put things on hold. During the 1950s and early 1960s, however, a tractor was acquired by almost every farm. Ploughing by horse now seemed slow: only seven acres could be covered per week. A tractor could do that in a day. But there was another compelling reason for the change: the introduction of a minimum wage forced a severe reduction of the farm workforce, which almost halved between 1945 and 1955. Then came combine harvesters and balers, powerful new artificial fertilizers, and a shift from hay to silage.

In 1945 there were over 500 Clydesdales in Bute. Twenty years later they had virtually all gone. There was a very special relationship between the men and the horses they worked. In the words of the island's vet, J. H. Duncan, 'the horse was much more of an individual than any cow could be and could make life for the man who worked him a pleasure or a misery. One got to know them personally.' Furthermore, 'in the stories told there was a warmth missing in discussion about tractors.' Who can doubt that we have lost something precious? This includes not only a relationship, but across today's farming community the skills that could, if necessary, be revived. Several of today's farmers remember

*A Bute harvesting scene,
c.1890.*

the Clydesdales of their childhood, before the tractor banished them.
One or two of them, for example, John Macmillan, refused to say a final
goodbye:

> I was born in 1947. When I was small I remember no tractors. The
> first tractors came in 1952. Alasdair Speirs was one of the last to
> work horses. He got a tractor in 1954-55, but he was still working
> horses into the late fifties. I was given the boyish jobs, like taking the
> horses to the smiddy to be re-shod.... At that time there were four
> mares on the farm, three working mares, and a show mare. That was
> at Eskechraggan. I was brought up there. I left home just before my
> sixteenth birthday in 1963. I worked in Lanarkshire for two and a bit
> years and when I came back in 1965 there were no horses.

John Macmillan missed them sorely, but so did his father who had got rid
of them. In 1978 his father suffered a stroke:

> He had a soft spot for a horse and I bought a Clydesdale from John
> Laird of Kilmacolm. That was the beginning. There were two other
> horses, one with Archie Murray and Tom Crawford had one also, so
> there were three Clydesdales in Bute.

Today John Macmillan keeps six mares, almost the last on the island. (His
brother, Tom, still at Eskacraggan, also keeps Clydesdales.) If you wish
to see them, they may be seen every year at the Bute Agricultural Show,
the second Saturday every August, or in the summer months Clydesdales
may usually be seen grazing at Greenan Mill.

Mixed farms slowly gave way to the economic imperative to specialise.

In the 1940s and 1950s every farm had hens, many also had pigs and sheep. There was a domestic routine too. All that has gone. Bobby Reid recalls life at Shalunt half a century ago:

> We used to slaughter a pig each winter, and make up four hams. We cured them, rubbing salt daily for two or three days, then we rolled and hung them up, cutting slices off them through the winter. There are no pigs on the island now.

AGRICULTURE TODAY

It was also economic pressure that reduced 90 farms in the 1960s (mainly engaged in dairying) down to 44 or so 'trading units' today, the change in vocabulary indicating the way in which specialisation has altered things. Of these 44 units, only 18 are dairy farms, but the herds are larger and the yield far greater, most of which goes to the Creamery (which can be visited, just above Townhead), to be made into Bute Cheese. But do not for a moment think that dairy farmers have it easy.

The pressure for the highest yields has led to the demise of Ayrshire herds, though one or two such herds may yet be found. Two farms have Friesians, adopted during experimental years, 1960-80. The majority, though, now have Canadian Holsteins, because they are heavy milkers.

Duncan Lyon at Drumachloy knows all about the economics of dairying, and the way the supermarkets forced the wholesale price of milk down. He inherited a famous herd of Ayrshires, as an official publication in 1962 reported: 'one family of North Bute farmers, Lyon of Drumachroy [sic] is known all over Scotland for its herds of this breed.' Like other dairy farmers, Lyon changed breeds for better yields. In 1995, in common with other farmers, he was getting 25 pence per litre. By the beginning of 2007 this had been forced down to 16½ pence per litre, a period in which diesel increased in price six fold, fertiliser two fold, and cattle feed by over one third. Supermarkets were able to force prices down because of a glut on the world market.

Two things have saved Bute's farmers going out of business. By converting to Canadian Holsteins they doubled their output. Meanwhile, China's sudden but enormous appetite for dried milk has eliminated the global milk surplus. In 2008 the price had reached 26 pence per litre, and is unlikely to fall.

The days – only half a century ago – when any man with a horse and implements could think of taking on a farm are now gone for ever, barring a global cataclysm. 'There are very few youngsters around the country today,' as Bobby Reid says, 'who have a farming future. There is virtually no chance of a young chap starting today, because he would be thwarted by land availability, start-up capital, and the quota system of the single farm payment.' There is also the problem in the global market of affordable labour. Where will it come from? Migrant labour seems to be replacing local labour because it is cheaper. The face of Bute farming will continue to change.

DRYSTANE DYKES

The drystane dykes, the field walls of Bute, date from the agricultural revolution in the second half of the eighteenth century, about fifty years after the first drystane dykes were constructed in Kirkcudbrightshire. Their principal purpose was to enclose, but their side benefit was to clear random stones off the land. Dyke construction demands skill and experience. Ian Fisher of Kilchattan (p.127) who loved his work, tells what is required:

> It's all in the eye, like putting a jigsaw puzzle together. You need a good eye for the stones – it's no use just looking around. There's a stone there that is the one, your eye must be the judge and you must trust it. The dyke must be thick at the bottom. A good base is the secret. For a 6-feet high dyke you would need a base that is two and a half to three feet wide at the bottom. Every three yards or so you must lay a through-stone half way up to hold the dyke together. I never liked anyone alongside me. It just put me off my concentration. There's a stone there that's the one to use, your eye must be the judge. As you worked you'd notice a good coping-stone, and set it aside for the end. After you'd finished, as you go away, looking back you'd think, "That's nice."

POACHING

The rules regarding poaching were fundamentally unfair. In 1621 the right to kill game was vested solely in the landlord. The poor did not dispute the property rights over enclosed animals, though they might still try to pilfer what they could. They saw wild game as an entirely different matter. Why should it belong to the landlord? Yet laws of 1829 and 1832 prevented tenant farmers from even shooting rabbits that were destroying their crops. It was not till the end of the 1870s that Lord Bute allowed tenant farmers to shoot such pests.

By the end of the nineteenth century rabbit poaching by the poor in the southern half of the island was rife, and significant numbers of young people ended up in court. Twelve year-old Patrick Shields found himself in court in December 1888, having already been subjected to 'a good licking with the stave of a barrel' by his dad. A few poachers violently assaulted the gamekeepers.

Ironically, however, the presence of rabbits owed little to the landlords. A pair, it seems, had been released on Ascog Hill by a steamer captain in 1825. That they had multiplied and spread across the island was, admittedly, probably due to the drained landscape and the improved ryegrass and root crops that were grown. To that extent landlords might honestly feel they had fostered the rabbit population. Yet it seems unfair that the poor, who frequently went hungry in the forty or so years of agricultural recession from 1870 to 1914, were criminalized.

DROVING

Droving, the long-distance driving of cattle, was Scotland's response to the demand for beef in Lowland Britain. The trade, dating back to the early 1500s, began to expand following the union of the two Crowns in 1603 and then grew rapidly on the abolition of tariffs following the Union of 1707. It is likely that Bute had joined the droving trade by 1650.

Small numbers of cattle must have been ferried across to the Ayrshire coast, but it seems that most Bute cattle walked to Rhubodach and swam the Kyles, presumably at the slack of low water, possibly via the Burnt Islands. Rhubodach may have been one of those places where a couple of experienced cattle were kept to lead the swim. The herd then began the long mainland journey, usually up to the head of Loch Fyne, through Glen Fyne to Glen Falloch (Crianlarich), or to the head of Loch Lomond, eastwards to Glen Dochart and Glen Ogle and thus to Crieff, where three 'trysts', or cattle markets, were held yearly until displaced by Falkirk sometime around 1770. There were several different routes that could be taken but the principal ones met at the north end of Loch Lomond.

English dealers attending the trysts make their choice from up to 30,000 cattle assembled there. Once a contract was concluded, many drovers took their cattle all the way to London (hence old pubs on the Great

North Road named, for example, 'The Highlander'). Many used dogs in droving herds. Extraordinarily, while some drovers sought summer work down south, their dogs sometimes returned home alone, a journey of 500 miles, knowing the stances, farms and inns of their southward journey at which they could stop to rest and be fed.

If he failed to obtain an acceptable price at the tryst, a good drover would return the herd intact to its owner. He would be highly regarded for his skill and trustworthiness, imbued, in Walter Scott's words, with 'patient endurance and active exertion', qualities which would disqualify most of us today. He knew to take an extremely leisurely pace so as to deliver his charges in good condition. Each night he pastured the herd in a stance, usually a grassy hollow set aside for droving, which until the end of the eighteenth century was usually available free of charge. Short cuts were not approved of. In 1774 Cowal drovers complained bitterly when compelled to take what they considered an exhausting short cut via the new military road over Rest-and-be-Thankful to Arrochar and thence to Loch Lomond. It took them two days *longer*, they complained, rest being necessary after the stress of the climb.

There was a smaller market at Kilmichael-Glassary, mid-way between lochs Awe and Fyne, just north of Lochgilphead. This tryst was principally for the cattle of Jura, Islay, Gigha and Kintyre. Yet it would also have appealed to some stockbreeders on the west side of Bute. They or their drovers would have gone via Kilmichael to land at Blair's Ferry, south of Kames, and driven their charges via Kilfinan to Otter Ferry, where they crossed Loch Fyne to Lochgilphead and thence to Kilmichael-Glassary, where there is still a last vestige, the 'Stance Pool' on the River Add. The journey would have taken three or four days. Here they may well have handed their cattle to other drovers to take to the Falkirk tryst, eight days away. Old folk in Kintyre in 1948 could still recall cattle landing from the Western Isles, presumably around 1880, by which time the trade from Bute must have virtually petered out.

Before the new improved breeds were introduced, cattle had a distinctive local look, acquired over very many centuries, perhaps over millennia. This led to the emergence of local variety, which made their provenance recognisable to the drovers. It may well be that like sheep, their lowing had also acquired a distinctive regional accent. We sense this local variety from a late eighteenth century Gaelic love song composed by a Perthshire drover, Duncan Comyn, and addressed to his sweetheart,

Peggy Cameron, who lived on the shore of Loch Rannoch:

> You move with your milkmaids
> Among the red cattle from Bute,
> The black cattle from Islay,
> The white cattle from Lewis –
> You are kin to the Drover of Hundreds
> He who is generous in dispensing wine.

Let us hope that young Miss Cameron, forsaking her milkmaids, was duly conquered by her poetic swain, and that Duncan Comyn did not simply have his eye on the benefits articulated in his last line. In this song lies not only an indication of local distinctiveness but also just how far north Bute kye were driven.

Singing was an essential part of the drover's skill, for it was pleasing to the cattle, which liked to walk in pace with measured cadences:

> May the herding of Columba
> Encompass you going and returning,
> Encompass you in strath and on ridge
> And on the edge of each rough region.

Buachailleachd Chaluim Chille

The flow of droving may have begun to change at the time that Lord Bute provided a livestock ferry from Scoulag to the Largs coast around 1760. Cowal drovers may also have begun to make use of this route, and also the one from Glencallum Bay to Ardrossan. Nevertheless, droving remained active. In Rothesay, No.66 The High Street was once known at Danny Lismore's Close. Danny, from Lismore (just offshore from Oban), was a widely known drover in the early nineteenth century of whom it was said, 'He was very illiterate, but in money matters he was all there, although in matters religious he was sadly deficient.' The corner house on the junction of the High Street and Stuart Street, between the Mercat Cross and the Museum, was an old drover inn dating back to the seventeenth century – but it has been so substantially re-faced that it certainly does not look that old now.

By the late nineteenth century droving in Bute may have been only of sheep. Flocks were brought down from Strachur and further afield, in all perhaps 2,000 sheep, to over-winter in the softer climatic conditions of Bute and presumably to complete their lambing, before returning north for the summer. Duncan Lyon claims descent from a Strachur shepherd, James Scott, unwise enough to bring his daughter Catherine on the autumn sheep drove to Bute in about 1913, where she inevitably fell victim to the charms of a strapping young Brandane by the name of George Lyon.

The last of the true Argyllshire drovers died on the shores of Loch Fyne in 1959, well within the lifetime of many of us. Bobby Reid recalls,

> When I was a lad [1950s], I befriended a retired shepherd, Neil Blair, at Rhubodach. He was in his late 70s or early 80s. He told me the old sheep fank [a ruined fold just up the track from Rhubodach Cottage] was in fact the remains of a bothy for the drovers.

That takes us back to around 1880.

Sheep still come south to over-winter in Bute. As Bobby Reid says, 'It's the 'hogs', female lambs kept for breeding, which will spend their first winter in Bute. They go mostly to the dairy farms and are put onto the pastures when the cattle are kept indoors over winter. So they come from nearby, like Glendaruel, but also as far afield as Oban.'

POTATO SOWING AND HARVESTING

Potatoes were introduced to Bute in about 1740. Unlike grain, potatoes did well in the acid soil. They demanded neither liming nor the same amount of manure, nor enclosing against livestock. They grew as well in the out-field as in the in-field. Kingarth parish became famed for its early potatoes, particularly after land drainage rendered the low loamy land between Kilchattan and Stravannan bays so fertile. By the middle of the nineteenth century Kingarth entered the keen competition to get the first new potatoes into the Glasgow markets.

Potatoes were sown in straight lines, by teams which drilled the furrows with a special plough, planted the seed potatoes and spread muck on top afterwards. The potatoes had to be planted at an exact distance apart. Harvesting, or 'howking', the potatoes involved back-breaking work and by the middle years of the nineteenth century cheap casual labour was brought in to do it, mostly from Ireland. We have a first-hand description of the travails of a howker, an Irish lad, almost certainly in the fields of Kingarth in 1905. Patrick MacGill had been sold by his father at the age of 12 as a bonded servant to a farmer in County Tyrone. Aged 15, MacGill ran away to join a howking gang bound for Greenock:

> The potato merchant hurried us off to Buteshire the moment we arrived, and we started work on a farm at midday. The way we had

Howking potatoes: it looks as if one field is done, but a large field lies behind: another round of back-breaking work.

to work was this. Nine of the older men dug the potatoes from the ground with short three-pronged graips. The women followed behind, crawling on their knees and dragging two baskets a-piece along with them. Into these baskets they lifted the potatoes thrown out by the men. When the baskets were filled I emptied the contents into barrels set in the field for that purpose….

The first day was very wet, and the rain fell in torrents, but as the demand for potatoes was urgent we had to work through it all. The job, bad enough for men, was killing for women. All day long, on their hands and knees, they dragged through the slush and rubble of the field. The baskets which they hauled after them were cased in clay to the depth of several inches, and sometimes when emptied of potatoes a basket [still] weighed over two stone [12.6 kg]. The strain on the women's arms must have been terrible. But they never complained……

We left off work at six o'clock in the evening, and turned in to look up our quarters for the night. We had not seen them yet…. A byre was being prepared for our use, and a farm servant was busily engaged in cleaning it out when we came in from the fields. He was shoving the cow-dung through a trap-door into a vault below. The smell of the place was awful. There were ten cattle stalls in the building, five on each side of the raised concrete walk that ran down the middle between two sinks. These stalls were our sleeping quarters… and the midden was situated in a grotto hollowed underneath.… in the corner of this vault we had to build a fire for cooking our food.… Around the blaze we dried our sodden clothes, and the steam of the drying garments rose like a mist around us…. We boiled a pot of potatoes, and poured the contents into a wicker basket which was placed on the floor of the vault. Then all of us sat down together and ate our supper like one large family, and because we were very hungry did not mind the reeking midden behind us.

Patrick MacGill, *Children of the Dead End*, 1914.

Tatty-howking was clearly not for cissies. Irish howkers were still coming for work in Bute in the early 1960s, as were Travellers (see p.189). Local school children were also co-opted for the late crop. As recently as the middle years of the twentieth century schools had a break in October for what was euphemistically called 'the Harvest Holiday'. Ian Fisher recalls 'girls and boys who wanted to make some money would do it, especially those who had left school. It was a back-breaking job because the farmer kept you going.'

Life at sea

FISHING

Bute's fishing industry only ended within living memory, as a result both of the depletion of stock in local waters and the introduction of mega-fishing vessels which virtually hoover the sea floor.

For Bute there has always been one species that has obsessed islanders: the herring, the 'silver darlings'. There must have been a herring trade in the Middle Ages but our first documentary evidence dates from the years around 1700. Fishing in Scotland was undeveloped. The imposition of a swingeing English salt tax following the Union of 1707 nearly led to the industry's collapse. That apart, barrels for cured herring were expensive. In a wood-starved environment, staves and hoops had to be imported. The Board of Fsheries, establshed in 1727 to develop Scotland's poten-tial, provided an incentive: a bounty for the construction of larger decked boats, or 'busses', on which both fishing and curing could take place. This measure was less successful than had been hoped, partly because boat builders collected the bounty for larger boats, which were then not necessarily used for fishing.

By the 1760s Rothesay harbour still contained so few fishing vessels that Lord Bute did what he could to encourage expansion. In 1764 he provided timber – principally Scots pine – from Mount Stuart planta-tions at a nominal price to a company of young men on the island for the construction of fishing vessels. It was, according to William Aiton, a wild success:

> many of the younger men (who had all acquired some knowledge of fishing) preferring the buss-fishing to farming, sunk their own money and what they could borrow in the trade, and prosecuted their fisher-ies with avidity. It was then deemed a want of spirit in any young man to prefer the farming to the sea-faring life.

The same year Lord Bute also seems to have used his influence (he more than anyone enjoyed the ear of the young king, George III), to have a Customs House established in Rothesay. This was temporarily housed in the Mansion House opposite the ruined castle. Siting the Customs House in Rothesay rendered the port the economic centre for the fishing indus-try over a wide area, as far afield as Islay.

By the end of the century, however, male ardour for the fishing had been discouraged by some catastrophic years. In 1785 the government withdrew the boat bounty and put in its stead a system of bounty per herring barrel, payable on certification at Rothesay's customs house, making the subsidy dependent on results, not on investment.

In retrospect, we can also see a moral shadow cast over Rothesay's expanding fishing industry that would have been apparent only to those aware of the growing slave emancipation movement. Local prosperity owed much to the fact that the West Indies' plantation slaves were fed with salted herring. In order to ensure quality control in gutting and packing – and it is likely that this followed complaints of rotten barrels by plantation owners – the government introduced a 'Crown Brand' in 1808, certified and stamped on every barrel, a practice discontinued only in the 1950s. Bute suffered a temporary reversal after the Emancipation Act of 1833, when the newly liberated slaves of the West Indies rejected their hated diet in favour of English ham. Within a decade this setback had been offset by demand from the rapidly expanding cities of industrial Britain.

As the strain on the fishing grounds began to be felt, the danger of over-fishing became a growing problem. The first factor was the new practice of ring-netting, which evolved in 1833, when a couple of shore-based men stretched drift nets across the mouth of a Loch Fyne bay and sensationally enclosed 6,700 barrels of herring. Tarbert fishermen began to 'play' and enclose inshore shoals. As the herring learnt not to come inshore, so the fishermen realised they could catch the shoals in deeper water from boats. Once a shoal was located, one boat would shoot the net, allowing the shoal to slip towards the net with the tidal flow. In the meantime, a second boat picked up the net's buoyed end and slowly took it in a large arc, eventually back towards the first boat, and then slowly but inexorably both vessels closed the net tighter. Ring-netters soon learnt, too, to weight the net to trawl the sea floor. This 'ring-net', or trawl, fishing became the standard method, even though it tended to destroy herring spawn and fry. Proscription of ring-net fishing between 1851 and 1867 met with 'sullen indifference', and so failed. It was impossible to police the fishing grounds effectively. A second setback for herring stocks was the replacement of hemp or linen nets with cotton. The latter provided a finer and lighter mesh, allowing boats to carry fivefold the area of netting previously possible.

Rothesay boats tended to fish in Arran Sound, the approaches to Loch

Loch Fyne skiffs moored in Rothesay Harbour.

Fyne, the Kyles and Loch Striven, all of which enjoyed a reputation for significant catches. By 1867 Rothesay boasted approximately 450 fishing boats, employing 1,475 crew. Ashore, this trade was supported by 25 coopers, 250 gutters/packers and 30 unskilled labourers. One can see how, if the industry still flourished today, it would dominate the economic life of Rothesay. Indeed, that year, 1867, Rothesay produced 28,500 barrels. Only Inverary and Stornaway exceeded Rothesay's catch.

Rothesay benefited from its proximity to the Glasgow railhead. Before dawn steamers were ready to take the night's catch straight to Glasgow. By mid-afternoon the catch could be in Billingsgate, London's fish market. Later landings fetched a lower price, since they could not reach their markets sufficiently fresh, and so were usually cured.

The fishermen's income was normally distributed on a share basis, after all the expenses had been met. The owner-skipper took two shares, one for the boat, another for the nets, and then a share was given to each crewmember. If the fishing was poor, crewmembers might go away empty handed and the skipper in debt.

By the 1880s, Bute fishing began to decline. Between 1882 and 1888 the price of herring halved, and in that latter year Rothesay's fishermen were starving, their weekly takings little more than five shillings (£14 in today's money). Yet the principal cause of decline was not a queston of price but of over-fishing. As a Loch Fyne fisherman had told the Royal Commission in 1877:

> When trawling was legalised, all the fishermen got trawls, and they fished Loch Fyne out; they then went to the Kyles of Bute and fished them out…. They got money for the fish at the time and did not care for the future.

In 1900 there were still 115 fishing boats in Bute, but less than half that number by 1914. Herring fishing had to be limited to May-February, to allow for spawning. The heyday of the silver darlings was over, thanks largely to human improvidence. It may be for this reason that some fishermen went much further afield. John Hogarth (see p.75) was sailing with his father around 1914 as far as the Outer Hebrides, Shetland, and Ireland. Like many other skippers, his father recruited men from Skye and other depressed Gaelic-speaking areas, since there were insufficient crew locally. He also went out line fishing in winter for whiting, haddock, as well as for lobster from smaller boats. A line one mile in length would carry 1200 hooks, each to be baited by hand, the women collecting the mussels and shelling them, the men baiting the hooks. Line boats only required a crew of three men. They would take turns rowing and looking after the line.

For much of the nineteenth century, fishermen had used open smacks, camping ashore in shacks on the beach. But in the 1880s, these were displaced by an improved vessel, the 'Loch Fyne skiff', 11m long, in three sections: the fo'castle decked over (providing sleeping quarters), the hold and a stern section. By 1900 these skiffs were being produced in substantial numbers. Some were built by James Fyfe, a member of the famous boat-building family of Fairlie, first at the Red Shed in Rothesay (p.64) but later at Ardmaleish. Oak was used for the keel, ribs and beam, and larch for the strakes, which stood up to saltwater well. Every year the skiffs would be scraped and varnished. Many families, like the Hogarths, made their own varnish from gum and linseed oil. On Scotland's east coast, such vessels were usually painted in jolly colours. On the west coast, fishermen preferred to use varnish, to show off the grain of the wood. Before 1914 such a boat cost £60 new, about £3,000 in today's money.

Powered boats in the twentieth century temporarily reversed the industry's decline. By 1912 six of these were registered in Rothesay, in search

Offloading the catch on Rothesay pier.

of the increasingly elusive herring. In the right place at the right moment, one could still make a bumper catch. In October 1928 a fleet of 300 ring-net skiffs left Rothesay for Loch Striven, a deep loch where it was reckoned that the herring were present in vast numbers. In fact they lay 70 fathoms below the surface. Thanks to the innovation of powered winches, it was possible to catch herring even at that depth. In retrospect mechanisation can be seen as a catastrophe for the fish, the fishing industry and finally for all of us.

Competition greatly increased with the arrival of German trawlers in the 1920s and 1930s, vessels which salted the fish on board, and continued fishing till the hold was full.

The Second World War created a hiatus. Many fishermen were taken into other duties. Tommy Hughes's family came over from Pittenweem on the east coast, partly because of the west coast shortage of crews, but also because it was forbidden to fish off the east coast after dark:

> Our big boat took a crew of seven, and had 55-70 drift nets, each 55 yards long. Up until the 1980s herring was fished in the dark in the Clyde. We'd fish inshore, top and bottom, in early summer. Fishing was full of surprises. You would close the net around a shoal and not pick up a bucketful. Presumably they plummeted into the depths. Loch Striven, for example is very deep.

During the war, Tommy Rae's father was called away to the Glasgow shipyards, but afterwards Tommy recalls joining his father's boat, one inch short of 40ft, the prescribed maximum for Clyde fishing:

> For two and a half years during the daytime we fished for lobster but

at night we took the mail from Gourock to Dunoon and Rothesay, where the mail had to be by 0530. During that time we only missed two nights. Once we put out from Rothesay Harbour at a quarter to midnight but so fierce was the sea we put back in. That night [31 January 1953], the *Princess Victoria*, the Belfast-Stranraer ferry, sank with a loss of 132 [out of 172] lives. The other occasion we just got out of Gourock when we saw the Customs Shed lifted off the ground by the wind, which was blowing at 113 mph. We turned back.

Meantime, Tommy Hughes was travelling great distances in search of fish:

From the first week of October we'd take the boat across to Whitby, which normally took 26 hours through the canal at Grangemouth. We usually went down to Yarmouth area. We'd take 50 cran [each cran = 28 stone/178kg] and take them in to Whitby.

He also went line fishing in the West Kyles, putting out 1,800 baited hooks a night, for cod, ling and skate:

You shot in the dark. You might come back with 70 boxes, each with five cod in it. Today they take £150 per box. Fifty years ago we settled for 30 shillings per box [in today's money £25]. We once fished for skate in Scalpsie Bay, which we reckoned were there in large numbers. We came away with only a box of skate, one of eels, a couple of boxes of dogfish, but no fewer than 82 boxes of cod. You could never be sure of what you will bring in. We took the cod into Tarbert, where Glasgow buyers were on the quayside. There were always lorries in Tarbert, Carradale and Campbeltown. We got £147 for the catch, the highest we had heard of.

Some gave up fishing in the summer to skipper the luxury yachts of Glasgow's magnate class. The work paid better. Many accepted a retainer to make themselves available for the following season. In the mid-1950s, Tommy Rae was still taking white fish in the Clyde, 'on one occasion we caught 68 boxes of cod, just north of Ettrick Bay.' But he gave up in 1956. Wooden boat fishing was being displaced by bigger boats from Ayr and Girvan which, as he said, 'caught more fish for fun than we could do in earnest.'

Ring-net fishing finally ended around 1980. Today there is not a single herring boat left in the Clyde. Herring fishing is now centred on Peterhead and Fraserburgh, where there are a small number of ships, some costing over £10 million. They pump live fish into holds filled with seawater, and pump them back out in port, still alive and fresh. 'No one,' as Tommy Hughes observes, 'can compete with that.'

THE FISHING BEACHES. Fishing beaches were instantly recognisable by wooden net hangers, on which nets could be dried and repaired. Nets needed painstaking preservative treatment before use. For many centuries they were tanned from birch bark which, unlike oak tannin, produces 'a softness and elasticity to nets, which cause fish to enter the meshes more readily than when they are preserved by any other material', as one manual put it. From the 1860s a product of Empire, 'cutch', the syrup extracted from Indian acacia trees, displaced birch bark. Sails were likewise tanned and then greased to keep them both waterproof and supple.

LOBSTER CREELS. Creels were traditionally made with a wooden base, usually pine, and a framework of hazel wands, on which thick cotton twine was woven to provide the funnel, through which a lobster would crawl. The hazel wands had to be cut green to be sufficiently pliable to shape the creel. The twine was woven with a bone needle usually cut from a bullock shinbone.

LOCATING THE SHOALS. Detection of herring depended on good seamanship, and a 'nose' for the prey, sometimes literally. Some men could detect the odour of fish oil on the surface, 'Are ye smellin' them? – ye've a damn good nose!' The best not only knew the fishing grounds intimately but also understood fish, bird and sea mammal behaviour, and were able to read the *coltais*, the 'appearances', as Gaelic crews called it. One watched for bubbles on the surface. Or one might hear a single 'plop' indicating a shoal. Once on the fishing grounds, therefore, total silence was observed. In the autumn, the shoal's phosphorescence in the sea could be seen, sometimes triggered by striking metal on the gunwale which made the shoal start. In the winter herring in abundance could give off a red sheen on the water, 'Ye'll see it fae a distance, a bloody colour.' As for a gannet's stupendous vertical dive, that gave the game away immediately. By the 1930s the fishermen were using a piano wire with a lead weight. An experienced fisherman would feel the fish striking the wire and be able to estimate the density of the shoal and its depth.

The only images of Rothesay's herring girls are poor. This view is from Kintyre. One woman in the foreground is busy laying the first layers of cured herring in the bottom of a barrel. Behind her the others work at speed, while in the background a pleasure steamer docks, just like at Rothesay.

DRESSED TO FISH. During the nineteenth century the common attire for Bute fisherman was an oilskin sou'wester, seaboots well-dressed with cod liver oil, a linen undershirt, a blue flannel shirt as thick as a blanket, a heavy waistcoat, thick blue trousers, a tam o'shanter bonnet or minister's hat, which gave way to a flat cap by the end of the century. Instead of the flannel shirt, some wore a 'guernsey-frock' or jersey. John Hogarth's father, at the turn of the twentieth century, wore heavy oilskin trousers and jumper, with a towel around his neck, and leather knee-length boots. As he often had to jump into the shallows to beach a boat quickly he always lashed his trousers tightly around his boots. Apparently, he never got wet.

GUTTING THE HERRING. Gutting teams, each of three women, waited on the quay, two to gut, one to pack. Many were migrant Gaelic workers. As an eyewitness in Rothesay noted in 1857:

> It is a bloody business; and the gaily dressed and dashing females whom we had observed hanging about the curing yards waiting for the arrival of the fish are soon most wonderfully transmogrified.

They, of course, put on a suit of apparel adapted to the business they have in hand – generally of oil-skin, and often much worn.

The gutters – 'their every bit about them, fore and aft, are sprinkled o'er with little scarlet clots of gills and guts' – relied on skill and speed. They 'performed with lightning rapidity by a mere turn of the hand, and thirty or forty fish are operated upon before you have time to note sixty ticks of your watch.' Gutted fish were tossed into a trough and sprinkled with salt, then packed with more salt into barrels. Tommy Hughes recalls:

They were still gutting and salting on the quayside in the 1930s. The pay was poor, but a skilled team could acquire a bonus for fast work. The cooper would fasten the lid, but the herring would always shake down [over 2 weeks], and the lid would be re-opened, and another couple of layers put in before finally sealing the barrel.

Robert McLellan, who also fished, remembered their stoicism:

'There used to be troughs on the promenade in winter, with the gutting girls there. These girls, I don't know how they did it, gutting in the bitter, bitter weather there. It was very tough.'

So far you have had the prosaic version, but Derick Thomson, the Hebridean poet, saw such women with the eye of love, an integral part of a disappearing world he deeply cherished:

An gàire mar chraiteachan salainn
> *Their laughter like a sprinkling of salt*

ga fhrosieadh bho 'm beul,
> *showered from their lips,*

an sàl 's am picil air an teanga
> *brine and pickle on their tongues,*

's na mairan cruinne, goirid a dheanach giullachd,
> *and the stubby short fingers that could handle fish,*

no a thogadh leanabh gu socair, cuimir,
> *or lift a child, gently, neatly,*

seasgair, fallain,
> *safely, wholesomely,*

gun mhearachd,
> *unerringly,*

's na sùilean cho domhainn ri fèath.
> *And the eyes that were as deep as a calm.*
>> From *Clann-Nighean an Sgadain/The Herring Girls* (1967)

Some herring, of course, were smoked on spits arranged on wooden frames for three weeks (see p.75). 'Tasty' is an inadequate description for the final product. It was a gustie kipper indeed that arrived on the Scottish breakfast table.

AFTERWORD. Two books offer a wonderful insight into the herring fishing business: *Gillespie*, a remarkable dark work of fiction, located in Tarbert, Kintyre, by John MacDougall Hay, first written in 1914 but still available; and a history, *The Ring Net Fishermen*, by Angus Martin, published in 1981, the source on which I have primarily relied. I am compelled by our present desperate straits to repeat some of Martin's concluding words:

> The most profound personal lesson of these five years of questioning and gathering has been this: that Western society, by its criminal contempt for the fellow creatures which share its corner of the planet, has brought itself to the edge of an ecological and moral crisis from which, without the exercise of immediate and unswerving restraint, there can be no withdrawal.

Today we know that the cruel truth of what he said over a generation ago applies with equal force to the portents of environmental catastrophe on the land and in the atmosphere also. Let us hope we are not too late for amendment of life.

THE ROYAL NAVY

Bute has had an intermittently intimate relationship with the Royal Navy. Its more recent history, 1939-57, may be found on p.19 and p.193. This section, however, is about the notorious period of the press gang.

In England men had been pressed into service for many years, but following the Union of 1707 the London government had refrained from extending the press to Scotland. In 1755, at war with France and with its vessels seriously undermanned, the Admiralty finally decided that Scots were fair game for pressing into the Navy. In an excess of zeal the commander of the local revenue wherry put in to Rothesay that April in order to round up fishermen to hand over to the Navy. He was met by a mob of extremely angry women who successfully blocked his way while their menfolk legged it into the hills. Thwarted of his quarry, he seized three old fishermen, of whom the youngest was over sixty, a man so lame he could not run away and a ship's boy from a visiting boat. In London Lord

Bute protested. While those so outrageously seized were released, the Admiralty remained determined to take those it could.

Intermittently over the next half century, able bodied men in Bute, like the rest of the Clyde estuary, had to take care not to be caught, unless they were willing to serve. Fishermen would put in at Kilchattan Bay, Kames Bay and probably Straad, and arrange for men too old for the press to take the catch to Rothesay. Sometimes they hid in Bible Cave around the back of Inchmarnock when they saw the Navy coming. Yet we know that with population growth and agrarian clearances, many young men sought their fortune, not merely by fishing but also by joining the Royal Navy or a privateer, with the hope of sharing in the prize money disbursed following the capture of enemy shipping.

From the 1790s the navy found itself competing with the army for the same men, the press versus the militia ballot. On the whole if forced to choose, the great majority of Brandanes saw naval service as the lesser evil, as one Rothesay official noted:

> Their insular situation…. and their frequent employment in fishing and other maritime business dispose them rather to nautical ideas and habits…. If the people of the County of Bute were allowed to choose between the Army and Navy they would universally prefer the latter.

Because ballot lists had been drawn up for the militia, anyone on that list who was then pressed was viewed as having been poached, leading to terse correspondence between the respective service chiefs in London. Because Lord Bute took a keen interest in the militia, he was quick to challenge the pressing of any of 'his' men.

Nevertheless the expansion of the Royal Navy from 20,000 men in 1793 to 145,000 seamen and marines by 1812 and the fact that only 25 per cent were volunteers indicates the success of the press gang. The press was abandoned at the end of the Napoleonic War, but having suffered shortages of experienced seamen, the Admiralty maintained a list of captains of vessels registered in Rothesay, just as they did with every other port of registration around Britain's seaboard.

SMUGGLING, CUSTOMS AND EXCISE

Virtually all Scots instantly resented the cascade of duties and tariffs introduced on goods following the Union in 1707. English duties had quadrupled in the period immediately prior to the Union, 1690-1704, principally in order to pay off debts arising from England's war against France. Scots could not see why they should pay duty for the financial scrapes into which England had landed itself before 1707. Proscription of, or high duties on, any commodity immediately creates its own black market and Scots were not alone in responding to it.

There was already bitter resentment, particularly in the Clyde Estuary, from where the Darien Scheme expedition had sailed, because of the way the English colonies had deliberately refused to assist the Scots colonists who were dying after the collapse of the Darien colony in 1698. The final Darien expedition fleet had sailed from Rothesay itself and must have been crewed by many Brandanes. Quite apart from the death of hundreds of Scots sailors, the failure of the Darien Scheme had virtually bankrupted Scotland. It was an act of profound insensitivity, to say the least, that the London government deployed English customs officials, reinforcing the impression not so much of a union as an English takeover of Scottish trade.

The principal smuggling networks radiated out along Britain's coastline from the Isle of Man, which lay outside the customs regime of the new state of Great Britain until 1765, affecting the whole coastline from Argyllshire to Anglesey. The principal commodities smuggled in Clyde waters were herring, salt, coal, sugar and tobacco. Salt was a particularly bitter issue, since the curing of herring depended on it. Local salt was inferior but imported salt was only available from a small number of customs posts and because of the heavy English duty imposed from 1707, it was extremely expensive. Indeed the new duty looked set to crush the herring fishery. Salt smuggling consequently rocketed.

Smugglers had a key advantage, since they enjoyed the wholehearted support of local people, even to the point of offering armed resistance to customs officers. They were also technically advantaged. The shift in the early 1700s from square to fore-and-aft sail rig enabled small swift vessels to drop goods in the smallest of inlets, an equivalent to the high-speed motorboats which have made it notoriously difficult to intercept narcotic traffickers today.

In 1764 the Mansion House in Rothesay was designated as a Customs House. The establishment of a customs house in Rothesay was part of the 3rd Earl's efforts to increase the regional importance and prosperity of the port. He had his eye principally on harbour dues on goods destined for Ireland, since at that time nothing could be exported to Ireland except via a British port. The increased traffic of vessels, however, also meant more trade and custom for the people of the burgh. Rothesay and Scoulag were the only two approved landing places for goods.

The principal concern of Customs in Rothesay was the herring trade and salt duty. The government sought to assuage the desire to smuggle salt by reimbursing the duty already paid on salt that was to be used to pickle herring. That, however, had its own pitfalls. Customs had to ensure that the government did not reimburse duty on salt that had in fact been smuggled, either from abroad or from Ireland. In Rothesay Customs already faced formidable odds simply dealing with the 200 or so fishing busses, besides other boats, bringing in substantial catches of herring. Each catch might fill up to 200 casks but each had to be assessed separately. It was a tall order to combat other forms of smuggling also, particularly as there could be armed resistance.

It was only after 1765 that the efforts of HM Customs had modest impact, with the official closure of the Isle of Man as a duty-free *entrepôt* and the equipping of revenue vessels at Millport in Great Cumbrae, Rothesay, Inverkip, Port Glasgow and Greenock to intercept suspect vessels. In October that year a Customs official was physically prevented from seizing a Rothesay boat loaded with salt. In December, however, the Revenue men struck lucky. They caught a couple of open boats off Bute, containing 213 bushels of salt (equivalent to almost 8,000 litres). From the 1760s two of the 'King's Boats', almost certainly cutters, were kept at Rothesay to intercept suspect vessels.

We normally think of liquor when speaking of smuggling. Liquor destined for Ireland found its way ashore in substantial quantities. Rothesay Lade was favoured for discharging the casks after dark, whence they were shifted to a nearby public house, 'The Shark of Loch Striven', to be stowed in the landlord's cellar. One such smuggler found a grating across the mouth of the Lade, perhaps placed there by Customs officers, but managed to discharge his cargo at Port Bannatyne without being caught.

Smugglers resorted to a variety of gambits. Sometimes they evaded the Revenue cutter by reversing port and starboard stern lights. Once ashore, casks were reportedly hidden at night in the High Kirk graveyard up the High Street. Small quantities were constantly being found around town. On 2 June 1771 John McNeil was brought to book, not by the Revenue men but by that more formidable body, the Rothesay kirk elders, for 'smuggling Rum upon the Sabbath.' Three times McNeil refused to

The Royal George, *the Millport-based cutter which made a spectacular capture of contraband in Bute. No other vessels were allowed so long a bowsprit, ensuring the Revenue could always put on more sail and thus hopefully catch their quarry.*

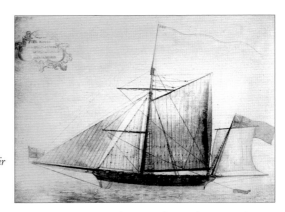

appear before the Session. The elders had ways of coercing attendance, for anyone defying them might well find every door in the parish shut against him. So in due course McNeill submitted. There were plenty of other such petty incidents, for example the small matter of a five-pint jar of rum being carried, all innocent-like, by a sailor down Montague Street.

One Customs officer, a Captain James Millar, landed a detachment of men from the *Royal George* in Bute and ambushed a train of 18 ponies with casks of whisky. He was lucky to face no opposition, for it was not unusual for smugglers to 'go about with Foreign spirits in gangs or companies armed with large clubs and attended with mastiffs and bid defiance to the officers of the revenue.'

Bute was also awash with locally brewed stuff, if you knew where to look. By the 1770s, Rothesay itself was reputed to have fifty or so of its own clandestine whisky houses. The east end of the then hamlet of Port Bannatyne was known locally as 'Grog Port'. Much illicit liquor was brought in by fishermen from distilleries along the shores of Loch Fyne (p.200). Most must have escaped detection, as suggested by Burns:

But the ae best dance e'er cam to the land

Was, the deil's awa wi' th'Exciseman.

A few were caught, however, as the revenue men slowly became more efficient. It is remarkable what kind of wholly implausible excuse a guilty party will come up with, once in a tight corner. We have all been there, if only in our childhood. Take the Rothesay Sheriff Court hearings of 1772. One defendant explained how it was really all the fault of the barley: some grain he had purchased had been of such poor quality it was simply unfit for sowing and thus it was wiser to steep it instead. He had only done what any intelligent person would have done with such inferior quality. Another admitted to the temptation of steeping a small amount of grain. Once he realised he was likely to be caught and that the fine would exceed the value of the whisky distilled, he decided the only sensible thing to do was to increase the quantity distilled in order to cover the cost of the fine. Anxious to satisfy the court that he had paid fully for all his crimes, he assured them that there had been no occasion on which, since his last recorded offence, he had not been caught, a confession which must have had them guessing at how many times he had, in fact, got away with it.

So long as duty on liquor was high, the black market continued to flourish, despite the risks of being caught. In May 1809 a court held in Rothesay heard no fewer than 52 cases of illicit brewing on the island. Another court was held that July for more cases, and in October there was another rich crop of 45 lawbreakers. Most, it seems, were incorrigible past offenders.

It was not until the government severely reduced the duty on imports in the early nineteenth century that smugglers found the illicit trade no longer worth their while, and their business shrank. In a sense, therefore, it was the smugglers, not Customs, who won. Yet, even in the mid-nineteenth century there was plenty of boot-legged alcohol around, either distilled in local shebeens or brought in from neighbouring districts. In December 1855, for example, a Rothesay eating-house keeper was caught selling whisky without any licence. He got off very lightly, with a £5 fine, equivalent to only £200 today. Perhaps the sheriff remembered he had himself consumed a drop or two of unlicensed liquor (who hadn't?), and did not wish to trouble his conscience unduly with a barefaced act of hypocrisy.

Industry

LINEN PRODUCTION

Linen was produced in the eighteenth century at both Rothesay and Wester Kames (p.179). Lint was a longstanding minor crop in Bute, the end product of a tedious process. Once the stalks had started to yellow in late summer, lint would be harvested by uprooting the whole plant. Bundles of plants first had to be 'rippled', by two men flaying them on a board with a comb of wooden or iron teeth until all the seeds had dropped out. It was hard monotonous work. Once rippled, lint was steeped in stagnant water for a week or so to allow the woody outer part of the stalk to begin to separate from the internal fibre, a task completed by another beating when still wet. Once dry, the fibres endured a third beating or 'scutching', this time with wooden mallets. It was machine-driven scutching which the mills at Wester Kames and Rothesay carried out. Finally, the remaining fibres were 'heckled', teased out on a comb of iron or steel teeth to render them ready for spinning. This was a highly skilled task if fine linen was required.

Traditionally lint fibres were spun by women with a distaff or spinning wheel. A full spindle contained 8 miles (13 km) of continuous thread. This work was poorly paid but most women were prepared to do it when times were hard. In years of glut when there had been a good harvest many women found the meagre payment not worth it. Yarn merchants identified Bute, Kintyre and Argyll as prime areas for investment in spinning partly for their proximity to the weaving centres of Paisley and Glasgow but principally because there was a large female labour surplus in the area. Women were supplied with improved spinning wheels in the 1750s. In the smug and calculating words of a Kinross clergyman writing in 1797 in *The Annals of Agriculture*, Britain's first agricultural journal:

> It [linen manufacture] affords many strong inducements to the female part of the community to be active and thrifty. It leads them to employ, with great advantage, every moment of their time which can be spared at home from the necessary business of the farm; and wholly preserves them from that sauntering and indolent life….

Weavers bought their yarn from spinsters trusted to have produced smooth thread with few knots. Linen production increased prodigiously across Scotland in the middle years of the eighteenth century. The reputation of Paisley and Glasgow for fine threads and linen was established in these years. Exports of Scottish linen increased fourfold between the 1740s and 1770s. By the 1760s there were at least 20,000 handloom weavers, supplied with thread by much of the female population. There was at least one female spinner for every three families in Scotland. Linen production collapsed at the end of the eighteenth century because cotton production was so much cheaper.

COTTON AND WATER

Between 1780 and 1850 it was cotton, more than any other commodity, which raised Scotland from acute backwardness to become a full player in Britain's industrial revolution. By 1820 the manufacture of cotton goods accounted for 89 per cent of all manufacturing employment in Scotland. By 1834 there were 134 spinning mills, virtually all within a 25-mile radius of Glasgow. The market was international, since by this time Britain governed 25 per cent of the world population. It was great for Britain, but largely smashed the indigenous cotton manufacturing industry of Asia.

Rothesay may, just possibly, have been the first place in Scotland to produce machine-spun cotton, using an old lint mill in 1779. Rothesay continued to spin cotton until about 1880, though from 1850 or so its output was in slow decline. Even though its production was significantly less than that of later larger mills, Rothesay holds a significant place at the heart of Scotland's industrial take-off.

Rothesay was perfectly placed for cotton spinning. It had several advantages. Raw cotton came from plantations in the New World and Glasgow was an obvious destination. Glasgow's tobacco merchants had already demonstrated the city's geographical advantage, compared with Liverpool and Bristol, to import from the New World, and also their ability to achieve a faster turnaround of their ships than any rival. Furthermore, Rothesay was close to the yarn market, for Britain's finest weavers were concentrated in Glasgow and Paisley.

Thus, despite being ten years behind England in spinning technology, everything seemed to fall into place to make the Firth of Clyde the centre of the cotton trade. It is a measure of the Clyde cotton industry's spectacular rise that while in 1774 it imported 150,000lbs of raw cotton, by 1801 the annual figure had risen to 7,500,000lbs, a fifty-fold increase in 27 years.

Rothesay's final stroke of good fortune was that the commissioner for the Earl of Bute also happened to be a commissioner on the Board of Trustees for Manufactures and Fisheries, and he offered facilities to a couple of Sheffield manufacturers looking to use Richard Arkwright's Water Frame machine for spinning yarn in Scotland, where it would be unrestricted by the English patent of 1775 and where it would also enjoy lower labour costs.

The first temporary site for the venture was a small building used for spinning lint, at the bottom of Queen Street on the course of the lade (stream), which ran approximately down John Street and Lade Street from the Kirk Dam. Two water frames were installed and were soon producing 300 spindles a week, enough to supply 30 looms. In 1780 manufacture moved to Rothesay's first purpose-built mill, a five-storey building, 40 metres in length. The owners also rebuilt the adjacent old corn mill to use the same lade. When the cotton mill was offered for sale with all its equipment in 1785, it was snapped up by two yarn merchants, one of whom, David Dale, is best known as the enlightened owner of New Lanark Mill (which well repays a visit). The new owners erected a second mill, of six storeys, in Mill Street (at the top of John Street) in 1791, almost abutting the first mill. Thus three mills, two for cotton and one for corn were all powered by the same lade, which had to be raised in order to provide a better head. By 1800, out of a population of approximately 3,500 in Rothesay, no less than 1,000 were employed in the cotton mills. Furthermore their productive capacity was rapidly expanding: in 1780 the single mill could turn out 1,000 spindles per week. By 1810 total output had increased to 13,000. The mills used their own boats to get the yarn to Glasgow.

In order to achieve such capacity, cotton workers worked long hours, from 6am to 7pm six days a week. They were roused by a horn or trumpet being sounded in the relevant streets and closes. A visitor to Rothesay in 1798 ominously remarked of the new cotton works, 'it contains some hundreds of children and seems to succeed very well.' Pity the little children.

In 1812, despite their apparent success, Rothesay's mills were declared bankrupt. At the heart of the problem lay the issue of guaranteed continuous power which the lade, even after elevation, simply could not provide. The demand for greater power stemmed from two principal factors, the increased number of spindles to be driven and the extension of mill hours

Rothesay's two cotton mills, c.1795.

from eight to twenty four per day. Steam engines had been provided to pump water back over the waterwheels during periods of drought or low water pressure. These engines demanded coal and this had to be imported. The added cost rendered the mills uncompetitive.

THOM'S CUTS. It was at this juncture that Robert Thom (1774-1847), along with a colleague, purchased the mills. In his late thirties, Thom was a man at the height of his powers. He had attended Anderson's Institution (which would later develop into the University of Strathclyde) in Glasgow where he had become fascinated by hydraulics. He was sure he could add enough water to Loch Fad and its head, the Kirk Dam, to drive the mills successfully without ever having recourse to steam power.

Between 1813 and 1822 Thom oversaw the canalisation of water from the west and south of the island to drain into Loch Fad, and then through the lade to the sea. This was achieved by six 'cuts' – canals which took the water virtually along the contour lines, with a drop of 1:1,200: the slightest decline imaginable. Thus his cuts meandered patiently, joining one stream with another, with culverts and bridges where necessary so as not to obstruct tracks and roads. He rejected freestanding aqueducts as an unnecessary expense. His most ambitious cut diverted water flowing naturally southwards to Kilchattan Bay and coaxed it north through

Thom's float-operated sluice (simplified): A is the wooden float fixed to the beam B-D, which turns on the fulcrum at C. This lowers the beam at D, pushing down the rod to close the sluice gate, E. Adapted from Thom's drawing in The Edinburgh Journal of Science, *1825.*

the Mount Stuart estate to the Scoulag Burn, thence through Kerrycroy and past the south end of Loch Ascog to join the Barnauld Burn, and then to flow south-westwards into Loch Fad. All told, Thom's engineering increased Rothesay's waterpower from 30hp to 70hp, equivalent to the steam engines used on the mainland.

So efficient were these cuts that Mount Stuart's own water supply ran dry. Consequently, in 1829 the Marquess took Thom to court. He lost, for the lease had specifically allowed Thom 'all the water that could be turned into Loch Fad.' The Marquess must have been stunned when his water tank ran dry. We are stunned by what the cuts achieved. Yet perhaps we should be stunned most of all that Thom achieved this for approximately £3,000 (hardly more than £120,000 in today's terms).

Having gone to such effort, it was understandable that Thom could not bear to see water wasted. Yet this is precisely what had been happening in Rothesay. When the mills stood idle, water first filled the lade then ran into the sea. Thom designed self-activating sluices to prevent this: when water was shut off at the mills, the lade would fill with water. A float-operated sluice at the top of the lade would close, thus preventing further let-down from the Kirk Dam into the lade. When the mills started operating again and the water level in the lade fell, the float would drop, opening the sluice again: simple and brilliant. Thom went on to refine his system further, with a couple of auxiliary reservoirs in the cuts to store water in periods of heavy rainfall: Dixon's Dam on Drumreoch Moor and Kilmory Dam, below Loch Dhu. These, too, were operated by automatic sluices.

Robert Thom is a prophet for our own time. We rip the planet apart in our desire for power and its potentialities with scarcely a thought for the consequences, but here was a man who worked with the grain of nature. Scandalously this colossus does not yet feature in *The Dictionary of National Biography*, nor in Scotland-specific encyclopaedias and biographical collections. Like his contemporary, Paisley's James Simpson, whose designs for slow sand water filtration plants saved millions of lives across the Empire by providing clean water, Thom remains a largely unsung hero of British engineering. He went on to construct the Great Reservoir, later known as Loch Thom, and its 11 kilometre cut to supply Greenock with water and water power, completed in 1827.

Robert Thom

The piped water was completely clean, since he had designed a slow sand filtration system for the city. If you wish to pay your respects (how, having read this far, could you not?), Robert Thom lies in Rothesay Kirkyard, by the door of the old session house on the right of the front door of the High Kirk (p.38).

Where Thom's cuts may be seen.

Traces of Thom's cuts survive and may be found while out on exploratory forays. In many places they have silted up and now seem unremarkable. But as you look at one or two of the culverts or bridges that survive, cling to the notion that however mundane these may look, they are humble manifestations of a brilliantly executed if simple idea. His handiwork can be admired at Ardscalpsie (p.159) and Lover's Walk (p.69).

Transport

CLYDE STEAMERS

Going 'doon the watter' to Rothesay has a 200-year history. One of the early tourists to make the trip was a Glasgow man, Robert Reid, and his family in 1778. He had nine children. He had taken, he told them, a house for the summer at 'Rosa' (Rothesay). He made his preparations, employing a tailor to 'clout' the family, and mend the five boys' old clothes. Having made enquiries, he warned his wife that no public baker existed in Bute. She therefore went out and bought three barrels of dry stores, one of coarse brown sailor's biscuits, a second of more dainty quality, and the third of bere meal, for making warm scones for breakfast. She also bought in a large stock of hams and herself kippered the salmon. They embarked with their baggage at the Broomielaw, and cast off at noon. The journey, as Mr Reid acutely observed, 'was tedious, as we did not arrive in Rothesay till three o'clock next morning.' When they got there they discovered themselves in a semi-foreign land, for 'the Gaelic language was generally spoken by the lower orders.' The visit does not sound much of a success, yet Reid was undaunted and made further visits. It took steam power, of course, to transform the scene into one of mass tourism.

In 1812 the first steamer, the *Comet*, came down the Clyde from the Broomielaw and scared the good folk of Rothesay witless, belching black smoke, its pistons clanging and groaning. By 1816 a couple of steamers, *Rothesay Castle* and *Dumbarton Castle*, were calling regularly. It was on approaching the pier that the *Dumbarton Castle*'s engine was intentionally thrown into reverse, a first in steamboat history. By the end of the 1820s there were nine steamers calling at Rothesay. By the 1850s there were many steamers calling, beautiful, fast and highly manoeuvrable, so fast, so highly manoeuvrable that many were bought by businessmen of the American southern states, to be used as blockade runners during the Civil War. Thus, a new fleet was built to serve the resorts. Some of the new steamers, connecting with the new railways, ran from Greenock, Gourock and Wemyss Bay, instead of Glasgow.

In the meantime, in 1853, in an attempt to reduce alcoholism, the Forbes-Mackenzie Act had fixed Scottish public house opening hours. No one thought to include the steamships that plied the Clyde within the

Act's provision, so these quickly became floating pubs, with the notable exception of the *Ivanhoe*, the one dry vessel. Really dry? Alas, human nature and the spirit of free enterprise determined otherwise and a Glasgow spirit merchant was soon purveying 'The Ivanhoe Flask', for the benefit of male passengers who foresaw they might be overcome by a raging thirst while on the *Ivanhoe*. Many coming by steamer to Rothesay would stumble off their conveyance, very much the worse for wear.

In the second half of the nineteenth century there were a large number of steamer companies competing for trade. The competition waxed so fierce that despite company orders, captains would race each other, in the sure knowledge that they enjoyed the committed support of their passengers at least until a collision, which occurred from time to time. So anxious was one steamer captain to best his rivals that in his zeal to steam into Rothesay Bay first, he skipped scheduled stops at Dunoon and Innellan. It is difficult not to wish one had been aboard, and equally to regret that this lapse required his resignation.

Rothesay harbour resorted to a system of signals for beckoning vessels in to the pier, to avoid unseemly and dangerous jostling between ships. By 1900 the companies had been reduced in number, by bankruptcies and mergers, until the Caledonian Railway and David MacBrayne dominated the business. Their ultimate marriage provided the single company to serve Bute. The Caledonian's emblem, the red lion rampant on a yellow field, part of the distinctively smart appearance of its vessels and crews, continues to adorn CalMac.

The apogee of Rothesay as a tourist destination was between the 1930s and 1950s. With a usual population of around 6,000, in its heyday the population expanded to 40,000 during the Glasgow Fair every July. The collapse, in the years 1959-63, was sudden.

In Rothesay it was possible to sub-let half one's humble dwelling and earn enough to cover the rental outlay for the whole year as Mary Miller, who lived on Hillhouse Road, remembered in her old age in 1991:

each summer we moved into the room and let the kitchen. We hung a printed card upon the window. This read "Kitchen to let, one bed." A couple was preferred and they had to supply their own sheets. It was £5 [about £100 in today's money] for the Fair fortnight, which everyone knew as the Glasgow Fair, i.e. the second fortnight in July. We also got the same for the Paisley Fair which was the first fortnight in

August and we could get maybe £4 for the first fortnight in July which was the Greenock Fair.... The kitchen had sole occupancy so we had no right to go in. Our room had no water so we had to go for water in a pail from the washhouse. The pail was kept on top of the table with a pail for slops below. We also had a small gas ring to cook upon.

Annie Cuzens remembered her accommodation in Rothesay for her holiday around 1920:

It had a wee room and kitchen....the room had two inset beds into the wall. We all slept in the one room... There was a wee gaslight going up the stairs, no electricity and there was a jaw-box [basin] and everyone used it. There were six lots using the sink and the dry toilet otherwise you did everything in a pail in the house and then carried it down to empty it in the dry toilet which the midden men cleared.

LAND TRANSPORT AND TRAMS

A regular horse-drawn bus service was not established until the second half of the nineteenth century. The bus from Kilchattan Bay was drawn by two horses and took over 1½ hours to reach Rothesay. With a full load, male passengers were asked to get out and help push the wagon up the braes. In summer the wagon was open, but covered in canvas, called a 'Tinker's Tent', in winter, it had straw on the floor, and guttering candles to provide a little cheer. Kilchattan was not served by motorised bus until 1919, which seemed an improvement but fatally foreshadowed the collapse of the Bay as an autonomous village with its own shops and trades.

Bute's first trams in 1872 were 4-foot gauge and horse-drawn. They ran from Rothesay to Port Bannatyne. In 1902 they were entirely replaced by a 3ft 6in gauge electric tramway. A depot, composed of car shed, offices and generator room, was built at Pointhouse, between Ardbeg and Port Bannatyne, and is now used as the bus garage. Electricity was generated with a coal-fired furnace, the chimney now demolished. The tram supposedly ran at only 8mph but it was fast enough to kill a six year-old boy five weeks after its inauguration, as he dashed across the track at Skeoch Wood to a sweetie machine on the far side of the road. In 1905 the tramway was extended to Ettrick Bay.

The last tramcar made its final run from Rothesay to Port Bannatyne, all 'lit up', at 11pm on 30 September 1936. Among those present was the ex-Provost who had attended the opening of the first horse-drawn tram

Kingarth's horse-drawn Star of Bute coach, c.1890, run by Messrs McKirdy & McMillan, outside the Kingarth Hotel. The run to Rothesay took 1½ hours. The smiddy stands behind the coach, now redeemed as the Hotel bar.

in 1882, the driver of the first electrically-powered tramcar in 1902, and the general manager who had managed the electric trams throughout. History does not relate whether they, too, were all lit up, but given how generally a dram was favoured, one may guess that they were.

CYCLING

If you are fit and enjoy cycling, it is a wonderful way to relish Bute, since you will travel slowly enough to savour the island's variety. The Bike Shed on East Princes St will sort you out.

It was cyclists who pleaded for a road to be laid around the north end of the island, from Rhubodach to Kilmichael in 1900, an idea which was strongly advocated again during the Depression of 1929, as a means for employment as well as for infrastructure. Mercifully, the idea fell by the wayside. There were far more pressing cases for laying roads elsewhere.

However, cycling proliferated as both recreation and a vital means of transport. In Kilchattan Bay, Ian Fisher and his father, Willie, used the Post Office bike to get to Rothesay to deliver outgoing letters and pick up incoming ones for delivery through the country. Then a local cycling club was formed.

The first ever Round Bute Race was run in October 1934. Ian Fisher takes up the story:

> I entered for the race. I was on the Post Office bike doing delivery of the mail that day. My mother had bought me a pushbike for £2 14s 6d for my 21st birthday. On the day of the race I was up at 6am to deliver the mail [in Rothesay] in time to catch the steamer. I asked my dad to finish doing the mail or I should miss the race. I cycled into Rothesay just in time to start the race. There were fifteen riders. I was the only one on an upright bike, the rest were on racing bicycles. We started at Gallowgate. We got to Ardbeg, all in a bunch. I did not like that, so I pulled out on the outside and went hell for leather and stayed in front. And I stayed in front all the way. We went around the far side of the island. There were prizes for the person in front at different stages. There was a crowd waiting at Albert Pier. I looked around and no other racers were in sight. I jumped off my cycle. I could'na feel my legs. My sister was there. One of the prizes was a one hundredweight of potatoes, and was that valuable to my mother or was it not?

Ian Fisher was 22 years old, at the peak of his fitness. The youngest competitor, however was Colin Zavaroni's father, David, aged only 14. It must have been quite an undertaking at that age.

Bygone cultures

GAELIC

Gaelic was fatally endangered from the moment the Lowland tongue became the language of government in Scotland. Stewart kings had spoken Gaelic until the mid-fifteenth century. Following the forfeiture of the Lordship of the Isles (1493), however, Gaelic began to be perceived as an obstacle to the integration of the Gaelic-speaking lands, the Gaidhealtachd, into centralising Scotland. The alliance between McDonald kinsmen in Kintyre and Ulster in the early 1600s had demonstrated the enduring and powerful political axis between Scottish and Irish Gaels, which threatened royal authority. James VI and his advisers reckoned that if one could break the cultural bridge the political links would also wither. He introduced legislation in 1609 requiring those in possession of sixty or more cattle to ensure that their heirs were educated in the Lowland tongue. In this the Crown was reinforced by the Kirk. The English language thus became associated with political, religious and economic well-being, an idea finally rammed home with the Union of 1707.

One local indicator of the withering of Gaelic was the way the English language recorded Gaelic names. In the mid-seventeenth century a fair number of women still used the Gaelic patronymic prefix 'Nic' (daughter of), rather than 'Mac' (son of), and were recorded as such. Within half a century or so, such niceties had disappeared, as McDonald, McKinlay, McKirdy and so forth were used indiscriminately for women as much as for men.

Then came the Jacobite risings. The use of Gaelic itself occasioned nervousness. From 1734 the minister of Kingarth had been James Stewart of Kilwhinleck (later 'of Stewarthall', close by Ballianlay). As a Stewart he understandably had Jacobite sympathies and routinely spoke to his flock in Gaelic, since this was the mother tongue of the parish. In 1746 he was required to read from the pulpit stringent government orders regarding sedition. He thought these orders were ridiculously excessive and was unwise enough to hint this as he read them out. There was inevitably a snitch in his congregation and he was smartly suspended from his duties and required to report to the Dunoon Presbytery for questioning. Eventually the panic over Gaels died down, and Stewart was reinstated, although they finally found a pretext to get rid of him in 1755, p.81. He was succeeded by ministers, the second an Englishman, who 'cannot speak Gaelic, which is the native language of the people, many of whom understand little or no English.' The belief prevailed south of the Gaidhealtachd that Gaelic symbolised obstinate backwardness and stubborn resistance to London. In other words, Gaelic was not civilised.

In the aftermath of the '45 Rebellion, several Bute families decided, in John Blain's words, 'to exchange patronymical names for others which they deem more conformable to modern idioms'. They changed the spelling, already very anglicised, to something easier for their cultural masters or changed their name altogether into something English. For example, MacConechy was replaced by Duncan; MacIlheran by Sharp; MacWilliam by Wilson; MacIntyre by Wright (more properly, perhaps, it should have been Carpenter); Garlie by Douglas; MacCaw by MacKay; MacVurathy by MacKirdy; MacHamish by Jamieson; MacLoy by Fullarton.

In the 1790s Gaelic was still the principal conversational language in Bute, but by then the population was largely bilingual and the then minister of Kingarth hinted at the need for 'progress':

> Most of the natives speak English very well; although in conversing with one another, they seem to be fond of the Gaelic, their mother tongue, which chiefly prevails among the old people and may have been an hindrance to the more easy and more ready introduction of new methods of improvement in the parish.

How easily we know best, when we wish to improve the lives of others.

The decline of Gaelic in Bute in the nineteenth century was swift. It moved from mainstream in 1800 to the tongue of an ageing minority by 1900. Rothesay parish church had provided a morning service in Gaelic and an English one in the afternoon. It was the abandonment of Gaelic in 1836 that had led to a mass walkout and the establishment of the new church at Croc-an-Raer (p.185). The parish church had made amends by building a dedicated Gaelic-only church in the Old Vennel, now Russell Street, where the decaying structure could still be seen in 2009. At the Disruption in 1843, however, the minister and congregation of the Gaelic church opted to join the new Free Church.

Yet in May 1858, just fifteen years later, Mr Anderson, the minister, took it into his head to introduce an English service in defiance of the majority wish of his congregation. He obtained the backing of his Free

Church principals. The Gaelic majority was outraged and demanded the keys of the church. When these were refused they took direct action, as *The Buteman* described at length:

> Their next step was to place an additional lock on the gate, which prevented the English party getting in. Both parties thus had their own locks on the church, and, in consequence, it remained shut for several Sabbaths, as neither would give in. The Highland blood was up, and it looked like a row each Saturday night and Sunday morning.

As the weeks passed, the English party decided on direct action, tiring of the process of civil law. They tried to smash the chains applied by the Gaels, only to find these promptly replaced. In late August word reached the Lord Advocate in Edinburgh, who threatened to send a company of Redcoats, a clear indication of whose side the Lord Advocate was on:

> Instead of soldiers, the Sheriff himself arrived. His coming was made known by the policeman who had been sent to Edinburgh to stop the red coats. Last Saturday night he arrived, and took up his quarters in the Victoria Hotel [which still has its handsome lamps on the pavement outside]. Here he held something like a council of war.

The Sheriff conferred with the Provost and the Fiscal. He heard the minister's case and that of the Gaels, represented by Charlie Mclean. The Sheriff advised Charlie to remove the Gaels' padlock and chain from the gate. Charlie complied. Butter, it seems, would not melt in his mouth. The Sheriff, however, was taking no chances. He had arranged for up to 40 constables to be on duty at 10am on the Sabbath, by which time, of course, persons unknown had placed yet another chain on the gate.

> Early in the morning the Sheriff was on duty, waiting at the [Mercat] Cross to receive his trusty men, to the number of about two score they arrived, ready for the fray. Their courage was up when they found that to save the town the country was left defenceless: even from the wild region of Arran, the county police were drafted so that there was not one left to save the rustic bacon... Without opposition the church gate is reached, the crowd who had assembled in the Vennel opening to let them in. About half a dozen young Highlanders are arrayed in front of the gate; the order to clear away is given by the Sheriff but not obeyed. A little force is used but resisted, when forth the Sheriff pulls from his pocket the Riot Act, which he distinctly reads. Again the order is given to the Highlanders to move off, which they leisurely do, laughing at the farce... [a] blacksmith is called who does the needful.

> The gates fall back, and the Sheriff announces the joyful sound, "the church is now open for the congregation." The crowds are soon dispersed, the Sheriff enters the church to hear the sermon in Gaelic, which very possibly he does not understand....In the afternoon the Saxon language was heard emanating from the pulpit of the Gaelic church, Mr Anderson having for once succeeded in realising the most important dream of his life.

The following week three hundred Gaelic speakers transferred their allegiance to Croc-an-Raer. Behind this Gilbert & Sullivan farce, however, was a well-founded passion. A whole culture was being ruthlessly swept away and those who belonged to it knew that much of their own identity was disappearing with it.

North Bute became the last redoubt of Gaelic in Bute, where a majority still spoke the language as late as 1879. The Education Act of 1872 dealt the final death blow to mother-tongue Gaelic, since it introduced compulsory English-medium schooling for all children, a real catastrophe. With hindsight one can see that Gaelic-medium education, but with English language instruction, might have saved Bute, and indeed the whole Gaidhealtachd, from becoming monoglot English.

Yet Gaelic lingered on well into the twentieth century, partly thanks to the influx of Gaels from Argyllshire and the Hebrides in the middle years of the nineteenth century. Some came to farm, others for the herring fishing. By 1901 there were only 550 Gaelic speakers left in Bute, barely 7 per cent of the population. The following year *The Buteman* reported that the Gaelic Church in Russell Street was virtually dead, as there were so few Gaelic speakers left. But it still maintained the tradition of sitting for hymns and standing for prayer. Moreover, it eschewed 'human' hymns, confining itself to psalm singing.

High up on Chapelhill was another Gaelic Free Church, but by the 1870s, the greeting of its heavily bearded incumbent, *'Ciamar a tha sibh an diugh?'* (How are you today?) struck passers-by either as archaic or simply baffling. Meanwhile, in the secular domain, An Comunn Gaidhleach Bhoid (The Gaelic Society of Bute) met periodically to hear again the Gaelic tongue, and to sing the songs they still knew, to listen to *na h'orain mhora*, the heroic songs of the Gaidhealtachd, and routinely to end the evening bidding each other good night in song, *oidhche mhath leibh*. The society was still just surviving in the 1950s, as was a Gaelic service on Chapelhill.

No one speaks Gaelic conversationally in Bute any more. As a living language it has gone and this must be reckoned a profound loss. The Celtic language group is probably the oldest in Europe, but it is slipping away fast except for Welsh and, just possibly, for Irish. The Isle of Man lost its last native Manx speaker in 1974. Less than 1 per cent of Bretons under the age of twenty still speak Breton. Likewise Gaelic is spoken by only 1 per cent of Scots, 60,000, all of whom also speak English. Compare that with the 300,000 monoglot Gaelic speakers in 1800, 20 per cent of Scotland's then population. Gaelic is rapidly turning into a consciously learnt rather than mother tongue language, but even that is infinitely better than its disappearance, or indeed the disappearance of Scots in the face of standard English.

We face a progressive decline in variety and difference worldwide, not merely linguistically but in a whole range of ways. The continued use of Gaelic is an act of defiance against the growing domination of a global culture, a conscious dissent that we should applaud.

THE KIRK SESSIONS

From the Reformation until the First World War, the Kirk remained a powerful force governing the social affairs of the parish. The kirk elders were chosen usually from the wealthier or better educated male residents. They were charged with ensuring Sabbath attendance and the proper ordering of social life. This boiled down to dealing with misconduct, mainly of a sexual kind, but also cases of slander and magic, and giving alms to the poor. Trying to control human behaviour has been an un-winnable struggle for the Church.

It was inevitable that the elders should come across as spoilsports whenever they tried to stifle the more exuberant inclinations of the parishioners. Weddings, of course, furnished the opportunity for merrymaking and were usually celebrated in the open. Almost anyone could attend on payment of one penny. Carousing ensued. The Kingarth elders were not pleased and in December 1658 ordained:

> for the better regulating of the disorders that fall out at Penny Brydells [the elders] appoint that there be no piping, no promiskuous dancing under the penaltie of the parties maryed losing their consignation money and that there be no sitting up to drink after ten o'clock at night under the phine of forty shillings to be paid by the master of the

family where the Brydell holds.

The Kirk routinely considered pipers as likely to undermine the morals and good conduct of the community.

The records reveal case after case of fornication in which the elders were required to bring the culprits to book. These make for dispiriting reading. Here, for example, is the doleful list of miscreants in the Rothesay kirk session record for 29 April 1772:

> Janet Stewart acknowledged her being with Child to a Mr Mann in Glasgow whither she went to be delivered.
>
> Compeared Mary McKiachan who professed her sorrow for not having yet Satisfied Church Discipline for her fornication with Charles McKochan in Atrick some years ago. The Minister says that Janet McKiachan, who was guilty of Adultery with John Montgomery about two years ago, has satisfied Church Discipline. In regard that John Montgomery left the country soon after his last Compearance before them and has not yet returned since, the Session appoint the Minister to write to the Minister of Dalray in whose parish he resides, that he may cause him to be Summoned to compear before the Session here.
>
> Compeared Mary Whyte guilty of fornication in the year 1700 and sixty eight, who charged one Angus McFarlane as father of her Child…. Now being informed that he is settled and married in Greenock, and is said to live on the east side of the Long Vennel in a house belonging to one Clerk, married to a woman of the name of McNiccol, therefore the Session appoint the Minister to write to the Minister of Greenock…..

Alongside the relentlessness of sexual misdemeanours, there is the equally relentless long arm of the Kirk. You could run but it was much harder to hide. Eventually the elders would catch up with you.

It is easy to think of the elders as disapproving men, with mouths shaped like cats' bottoms. Yet this would be unfair. They were more often men of charity. Here is the final entry for that same day, 29 April 1772. It deals with a 'clandestine marriage', an act that was legal but performed outwith the parish and liable to a standard fine because the parish had not been properly intimated:

> Compeared Samuel Sanders a Negroe Man late the property of Mr Campbell South-hall [just south of Colintraive] and Mary McDonald resident in this parish who were delated to the Session

for being Clandestinely married. They produced Marriage Lines of date the 29th January last, signed Andrew Duncanson, Minister being required to name what witnesses he had he named two or three Witnesses. With which Marriage Lines and Witnesses the Session were satisfied as to their being married.

Sanders was one of only seventy or so Black people in Scotland at this time. His owner, possibly a retired Tobago planter, James Campbell, who died in Rothesay in 1784, had probably had a lifetime's service out of Sanders before deciding to let him go. Sanders had clearly spent sufficient time in Rothesay to forge a bond of love with a local woman, Mary McDonald. They may have feared public disapproval. Perhaps they knew Andrew Duncanson (who lived at Roseneath) to be a man of liberal persuasion, or even a sympathiser with the Emancipation movement. They probably did not know that he had a skeleton in his cupboard, having been caught some years earlier with his fingers in the poor box.

Yet it is the elders who catch our attention. Beyond the formality of the record, there is a softness about their handling of the case. It is clear that they wanted Samuel and Mary to be happy in their new life and did not wish to lean too heavily on them, for the record continues:

Being asked if they were resolved to adhere to their marriage and mutually perform all the duties of that State; Upon their answering in the affirmative, they were suitably exhorted and dismissed, without imposing any fine upon them in consideration of his having been all his lifetime still within these few months a Slave and had nothing to pay.

The marriage of Samuel Sanders and Mary McDonald is a touching and early herald of multiracial Britain.

Finally, the Kirk had to settle disputes between parishioners. On 1 April 1814 Betty McFee put it about that Mary Crawford of Low Kilchattan had secretly given birth to a baby girl, the father being a neighbour, John Blue. It turned out to be an April Fool's Day jape. However, neither the victims nor the elders found it funny since it rapidly went the rounds of the parish as established fact. The elders duly investigated and found Betty McFee guilty of slander. On 17 April they instructed both sides of the dispute exactly what they must do in their presence:

Betty McFee, taking Mary Crawford by the hand and looking her in the face, said, "Mary Crawford, for what I have said against your character, I beg your pardon as I hope for forgiveness from God." Mary Crawford replied, "Betty McFee, I forgive you from the heart."

Insistence on the injured party accepting the apology graciously was an essential ingredient of the remedy. This was followed by an announcement from the pulpit that Mary Crawford was innocent of the slander, reconciliation was made and the matter now closed. How much healthier it sounds than today's willingness to rush to litigation, the foolish words of angry litigants fed by ravenous journalists to a voyeuristic public.

WITCHCRAFT

We are still mesmerised by the witch-hunts of the seventeenth century. In 1662 four witches were tried and executed at the Gallowscraig, Rothesay. A fifth, Janet NcNicol, escaped from the Tolbooth and took refuge in Kilmarnock where she evaded capture for twelve years, no mean feat when one considers the difficulties of securing food and shelter and escaping the watchful eye on strangers in any parish. When she returned to Rothesay, either by her own ill-judgement or in custody, she was brought before the dempster in October 1673. She was charged with having consorted with the Devil at Halloween, 1661, making a covenant of service wherein he had promised 'she should not want for gear enough'. A pact of this kind with the Devil was not infrequent, for 'gear enough' meant a sufficiency of food and shelter, the lack of which constantly threatened all poorer members of the community in Scotland. She was duly strangled and her body burnt, presumably at the Gallowscraig (an outcrop of rock very close to where the statue of A. B. Stewart now stands at the end of the Esplanade gardens).

The 1662 witchcraft cases of Bute are of interest as a glimpse of a much wider Scottish canvas. Why were 95 per cent of those Scottish witches who are known to have been condemned of peasant status? And why were 80 per cent of them women? Calvinist theology posed a set of notions: that both men and women enjoyed a holy covenant with God. Those who broke this covenant did so by associating with the Devil, an idea closely associated with social breakdown.

Who was responsible for preventing social breakdown? The minister and kirk elders were drawn from the more educated and prosperous of the community, and were consequently powerful. Their victims were, almost inevitably, weaker, poorer people, possibly inarticulate, usually unmarried, unpopular, eccentric, bolshie, or practitioners of traditional folkloric medicine, something which the 'educated' class found difficult to control (as health professionals today can still dislike alternative medicine).

How was the Devil most likely to engineer sin and social breakdown? One need only glance at kirk session records to note that fornication was the principal issue with which the elders dealt. So, it was a short step to thinking of the original biblical means of Man's downfall: in James VI's words, the devil was 'the homelier with that sex [Woman] ever since [Eve]'. Woman was the route to Man's downfall. Thus, in a countryside still replete with long-standing superstitions and 'magical' practices, poorer women were at greatest risk. (It was entirely consistent, incidentally, for hardline Presbyterians to condemn the Episcopalian Church as 'the Mother of Harlots and Witchcrafts'.)

Furthermore, like the populist anxiety to identify paedophiles in the community today, witch hunting had a dreadful momentum of its own, driven in considerable measure by fear. As one dismayed Edinburgh lawyer observed in 1672, judges were 'afraid to suffer such to escape as are remitted to them, lest they let loose an enraged wizard in their neighbourhood. And thus poor innocents die in multitudes by an unworthy martyrdom.'

The process was simple, a victim was first reported to the kirk session, and duly detained in the tollbooth. If release did not happen quickly, there was the danger that a confession would be obtained by sleep deprivation. If that failed, there might be torture, or a professional might prick for the witch's 'mark'. This 'mark' was usually no more than a needle prick that drew no blood. For anyone with some idea of human anatomy this was easily done and such experts found themselves in demand, the payment making a useful income supplement. So there was no want of 'experts'. Fraudulence was inevitable. Indeed three such prickers were unmasked in Scotland in 1662, two of whom inexplicably turned out to be women dressed as men. Following a confession, the kirk sessions would apply to the Privy Council for a commission to try the witch who, if then found guilty, would normally be strangled and her body burnt.

The year 1662 was by far the worst in Scotland for witch trials. A wave of hysteria swept across the whole of the Lowlands and the fringes of the Gaidhealtachd where Kirk rather than clan dominated. A likely explanation lies in the fact that from 1652 Scotland had been under the English Protectorate. Cromwell deliberately installed English judges to sit alongside Scottish ones in court. English judges were more reluctant to condemn witches because torture for alleged witchcraft was forbidden under English law, so most cases were summarily dismissed. English judges were, like English society generally, a good deal more sceptical about witchcraft than their Scottish counterparts. Ardent Covenanters, like Robert Baillie, were frustrated, 'There is much witcherie up and downe our land... the English be but too spareing to try it.' The Protectorate ended in 1659, and was followed by almost two years' hiatus in the administration of the law. The Earl of Haddington complained 'Because the laws ar now silent, this sin [witchcraft] becomes daylie more frequent.' It was also a bad time in Scotland's economy. Resumption of the Scottish courts thus coincided with growing anxiety about the state of the nation and presented an opportunity for those who wanted to apply a purgative.

The hunt of 1662 faltered as judges became increasingly sceptical of the cases brought before them, with their concomitant acts of torture. So, after an unparalleled orgy of executions, they found an increasing number innocent. There were only four notable years when localised witch hunts occurred in Scotland after 1662, and the issue petered out in the early decades of the eighteenth century.

The very last case in Bute shows how half-hearted the witch-hunt had become. In 1706 Elspeth NcTaylor of Rothesay was in trouble for 'charmeing to find out and recover a gown that was lost' She got off scot-free because she 'is notourlie known to be most intractable, incapable and infamous and irreclaimable, the Session waives troubling themselves with her.' In short, no one had the bottle to take her on. Hurrah.

Nature

BIRDS

A confession is in order at the outset. The world is divided into those
who watch birds and those who do not, and I fall into the latter category.
Birders are welcome to avert their professional gaze.

PRACTICAL INFORMATION. If you wish to bird watch, there are four hides
worth using:

   (a) at the north end of Loch Fad, by the Causeway dividing the loch
      from the Kirk Dam (reservoir);
   (b) at the south end of Loch Ascog, accessible off the Moor Road;
   (c) one yet to be built: on the south bank of Loch Quien;
   (d) on the south edge of Ettrick Bay, close road and to the high water
      mark.

Good birdwatching is also to be had, according to Michael Thomas, one
of Bute's leading birders, at Ettrick, Kames, St Ninian's and Kilchattan
bays, and also at Kerrycroy, and at the south end of the island, looking
out westwards from the Dunagoil – Dunstrone area.

ABOUT BUTE'S BIRDS

Out of roughly 560 bird species ever recorded in Britain, approximately 220 species breed in Britain regularly. Of these about 150 are present
in Bute. The most recent published work, available from the Museum,
is Michael Thomas' *Ornithological Tales* (Rothesay, 2007). It deals with
39 of these species. The single best overall study of Bute's birds remains
John Morell McWilliam's *Birds of the Island of Bute* (1927). McWilliam
was the minister of St Brendan's Church, Craigmore.

I have, I must confess, been drawn irresistibly backwards and resorted
to the father of Scottish ornithology, William MacGillivray (1796-1852).
MacGillivray was brought up in Harris and Aberdeen. He virtually lived
out of doors, walking and observing nature. He attended Aberdeen gram-
mar school and university but spent his vacations in Harris. He routinely
made the journey on foot, a round trip across the highlands of 650km
(360 miles). You will therefore not be surprised that when he decided
that he should certainly see the bird collection at the British Museum in

London, he resolved to walk. And since there was plenty of the Highlands he had not yet seen, he first walked cross-country from Aberdeen to Inverary before walking south, so that he had walked over 500 miles before reaching the English border. He kept a journal as he travelled, watching birds as he went. Between 1838 and 1840 he published three volumes of *A History of British Birds*, and a couple more volumes appeared shortly after his death in 1852. It was a massive achievement, almost entirely based on personal observation.

Finally, I have also drawn on the delightful work of a modern birder, Mark Cocker, Birder Extraordinary, a man able to render ornithology a matter of fascination and fun for anyone.

If, like me, you do not watch them, birds can still astonish. Take, for example, the swift, a common sight in Bute during the summer months. From the time it hatches in the nest, it may well remain airborne for its first three years till maturity. Even then it will avoid landing on the ground, since becoming airborne again presents such a major challenge that a jumbo jet is sprightly by comparison. It always nests in cliffs, roof spaces or crevices in walls, whence gravity gives it a start in flight. Yet the really astonishing thing is its proportion. A mature swift weighs about 45 grams, but has a wingspan of 48cm. According to Mark Cocker, 'In order for a man weighing 65 kilos (about ten stone) to have the same ratio of weight to wing length he'd need wings that were 635 metres long. That's almost ten times the length of a jumbo.' And if, like me, you associate swifts with swallows, then McWilliam warns that 'the two species are as distantly related as birds could be.'

Or take avian navigational and homing skills. According to Cocker, a Leach's Petrel (essentially a Canadian bird) weighs no more than a small tomato. To prove its navigational prowess a couple were kidnapped in their nesting grounds in New Brunswick and released on a Sussex beach. A fortnight later they were back in their nest burrows. No rehearsals, no 'memory', just homing instincts over 4,800km distance. And here's another Cocker favourite, warblers, 'those tiny sheaves of feathers wrapped around a thimbleful of blood, a few grams of wing muscle and some twiglets of hollow bone'. They fly from sub-Saharan Africa, across the Sahara, across Western Europe and its Atlantic waters to Bute, landing at intimately known staging posts en route.

BIRDS OF CONSERVATION CONCERN

The following birds are present and breeding in Bute, but of general conservation concern:

Golden Eagle (*Aquila chrysaëtos*). There may be a breeding pair in some unfrequented part of the island, but the eagle's presence remains fragile. Unless you are expert, if you think you have seen one, you have almost certainly seen a common buzzard, of which there are now plenty, roughly 30 breeding pairs and their offspring. The gamekeepers, it seems, never quite managed to kill buzzards off.

Hen Harrier (*Circus cyaneus*). Like the golden eagle, the hen harrier is rare, having been eliminated from the island for much of the last century.

Peregrine Falcon (*Falco peregrinus*) Around 1900 its nests were routinely destroyed. Since it was the bird of preference during the Middle Ages for falconry, one may imagine them being flown by hunting parties over Bute Forest, the moorland north of the Ettrick road.

Merlin (*Falco columbarius*). If highborn women hunted alongside their spouses, their bird of choice was the merlin, small (no larger than a mistel thrush), and with deadly skills to catch small birds.

Red throated diver (*Gavia stellata*). This is one of only four species of diver in the world. Here it is more or less at the southern extremity of its range, more common further north. You get the picture of its fragility here from McWilliam's tight-lipped stricture: it 'still nests in the Clyde Area, though I am not permitted to name the locality.'

Black Grouse (*Lyrurus tetrix*) If black grouse are endangered, it is because so many were shot throughout much of the last century. For example, 150 black grouse were shot in Bute in the 1910-11 season. McWilliam found them nesting on the Burnt Islands by Colintraive, a relatively safe retreat from chaps with guns.

Skylark (*Alanda arvensis*). Skylarks are wonderfully common in Bute, given their steep decline in mainland Britain. Their loss on the mainland is attributable to modern farming methods, the destruction of good ground nesting habitat and, in publicly frequented areas, prying dogs. As with hares, their presence is a good monitor of the health of a landscape.

BIRDS COMMONLY SEEN AROUND BUTE

It is impossible to provide space to mention more than half a dozen species which you are bound to see, ones which have gripped my attention because of some particular quality.

Curlews. The curlew is present in Bute throughout the year, its haunting melancholy call a familiar sound. It nests on the high moorland above Glenmore, and also in grassland near the shore. In autumn and winter curlews congregate in large numbers on the shores of the island's bays. In his *History* MacGillivray imagines stalking one:

> There, twenty paces off, stalks an old Curlew, cunning and sagacious, yet not conscious of our proximity. He has heard or fancies he has heard an unusual sound, and there he moves slowly, with raised head and ear attent; but some appearance in the soft sand has attracted his notice, and forgetting his fears, he thrusts or rather works his bill into it, and extracting something, which he swallows, withdraws it, and proceeds, looking carefully around…. There he has dragged a small crab or insect. But now two others have come up; they are all within range; let me fire:- there they are, two are dead, the other with broken wings runs off screaming loudly…. The curlew,' MacGillivray concludes with an air of surprise, 'is extremely shy and suspicious.

Gannets. You will see Bute's gannets out at sea, particularly around Craigmore. They come from Ailsa Craig, one of only about twelve breeding gannetries in Britain. Gannets are extremely sociable, hence the gannetries, yet also extremely aggressive. Their behaviour is reminiscent of the mores of a school class (in MacGillivray's words, 'When seated together they have frequent quarrels,') or sometimes even of a gentlemen's club (sit in the wrong place and you may get pecked to death). They also have criminal tendencies for, in MacGillivray's words, 'They take advantage of the absence of neighbours to pilfer the materials of their nests, frequently two join in the act….' So they go in for collusion as well. Moreover, the gannet is also guilty of gluttony, 'When it meets with a shoal of herring, it gorges excessively, so as sometimes to be unable to rise from the water for a time.'

Here, though, it is their startling diving skill that grips. Having spotted its prey a gannet dives, but with only half-retracted wings. As it drops, it adjusts its aim as its prey swims. There is no escape. Only at the last instant does the gannet fully fold its wings, its prey left to face a lot of speed and a very sharp bill. As MacGillivray also noted, it descends with such force that it can drive its bill through a plank of wood. The old form of execution in the Outer Hebrides was to bind a criminal to a stake, with a herring tied to his head. Do not let this distressing thought make you wince as you watch their astonishing and dramatic diving skill.

Oystercatchers (or sea pies, as they used to be known hereabouts). These birds, black backed with white underparts and a striking long orange-vermilion beak, will be found sociably gathered on most shores around the island. It is impossible not to see them. They live largely off bivalves, mussels, and limpets. But oysters? William MacGillivray observed, 'Although they have been said by many to eat oysters and other large bivalve mollusca, I have not found such animals in their stomach.' MacGillivray was thorough. Instead of pretty pictures of birds, most of the illustrations in his great work were of the digestive tracts and other organs, of the different species. Thus, he also noticed of the oystercatcher, 'One of the most remarkable circumstances connected with this genus is the attenuated wedge-like form of the bill, which is produced by attrition.' If a shell is open, an oystercatcher will insert its bill to cut the muscle whereby the shell snaps shut. Then it chisels with the bill's wedge end.

The last word on oystercatchers, however, must go to McWilliam, or rather to one of his correspondents, a Mr Budge, lighthouse keeper on Pladda, who reported in 1923 an oystercatcher flying through the lighthouse plate glass. 'It sounded,' he wrote, 'like a high explosive and fairly made me jump.' It must have made the oystercatcher fairly jump too. Mr Budge relates that it 'landed inside on the grating, not much the worse, except that it was dead.'

Rooks. 'There are few birds that deserve or have received closer studies by naturalists than the Rook', wrote McWilliam eighty years ago. Nevertheless, there is plenty about them that remains a mystery. Bute's rooks routinely fly in small parties to the mainland shortly after dawn to feed. They depend on open fields and presumably have had a close relationship with humankind since Neolithic times. The rooks return at dusk when, in Macbeth's words, 'Light thickens and the crow makes wing to the rooky wood.' Less poetically, McWilliam notes, 'Their usual custom is then to go to their rookeries, and afterwards they set off for the great winter roost at Ascog Loch, where, for several months, all the rooks of the island sleep. This roosting place is in a small section of the wood at the south end of Ascog Loch.' These rooks assemble towards dusk at various meeting points, often a couple of kilometres apart. 'When all the Rooks from different directions have joined the flock, immediately before dark the flock rises and goes to the roosting-place. Sometimes they circle for a considerable time and on other evenings they enter it without delay.' It is part of the autumnal rural scene, so deftly captured by Burns:

> November chill blaws loud wi' angry sugh;
> The short'ning winter-day is near a close;
> The miry beasts retreating frae the pleugh;
> The black'ning trains o'craws to their repose;
> The toil-worn Cotter frae his labour goes, –

Rook roosts, mass assemblies of this species, have vanished completely by March, all effort devoted to nesting in the rookery. No sooner are the young fledged than the rookery is again abandoned in favour of the roost, and so the cycle starts again. But why do they roost communally? Mark Cocker believes roosts act as information centres, places that impart information about feeding sites. The principal 'informer' rook will always be found at the very centre of the roost. And what of the collective circling before roosting? Perhaps it is an advertisement to other corvids to join the roost.

Swallows. The swallow arrives from southern Africa each summer and is a common sight in Bute during the summer months. Their swift, unpredictable and swooping flight is a delight to the eye. McWilliam liked their persistence:

> In the early autumn about the year 1922, a young Swallow came each evening for about a week through the open window of a bedroom in my house, sleeping on a picture frame, and before morning it would sit on the bed of the little child. The incident ended by the window being accidentally closed one evening... Mrs Myles told me that at Wester Kames a brood of Swallows left the nest on her staircase on 12th July 1917. The parents tried to rebuild the nest on the 17th. She shut them out. They tried to build in the tower on the 19th, in the drawing room on the 22nd, and in a bedroom on the 23rd. All windows were shut for a week. The birds built under a hanging stone on the 30th.

A FINAL WORD ABOUT HUMANS. To an outsider, there can sometimes be something bizarre about the human relationship with birds, in particular the human impulse to shoot dead the object of desire (now, thankfully, an urge in abeyance). Here, however, are two examples which baffle. The first concerns a wader, the Bar-tailed Godwit. It does not breed in Britain but in Scandinavia, and tends only to visit coastal locations. McWilliam recounts:

> The only Bar-tailed Godwit that I know to have been shot on Bute is in the Museum. It was shot by Mr Dan Wallace at Port Bannatyne about 1914. Mr Wallace was struck by the tameness of this bird. He saw it on the shore and went to his house for a gun, and came back and secured it. He told me it was the only one he had seen on the island.

One has to admire the word 'secured', so tidy and hygienic, the kind of word one can imagine tripping off the lips of a politician, an anodyne description for some fell deed. Dan Wallace liked his birds peppered with lead.

The Whimbrel is one of Britain's rarest breeding waders. Dan managed to shoot four of them in the last decade of the nineteenth century. He was by no means alone. The Great Skua was in danger of extinction around 1900: 'There is a Great Skua in the Bute Museum, an immature female, which was shot… at… Ardmaleish on 13th November 1912. This is the only record for the island.' We can be grateful that human values have changed.

LAND MAMMALS

Foxes. Foxes are a recent introduction, either by misplaced affection for them or malice towards the farmers of the island. They are a damaging presence. There is no record of foxes prior to the last ten years or so, but they are now firmly established.

Hares. It is impossible to walk this island and not to see brown hares. They are a good measure of the environmental health of our landscape. In mainland Britain their numbers have decreased in the past century by 75 per cent, an indictment of modern farming methods and what it has done to our wildlife. In Ancient Egypt the hieroglyph signifying the verb 'to exist' was a ripple of water, and above it the hare. It was closely associated with the idea of Creation. Bute has plenty of water and plenty of hares. We should rejoice.

The hare has always occupied an ambiguous place in man's imagination: bewitching in the sense of delighting us, but also in the sense that, as even Gerald of Wales, in about 1200, noted, certain witches in Scotland changed themselves into hares to escape. This belief survived into the eighteenth century and possibly later. But listen to the delightful descriptive phrases for the hare in a thirteenth century English poem: 'the way-beater', 'the hedge-frisker', 'the stag-of-the-stubble', 'the sitter-still', 'the light foot', 'the one who does not go straight home'. The creature is embedded in our folk memory in connection with Easter, for it was the hare, not the rabbit, which was the true symbol of this Rite of Spring.

If you surprise one in its form, it may well flatten itself on the ground, hoping you will walk past without noticing it. If it knows it has been seen it will make off uphill, its long hind legs giving it an advantage uphill over predators. If necessary it can attain a speed of 45mph.

Roe Deer. These are native to Britain, having been here for at least 10,000 years. They were hunted to extinction in England in the eighteenth century but survived in Scotland where re-afforestation has led to their increase over the past century. They have now re-established themselves in England. They can be seen all over Bute, but particularly at the north end. They probably colonised the island when it was still joined to the mainland.

Red Deer. There may well have also been Red Deer here in the Middle Ages, when the north end of the island was a hunting forest. Red Deer are still occasionally seen, thought to be temporary visitors, having swum the kyles. Deer rut in August-September, the does giving birth the following spring. Never approach a kid, even if it appears abandoned. No doe will go near its own kid once it smells of human.

Voles, field mice, weasels and **stoats** are present but seldom seen.

Wild Goats. A herd of feral goats established itself at the north end of the island in the 1980s, so keep a look out if you are walking.

Red Squirrels. These have occasionally been seen at the north end.

WATER AND SEA MAMMALS

Water shrews. These have bodies only about 7 or 8cm long, with tails a similar length. They have velvety jet-black hair, with off-white undersides. You are unlikely to see one of these, but a small community is known to exist in Beaver Wood (the woodland just north of Langalchorad and the Kingarth Inn, where Lord Bute experimented unsuccessfully keeping beavers in the 1870s).

Water voles. These are probably extinct, killed either by the American mink which either escaped or was introduced in the 1980s, or by the outflow of pesticides from farmland.

Otters. You will be lucky to spot one on the shoreline but keep an eye out, for they certainly visit Bute's shores. They are dependent on clean fresh water, partly to keep their coats in good condition. They suffered steep decline as a result of hunting and the use of organo-chlorine pesticides in the 1960s and 1970s, but are slowly increasing in numbers. They are deeply embedded in Gaelic folklore, as *an dobharchu*, the water-dog, a creature with healing properties.

Seals. The Common Seal is usually under 2m in length, with fine spot-patterned grey or brown fur and a rounded head. Ninety per cent of Common Seals are to be found in Scottish waters. However, there has been a serious decrease since the mid-1970s, the result of phocine distemper. Cows can most easily be seen from July to September at Scalpsie Bay (there is a viewing point just below the Ardscalpsie car park), but they can also be seen off Garroch head and Rhuboadach. Their pups are born in June-July and are suckled for a month. The Grey Seal is about 2m in length, with grey-brown fur, sometimes with blotches, and has a longer muzzle. Their numbers are increasing as a result of protection by law and public opinion. They are less susceptible to distemper than the Common Seal. Frank Fraser Darling, the great naturalist, learnt how to communicate with grey seals on the island of Rona:

> in their confidence they have come out of the water to my feet as I have sat there on the rock, using my voice in the way I have learned…. And now the mother seals are high on Rona near the door of our hut and our own child plays among them.

There are endless stories of 'selkies' over the centuries. These are changelings with humankind, people under spells as poetically described by George Mackay Brown in his wonderful stories.

Dolphins. Both the Common Dolphin, which seems to be on the increase, and the White-beaked Dolphin, which is decreasing in numbers, are occasionally seen off the south end of the island.

Porpoises. These can be seen frequently, off Kerrycroy and off the south end of the island.

Killer Whales. These have increased in frequency, and if you are lucky you might see one off Garroch Head or in the Sound of Bute on the west side of the island.

TREES AND WOODLAND

INTRODUCTION. Bute's oldest parcels of woodland lie north of the Highland Boundary Fault line. Trees have been important in the Highland imagination since the era when Irish and Scots Gaelic were one. Everyone was familiar not only with the practical value of each species (see the list of principal ones on Bute, p.331) but with their abstract qualities, a way of looking at trees we have almost entirely lost in the past 150 years. When Alasdair of Glengarry died in the early 1720s, Sìleas na Ceapaich (Julia McDonald of Keppoch) composed a lament, in which one translated verse runs:

> You were the yew above every forest,
> You were the strong steadfast oak,
> You were the holly and the blackthorn,
> You were the apple tree, rough barked and many-flowered.
> You had no kinship with the aspen,
> You owed no bonds to the alder; there was none of the lime tree
>   in you;
> You were the darling of beautiful women.

Her listeners would have known precisely what she meant. Alasdair was identified with noble tree species but not with undesirables: the aspen that supposedly provided the timber for the Crucifixion; the alder, so 'common'; the lime suggestive of feebleness.

So deep were trees in the Gaelic mind that even the alphabet was learnt by native tree names, A *ailm* (elm), B *beith* (birch), C *coll* (hazel); D *darach* or *dair* (oak), E *eadha* (aspen), F *fearn* (alder) and so on. In the Gaidhealtachd, it seems, one cannot get away from trees or, rather, from the idea of them.

It is, therefore, an irony that Scotland is nearly the most treeless country of Europe. It is tempting to assume that this is because of the wanton destruction of 'the Great Wood of Caledon'. In fact the landscape was damaged more by climate change than by human activity. The weather became progressively wetter and colder around 5500-5000BC. Deforestation caused by climate change was accelerated particularly during the Bronze and Iron Ages, by clearance for livestock rearing and arable. There were later phases of climate deterioration, of which the most significant was the Little Ice Age, which commenced just as Scotland also faced its fight for survival against the English at the end of the thirteenth century. Cold and unpredictable summers persisted until the nineteenth century. To give some idea of the severity of the weather in the fifteenth century, Greenland was abandoned by its settlers, while in Switzerland steadings were crushed beneath advancing glaciers.

From the sixteenth century climatic deforestation was accelerated by the demands of population growth for both timber and underwood. The distinction has been lost today, but timber was the term for load-bearing pieces of wood, i.e crucks or roof beams, and keels of boats. 'Wood', or underwood, provided smaller items: oars, agricultural implements, fences and hurdles for livestock, fish traps, barrels, kists, platters and spoons. The principal means of producing underwood was by coppicing: cutting shoots at ground level every seven to ten years. The remaining 'stool' would rapidly produce more shoots to be harvested in due course. But it was vital to protect coppice from grazing livestock and so it had to be fenced in with hazel hurdles or hedging. Underwood was also a valuable fuel, for compared with peat, it burnt fast and hot and was thus, along with whin, an essential for baking. Then there was the need for charcoal for smelting and bark for tanning. Without wood and timber one could do nothing.

Repeated and increasingly urgent legislation indicates that tree cover all over Scotland became much scarcer in this period. Part of this denudation may have been the consequence of recklessness, the failure to enclose vulnerable areas following timber felling or the opening of woodland to grazing, thus preventing regeneration of seedlings and saplings. By 1500 large oak trees, essential for large houses or ships, were a real rarity. Scottish landlords only learnt to be more systematic in felling sections of woodland in the eighteenth century. Increasing demand was only satisfied by massive importation of timber from Scandinavia. By the mid-eighteenth century, Greenock was second only to Leith in the importation of Scandinavian or Baltic deal. The destination for some of it must have been for house construction in Rothesay.

TREES IN BUTE

The principal areas of Bute's natural and semi-natural woodland are slopes and gullies: Barmore Wood on the north-west side of Loch Fad; the raised beaches on the north-west coast around Lenihuline; on the north-east side at Shalunt, and in the very north, on the slopes below Balnakailly, Gaelic for 'settlement in the woods', indicating that the oak woodland here is ancient – several centuries old. The dominant native species in Bute is the sessile, or durmast, species of oak but of course, like the rest of the plant world, each tree species flourishes in the specific terrain to which is suited.

The remaining woodland is almost entirely plantation, the earliest being integral to the agricultural improvements of the eighteenth century. The valuable trees were oak, ash, elm, sweet chestnut, sycamore, maple, hazel, birch, poplar and alder, all of which grew vigorously in Bute and were mostly good for coppicing. Alexander Carlyle noted on his visit in 1766 that 'every little cottage had a dozen of trees around it. Lady Bute (widow of the 2nd Earl), had got them planted in every kailyard…' Tree planting was a frequent condition of a tenancy.

On farms trees served as windbreaks protecting crops from the worst of Atlantic gales. They were used for construction (not least for fishing vessels) and as a source for fuel. Large scale planting occurred at Mount Stuart and was imitated at Kames.

In the nineteenth century Skeoch and Skipper (Bogany) woods were also planted, mainly with beech, essentially an ornamental tree. Both were felled almost in their entirety during the First World War, but have been replanted. The nineteenth century also saw a dramatic increase in planting conifers, notably larch, Norwegian spruce and Douglas fir. Since 1950 large tree plantations of Sitka spruce have been established, for example above Balnakailly in the north.

NOTES ON INDIVIDUAL TREE SPECIES

Alder was valued neither in mythology nor in practice. Yet resilience to wet rendered it useful for things like fish traps. James Macdonald's *General View of the Agriculture of the Hebrides or Western Isles of Scotland*, published in 1811, stated why it was of value here:

> this tree is also indigenous, and grows in the wettest mosses.... Its wood is not valuable any where else; but any thing in the shape of wood is so precious in the Western Isles that even the aller [*sic*] ought to be carefully propagated.

Furthermore, alder could be rendered into fine charcoal for smelting iron and for gunpowder production. Alders create a rich soil habitat for other plants: primroses, garlic, mint, wood violets, worth bearing in mind as one walks.

Ash seems to have been venerated all over Britain for its magical properties. Even in the mid-nineteenth century, within ten miles of Westminster, certain ash trees were still believed to hold curative properties for sick children and animals. The Vikings viewed the ash as 'the World Tree', its roots in the underworld, its trunk on earth while its crown held up the sky. The Gaels considered it the Tree of Life, with life-giving properties. In 1772, as he toured the Western Isles, Thomas Pennant described how a midwife gave newborn babies 'sap from a green stick of ash held in the fire so that the juice oozed out onto a spoon held at the other end.'

Macdonald knew its value:

> This tree, perhaps the most useful of all for agricultural purposes, grows pretty fast, and spreads its branches widely.... grows most vigorously in gravely stony ground, on the banks of running streams; and provided it be protected from the storms, can endure any degree of cold without injury.

In fact, right across Britain, probably ever since Neolithic times, the ash had been grown in coppice for the production of most agricultural tools. Ash poles are strong, springy and resilient. No other wood has quite the same useful qualities.

Aspen was traditionally identified with the Crucifixion (just as other poplar species were similarly associated with the Crucifixion elsewhere in Britain). Using it courted disaster, so Gaels tended to shun its use, particularly for anything to do with boat building. Never offend the Almighty on a turbulent sea. Yet while they cursed the aspen, *an chritheann*, the 'trembling tree', they used it for making herring casks. But by then one was safely on *terra firma* and perhaps there was a dearth of alternatives.

Beech is not a native species in Bute. It was deliberately planted from the eighteenth century onwards, essentially as ornament. It is of little use except as a windbreak and for burning. Macdonald deprecated cultivation of beech, because it did not stand up to salt spray:

> it is unquestionable that every attempt to rear this tree hitherto made in the Hebrides, excepting in Bute and Islay, has been in a great measure unsuccessful.

Yet in Bute, it flourishes and lives up to its promise of great beauty.

Birch is the only broadleaf which grows happily on nutrient-poor acid soil. It helps create a habitat for species requiring somewhat richer soil, for example, the oak. It was particularly valued for the tannin derived from its bark. It was also used, like alder, to produce charcoal suitable for gunpowder. It was a symbol of fertility in Gaelic mythology, possibly on account of its ability to flourish where other broadleaf species would not.

Elder, known as 'the stinking tree' for its malodorous quality, is an embarrassment to its more fragrant relatives in the honeysuckle family. It is one of nature's urchins, frequenting the rich soils of refuse tips, dunghills and graveyards. It was supposedly a magically powerful plant, so it enjoyed an ambiguous status, reviled and revered at the same time. It may be a scrubby ragamuffin, but it had its uses. Drovers used switches of elder, as its unpleasant guff kept the flies off the cattle and themselves. Draught horses might have elder stuck in their harness for the same purpose. Drovers, shepherds and travellers would fashion pipes out of the stem either for musical instruments or for bellows, since the pith is so easily hollowed out.

Elm, usually wych elm in Bute, does well on wet soils, where rush and bracken grow. Like the alder, it was useful because of its tolerance of persistent wetness.

Hawthorn means 'hedge thorn' in Anglo-Saxon, precisely what the plant has been used for, for it grows quickly and, if properly maintained, provides an impenetrable barrier for livestock. Thus, while drystane dykes were built where there was a plethora of stones, in the softest landscapes in Bute the fields are bounded with hawthorn hedgerows. It was the great enclosure plant of the agricultural revolution.

Hazel flourishes where the soil is richer and less acid, so it is to be found at the bottom of slopes where there are still sufficient nutrients and the ground tends to be less acid. It grows well in hedgerows and also on the edges of oakwood, enjoying the same quality of soil but needing more light. Hazel is of great practical value, for its wands split well down the middle and accept being woven, thus making it an invaluable material for hurdles, for fencing and the wattle of housing. 'Creel' houses, the kind of thing referred to by Froissart (p. 253), made out of hazel or willow wands covered with turf, may well have been used in Bute. A creel house could last up to ten years or so.

Holly is our only broadleaved evergreen. It is essentially a woodland plant, able to flourish in the penumbra beneath the canopy of, for example, oaks. It can achieve dominance, enduring greater shade than other species. Its decline must be ascribed to the selective grazing of sheep and deer, which proliferated in the eighteenth century.

Oak is the dominant native species, principally the sessile or durmast oak (*Quercus petraea*). Its strength and durability was symbolic and it was used for house and boat construction, since it stood up well to both wetness and to drying winds. Most types of wood lack that quality. There must have been much more oakwood once, but it has been denuded by climate and human demand. Much was used, particularly across the Kyles in Cowal, for iron smelting. Yet by the nineteenth century the bark was rated even more valuable than the timber, used for tanning leather and curing sails and nets. As one mainland forester noted in the 1860s, 'The bark of a young oak of about 40-50 years is more valuable than the tree itself.' Sure enough, on 4 May 1861 *The Buteman* reported:

> On Tuesday evening last about sixty persons, principally females passed Rothesay, per mail steamer for Ormidale [just beyond Bute, at the top of Loch Riddon]. Most of them are from Greenock, and two or three of them are from this place. During the summer months they will be employed stripping bark off oak.

Spring was the moment for flawing off bark, for the timber was also at its most workable, with the sap rising. There could not have been many seasons left for bark stripping, for by then chemical substitutes had been invented that would destroy not only the bark economy but the value of oak as a tree to plant.

Rowan, widely known as the 'wicken tree', was planted by the door to protect against witchcraft, a persistent ancient belief stretching across Ireland and western Britain. People still grow rowan outside their door. There is an old example at the ruins of Ardnagave in the hills east of Kilmichael. To fell a rowan was asking for trouble. Yet, connected with the afterlife, its wood was used to make funeral biers. With its bright berries and its ability to grow parasitically on other trees, like mistletoe, the rowan caught the Gaelic imagination:

> Glen of rowan with scarlet berries,
> With fruit fit for every flock of birds;
> A slumberous paradise for badgers in their quiet burrows with their young.

> 'Deirdre remembers a Scottish Glen', Anon, 14th cent.

Sycamore or **Scots Plane** (*Acer pseudoplatanus*) is misleading in both its English and Scots names. It is, of course, a maple. Open any book on trees in Scotland and the sycamore is described as a *parvenu* from Central Europe, its introduction dated usually to the sixteenth or seventeenth century. Yet there is evidence that it was present in Britain before AD 1300. One or two dendrologists think it may have been used by the Romans in Scotland. Could it be a native? Scotland hosts the oldest specimens in Britain, possibly because they do best in the north and west of the country. The most northerly wood of Britain, on the north Caithness coast, is sycamore. If this tree were a native then, surely palaeo-botanists would have found pollen evidence. But sycamores produce only a small amount of pollen which, unlike other tree pollens, does not preserve well. Moreover, its pollen is indistinguishable from that of the field maple. (Could it be, for example, that the Bute Mazer is made of sycamore, since field maple does not grow this far north?) Yet on the other hand native tree species seem to feature in Gaelic folklore, whereas the sycamore does not. This suggests that it is, after all, an exotic, but perhaps in Scotland by the early Middle Ages.

The improvers of the eighteenth century started using the syca-more as a windbreak. It has become the principal hedgerow tree north of Durham and often surrounds steadings. It had a real claim to a place on the west coast of Scotland for, in Macdonald's words, the sycamore:

> ….has the invaluable advantage of buffeting the storms better than any other species of hard wood. It ought therefore to be placed in the advanced guard, and on the outpost piquets of our sylvan host in its perpetual conflict with the Atlantic tempests.

Macdonald did not rate the wood of much value. He may have been right, until it became popular for veneer work in the early twentieth century. Sycamore produces an off-white veneer beautifully sugges-tive of watered silk. Half a century ago, a single sycamore tree sold for over £1,000 (roughly £14,000 in today's money). The purchas-er knew he could cut veneer from it sufficient to cover five football pitches.

Whin, **gorse** or **furze**, is common on acidic soil, moor and rough pas-ture. It used to be harvested for its value as kindling and for roaring up a fire to the high temperatures necessary for baking. Yet it also has an important agricultural use. In 1811 James Macdonald extolled its value:

> …whins, or furze, would not only prove highly serviceable in pro-tecting sheep and cattle from the fury of the storms, but also in gradually helping to inclose and shelter the most exposed fields. They would facilitate the rearing of wood [as a seedling protected by whin prickles], check sand drift, and consolidate and strength-en earthen dykes and fences in places where stones cannot be easily procured; in short, they would prove a most precious acqui-sition to those islands. They grow luxuriantly in Bute, Islay and Arran.

Willow. Goat ('pussy') and crack willows are common in Bute. Willow wands were invaluable for weaving lobster creels, baskets and bee-hives. After three years' growth, planted goat willow-cuttings could grow to 10 feet (3 metres) in length, more than sufficient for herring barrel hoops. In Macdonald's day the purchase price for one thou-sand such willow wands was £2 (£75 in today's money):

> It is astonishing that a plant so very useful for making creels,

baskets, hoops for casks and barrels, &c. and for innumerable purposes equally obvious and necessary in this country, has hitherto been so deplorably neglected.... It thrives on moist sands, and even among *blowing sands*, and wherever sea-bent is met with. An acre may contain 10,000 plants. Scarcely any vegetable can vie in point of profitableness with the willow on moist land.

Willow was widely known to be health giving. Presumably Gaels were aware that willow yielded salacin, the drug from which aspirin is made. Catkin wool was used as lint, healing damaged skin, and used medicinally by St Bride: 'The lint the lovely Bride culled through her palm....' Willow was also associated in the Gaelic mind with justice. The Lord of the Isles would administer justice holding a willow wand in his hand.

The day of the willow is not necessarily over. In 2009 scientists working on renewable energy realised that second generation biofuel may be best produced by breaking down willow wood with the enzymes used by the gribble, a marine woodlouse that bores ships' timbers. We may yet see marginal farmland converted to willow coppice.

AND TWO EXOTICS....

The Monkey Puzzle Tree. One cannot fail to notice monkey puzzle (*Araucaria araucana*) trees in the gardens of Bute. They are native to Chile and Argentina, in nature confined to the southern hemisphere, living fragments of the ancient continent of Gondwana. Forget about monkeys, for these trees predate primates by a good 120 million years and probably evolved their unappetising leaves to deter dinosaurs. The first monkey puzzle was introduced to Britain by the collector and surgeon Archibald Menzies who, against the odds, brought five seedlings to Kew in 1795.

Menzies had travelled as naturalist and surgeon on HMS *Discovery* in 1791 under Captain George Vancouver, himself a veteran of Cook's voyage to the south Pacific. When the *Discovery* put in at Valparaiso, Menzies and Vancouver rode inland to Chile's capital, Santiago. They had been forbidden to explore, for the Spanish were understandably suspicious of Britain's acquisitive intentions. They dined with the governor, a man with the improbable name of Don

Ambrosio O'Higgins (father of the more famous Bernardo, destined to become the hero of Chilean independence). It was in his dessert that Menzies struck lucky, for there he espied the seeds of the monkey puzzle tree. Possibly too challenging to swallow whole (the seed can measure up to 4 x 2 cm), he must have pocketed those on his plate.

However, Menzies' troubles began at sea. His instructions to his manservant for nurturing his seedlings under their glazed frames on the *Discovery*'s quarterdeck were countermanded by Vancouver, who co-opted this man to help crew the ship. The consequence was that many plants perished. When Menzies expressed his dismay, Vancouver, mindful of his absolute powers on board his own vessel, had him arrested. There must be more to this tale than meets the eye. They had spent five years in close confinement together, so one can imagine that there were simmering tensions. Menzies' journal of the voyage ends very abruptly in February 1794, eighteen months before their safe return to these shores. Did Vancouver remove the later entries while Menzies was under arrest? If so, what did he wish to remain secret? We shall never know, but each time you see one of these trees, think of the good fortune whereby these seedlings survived.

The Cabbage Tree (*Cordyline australis*). This tree, frequently thought of as a palm, is widespread on the western seaboards of Britain and Ireland, where it flourishes in the maritime climate, and enjoys swampy ground. Like the Monkey Puzzle it belongs very firmly to the Southern Hemisphere, in this case New Zealand. It was first introduced to Britain in 1823. The flowers are creamy white, turning into immense clusters of white berries, each up to 7mm long with a high carbohydrate content. In New Zealand the roots and the base of young shoots were harvested by the Maori, cooked in pits and eaten. Its leaves were used for garments, baskets, mats and twine. It may yet have commercial value, as a low-calorie sugar or possibly as a source for ethanol, though it is difficult to see this happening in Bute.

MOORLAND AND MOSS

The loss of trees not only denuded the landscape but removed a vital means of drainage. For trees not only absorb large quantities of water through their root system, but discharge it into the atmosphere by transpiration. They also provide a sheltered habitat, creating rich humus in

Volunteers for the Red Cross collecting sphagnum for the treatment of wounds during the Second World War.

which other shrub species can grow.

Before the draining of the land at the end of the eighteenth century, most of Bute must have been moorland. With drainage, manuring and the sowing of improved rye grass, it was possible to create a highly productive landscape.

The high ground at the north end of Bute represents the unimproved landscape: rough moorland with areas of moss, or bog. On the better drained areas one finds heather, bilberry and rough grasses, like purple moor grass, that do well on this impoverished terrain. Heather would have been harvested for bedding, probably for humans as well as animals, and for thatching roofs. Bracken and whin both grow on poor but dry sandy acidic soil. The proliferation of bracken is sometimes associated with overgrazing.

Bracken was, however, valued as litter for livestock, for manuring and covering potato beds, and as fuel and tinder. In the Western Isles in the mid-eighteenth century, according to the naturalist, John Lightfoot, 'the inhabitants mow it green, and burning it to ashes, make those ashes up into balls with a little water which they dry in the sun, and make use of them to wash their linen instead of soap. In many of the western isles the people gain a considerable profit from the sale of the ashes to soap and glass makers.' A swingeing tax on soap, not abolished until 1853, was a particular inducement to homemade substitutes.

In poorly drained areas one finds wet and acid-tolerant species: cotton grass, sedges, rushes and, above all, sphagnum. Sphagnum thrives in the wettest parts of a moss, and is the living surface of peat bog, for it is sphagnum's lower roots that create the peat. Sphagnum was discovered to have an important medicinal value in the dressing of wounds: it tended to prevent bacteria and fungi entering the wounded area.

The chief merit of the landscape at the north end of Bute today is that it is so little frequented by humans, allowing it and its wildlife to remain largely unruly and untamed:

What would the world be, once bereft

Of wet and of wildness? Let them be left,

O let them be left, wildness and wet;

Long live the weeds and the wilderness yet.

Gerard Manley Hopkins, *Inversnaid*

Index